First and
Second Peter

First and Second Peter

DUANE F. WATSON
AND
TERRANCE CALLAN

Baker Academic
a division of Baker Publishing Group
Grand Rapids, Michigan

First Peter © 2012 by Duane F. Watson
Second Peter © 2012 by Terrance Callan

Published by Baker Academic
a division of Baker Publishing Group
PO Box 6287, Grand Rapids, MI 49516-6287
www.bakeracademic.com

Printed in the United States of America

Library of Congress Cataloging-in-Publication Data
Watson, Duane Frederick.
    First and Second Peter / Duane F. Watson and Terrance Callan.
        pages   cm — (Paideia: commentaries on the New Testament)
    Includes bibliographical references and index.
    ISBN 978-0-8010-3227-1 (pbk.)
    1. Bible. N.T. Peter—Commentaries. I. Callan, Terrance, 1947– II. Title.
BS2795.53.W38 2012
227′.9207—dc23   2012002599

12   13   14   15   16   17   18   7   6   5   4   3   2   1

In honor and memory of Professor Cullen I. K. Story,
of Princeton Theological Seminary,
who instructed and inspired me to look carefully and reverently
at sacred texts
D. F. W.

For my students,
whose questions have often shown me what I did not know
T. C.

Contents

Contents

Figures

Foreword

Paideia: Commentaries on the New Testament is a series that sets out to comment on the final form of the New Testament text in a way that pays due attention both to the cultural, literary, and theological settings in which the text took form and to the interests of the contemporary readers to whom the commentaries are addressed. This series is aimed squarely at students—including MA students in religious and theological studies programs, seminarians, and upper-division undergraduates—who have theological interests in the biblical text. Thus, the didactic aim of the series is to enable students to understand each book of the New Testament as a literary whole rooted in a particular ancient setting and related to its context within the New Testament.

The name "Paideia" (Greek for "education") reflects (1) the instructional aim of the series—giving contemporary students a basic grounding in academic New Testament studies by guiding their engagement with New Testament texts; (2) the fact that the New Testament texts as literary unities are shaped by the educational categories and ideas (rhetorical, narratological, etc.) of their ancient writers and readers; and (3) the pedagogical aims of the texts themselves—their central aim being not simply to impart information but to form the theological convictions and moral habits of their readers.

Each commentary deals with the text in terms of larger rhetorical units; these are not verse-by-verse commentaries. This series thus stands within the stream of recent commentaries that attend to the final form of the text. Such reader-centered literary approaches are inherently more accessible to liberal arts students without extensive linguistic and historical-critical preparation than older exegetical approaches, but within the reader-centered world the sanest practitioners have paid careful attention to the extratext of the original readers, including not only these readers' knowledge of the geography, history, and other contextual elements reflected in the text but also their ability to respond correctly to the literary and rhetorical conventions used in the text. Paideia commentaries pay deliberate attention to this extratextual repertoire in order to highlight the ways in which the text is designed to persuade and move its readers. Each rhetorical unit is explored from three angles: (1) introductory matters; (2) tracing the train of thought or narrative or rhetorical flow of the argument; and (3) theological issues raised by the text that are of interest to the contemporary Christian. Thus, the primary focus remains on the text and not its historical context or its interpretation in the secondary literature.

Our authors represent a variety of confessional points of view: Protestant, Catholic, and Orthodox. What they share, beyond being New Testament scholars of national and international repute, is a commitment to reading the biblical text as theological documents within their ancient contexts. Working within the broad parameters described here, each author brings his or her own considerable exegetical talents and deep theological commitments to the task of laying bare the interpretation of Scripture for the faith and practice of God's people everywhere.

Mikeal C. Parsons
Charles H. Talbert

Preface to First Peter

First Peter is a rich source of instruction, motivation, and hope for the Christian life. Its rich images and metaphors of the family and household of God, suffering resident foreigners, and people of covenant and priesthood, to name a few, enrich and inform our understanding of what it means to be a Christian. It is my hope that this commentary clearly conveys this epistle's powerful message to its readers.

This commentary was nurtured during more than two decades of teaching the Hebrews and General Epistles class at Malone University. I want to thank my students for their interaction and the Malone Board of Trustees for granting the sabbatical leave that made the completion of this commentary possible.

I particularly want to thank Charles Talbert and Mikeal Parsons for inviting me to contribute to the Paideia series, and James Ernest and the editorial staff at Baker Academic for their careful reading and refinement of the manuscript.

I also want to thank my wife, Dr. JoAnn Ford Watson, for her continued love and support, and my daughter, Christina, who is beginning to ask hard questions of the biblical text.

The translation of 1 Peter is my own. All quotations from elsewhere in the Bible are from the NRSV. All quotations from Greek and Roman sources and the church fathers are from the Loeb Classical Library editions.

Duane F. Watson
Malone University

Preface to Second Peter

I began intensive study of 2 Peter in 1997. In the spring quarter of that year, I had as usual described the relationship between Jude and 2 Peter as part of my course introducing the NT. The students in that course made me realize that my own understanding of the relationship between Jude and 2 Peter did not go very far, so I started to investigate the relationship more carefully. That began a period—still not ended—during which 2 Peter has been a major focus of my research and writing, as I have looked into more and more aspects of that very interesting text.

I am grateful to the Athenaeum of Ohio for two quasi-sabbaticals largely devoted to study of 2 Peter. I am grateful to the editors of Paideia for this opportunity to present some of what I have learned. And I am grateful for the way preparing this commentary has given me further opportunity to develop my understanding of 2 Peter.

I find 2 Peter a fascinating document and think it has more to say to the church than the church has yet heard. I hope this commentary helps bring readers into the world of 2 Peter more fully and increases their ability to understand its message. The commentary's translation of 2 Peter is my own.

Terrance Callan
The Athenaeum of Ohio

Abbreviations

General

//	indicates textual parallels	e.g.	*exempli gratia*, for example
AT	author's translation	esp.	especially
BCE	before the Common Era	i.e.	*id est*, that is
ca.	circa, approximately	lit.	literally
CE	Common Era	n	note
cf.	compare	NT	New Testament
contra	in opposition to	OT	Old Testament
ed.	edition, editor	par.	and parallel(s)

Bible Texts and Versions

LXX	Septuagint	NIV	New International Version
MT	Masoretic Text	NRSV	New Revised Standard Version
NEB	New English Bible	RSV	Revised Standard Version

Ancient Corpora

OLD TESTAMENT		Judg.	Judges
Gen.	Genesis	Ruth	Ruth
Exod.	Exodus	1–2 Sam.	1–2 Samuel
Lev.	Leviticus	1–2 Kings	1–2 Kings
Num.	Numbers	1–2 Chron.	1–2 Chronicles
Deut.	Deuteronomy	Ezra	Ezra
Josh.	Joshua	Neh.	Nehemiah

Esther	Esther
Job	Job
Ps./Pss.	Psalm/Psalms
Prov.	Proverbs
Eccles.	Ecclesiastes
Song	Song of Songs
Isa.	Isaiah
Jer.	Jeremiah
Lam.	Lamentations
Ezek.	Ezekiel
Dan.	Daniel
Hosea	Hosea
Joel	Joel
Amos	Amos
Obad.	Obadiah
Jon.	Jonah
Mic.	Micah
Nah.	Nahum
Hab.	Habakkuk
Zeph.	Zephaniah
Hag.	Haggai
Zech.	Zechariah
Mal.	Malachi

DEUTEROCANONICAL BOOKS

1–2 Esd.	1–2 Esdras
Jdt.	Judith
1–4 Macc.	1–4 Maccabees
Sir.	Sirach
Wis.	Wisdom of Solomon

NEW TESTAMENT

Matt.	Matthew
Mark	Mark
Luke	Luke
John	John
Acts	Acts
Rom.	Romans
1–2 Cor.	1–2 Corinthians
Gal.	Galatians
Eph.	Ephesians
Phil.	Philippians
Col.	Colossians

1–2 Thess.	1–2 Thessalonians
1–2 Tim.	1–2 Timothy
Titus	Titus
Philem.	Philemon
Heb.	Hebrews
James	James
1–2 Pet.	1–2 Peter
1–3 John	1–3 John
Jude	Jude
Rev.	Revelation

DEAD SEA SCROLLS

1QH	*Hodayot*, or *Thanksgiving Hymns*
1QS	*Serek Hayaḥad*, or *Rule of the Community*
4QFlor	*Florilegium*
4QpNah	*Pesher Nahum*

TARGUMIC TEXTS

Tg. Neof.	*Targum Neofiti*
Tg. Onq.	*Targum Onqelos*
Tg. Ps.-J.	*Targum Pseudo-Jonathan*

OLD TESTAMENT PSEUDEPIGRAPHA

As. Mos.	*Assumption of Moses*
2 Bar.	*2 Baruch*
1–2 En.	*1–2 Enoch*
Jos. Asen.	*Joseph and Aseneth*
Jub.	*Jubilees*
Let. Aris.	*Letter of Aristeas*
Odes Sol.	*Odes of Solomon*
Sib. Or.	*Sibylline Oracles*
T. Benj.	*Testament of Benjamin*
T. Reu.	*Testament of Reuben*

APOSTOLIC FATHERS

Barn.	*Barnabas*
1–2 Clem.	*1–2 Clement*
Did.	*Didache*
Diogn.	*Diognetus*
Herm. Mand.	*Shepherd of Hermas, Mandate*
Herm. Sim.	*Shepherd of Hermas, Similitude*

Abbreviations

Herm. Vis.	Shepherd of Hermas, Vision
Ign. Eph.	Ignatius, To the Ephesians
Ign. Magn.	Ignatius, To the Magnesians
Ign. Phld.	Ignatius, To the Philadelphians
Ign. Pol.	Ignatius, To Polycarp
Ign. Rom.	Ignatius, To the Romans
Ign. Smyrn.	Ignatius, To the Smyrnaeans
Ign. Trall.	Ignatius, To the Trallians
Mart. Pol.	Martyrdom of Polycarp
Pol. Phil.	Polycarp, To the Philippians

NEW TESTAMENT APOCRYPHA AND PSEUDEPIGRAPHA

Ep. Apos.	Epistle to the Apostles
Gos. Thom.	Gospel of Thomas

Ancient Authors

ARISTOTLE

Pol.	Politica
Rhet.	Rhetorica

CLEMENT OF ALEXANDRIA

Strom.	Stromata

DEMETRIUS

Eloc.	De elocutione

DIO CHRYSOSTOM

Or.	Orationes

DIODORUS SICULUS

Hist.	Bibliotheca historica

DIOGENES LAERTIUS

Lives	Lives of the Philosophers

DIONYSIUS OF HALICARNASSUS

Ant. rom.	Antiquitates romanae

EPIPHANIUS

Pan.	Panarion (Adversus haereses)

EUSEBIUS

Hist. eccl.	Historia ecclesiastica

HESIOD

Op.	Opera et dies

IRENAEUS

Haer.	Adversus haereses

ISOCRATES

Ep.	Epistulae

JEROME

Vir. ill.	De viris illustribus

JOSEPHUS

Ag. Ap.	Against Apion
Ant.	Jewish Antiquities
J.W.	Jewish War

JUSTIN

1 Apol.	Apologia i
Dial.	Dialogus cum Tryphone

JUVENAL

Sat.	Satirae

LYSIAS

Or.	Orationes

MUSONIUS RUFUS

Or.	Orationes

OVID

Ars	Ars amatoria

PHILO

Ebr.	De ebrietate
Migr.	De migratione Abrahami
Mos.	De vita Mosis
Opif.	De opificio mundi

Sacr.	*De sacrificiis Abelis et Caini*	
Virt.	*De virtutibus*	

PLATO
Leg.	*Leges*
Resp.	*Respublica*
Tim.	*Timaeus*

PLINY THE YOUNGER
| *Ep.* | *Epistulae* |
| *Pan.* | *Panegyricus* |

PLUTARCH
| *Alc.* | *Alcibiades* |
| *Mor.* | *Moralia* |

POLLUX
| *Onom.* | *Onomasticon* |

PSEUDO-ARISTOTLE
| *Oec.* | *Oeconomica* |

SENECA
| *Ep.* | *Epistulae morales* |

TACITUS
| *Ann.* | *Annales* |
| *Hist.* | *Historiae* |

TERTULLIAN
| *Apol.* | *Apologeticus* |

XENOPHON
| *Cyr.* | *Cyropaedia* |
| *Oec.* | *Oeconomicus* |

Modern Works, Editions, Series, and Collections

APOT   *The Apocrypha and Pseudepigrapha of the Old Testament.* Edited by R. H. Charles. 2 vols. Oxford: Clarendon, 1913.

BDAG   W. Bauer, F. W. Danker, W. F. Arndt, and F. W. Gingrich. *A Greek-English Lexicon of the New Testament and Other Early Christian Literature.* 3rd ed. Chicago: University of Chicago Press, 2000.

BDF   F. Blass, A. Debrunner, and R. W. Funk. *A Greek Grammar of the New Testament and Other Early Christian Literature.* Chicago: University of Chicago Press, 1961.

CIG   *Corpus inscriptionum graecarum.* Edited by A. Boeckh et al. 4 vols. Berlin, 1828–77.

OTP   *The Old Testament Pseudepigrapha.* Edited by James H. Charlesworth. 2 vols. Garden City, NY: Doubleday, 1983–85.

TDNT   *Theological Dictionary of the New Testament.* Edited by G. Kittel and G. Friedrich. Translated by G. W. Bromiley. 10 vols. Grand Rapids: Eerdmans, 1964–76.

First Peter

Duane F. Watson

Introduction to First Peter

Authorship

First Peter makes only two references to its author: "Peter, an apostle of Jesus Christ" (1:1) and "a fellow elder, witness of the sufferings of Christ, one who shares the glory to be revealed" (5:1). These references and the authority that the author assumes in the letter seem to indicate that the author is the apostle Peter himself. He was an apostle, elder, and witness to Christ's sufferings. The traditional view of the church is that the apostle Peter wrote 1 Peter, an attribution well attested from the second century to the present and undisputed in the early church.

The earliest reference to 1 Peter is found in 2 Pet. 3:1 (ca. 80–90): "This is now, beloved, the second letter I am writing to you." The author of 2 Peter is probably a disciple of Peter, and his assumption that Peter wrote 1 Peter may come from firsthand knowledge. In the late second century, Irenaeus is the first to explicitly cite Peter as the author of 1 Peter (*Haer.* 4.9.2 and 5.7.2 cite 1 Pet. 1:8; 4.16.5 cites 1 Pet. 2:16). In the third century, Eusebius cites a tradition from Clement of Alexandria (ca. 150–ca. 215) that Peter was the author. "He [Clement] also says that Peter mentions Mark in his first Epistle, and that he composed this in Rome itself, which they say that he himself indicates, referring to the city metaphorically as Babylon, in the words, 'the elect one in Babylon greets you, and Marcus my son'" (*Hist. eccl.* 2.15.2; cf. 1 Pet. 5:13). Eusebius also cites a lost portion of Origen's commentary on the Gospel of John that refers to Peter as leaving one acknowledged and one suspect epistle, that is, 1 and 2 Peter respectively (*Hist. eccl.* 6.25.8). Though the author of 1 Peter did not found the churches addressed (1:12), church tradition assumes that Peter did visit the churches of Asia Minor (Eusebius, *Hist. eccl.* 3.1, citing Origen;

Epiphanius, *Pan.* 27.7; Jerome, *Vir. ill.* 1). Thus the assumption that Peter wrote a letter to these churches is quite plausible.

Modern biblical scholarship has proposed that 1 Peter is pseudonymous, that is, written by someone using Peter's name and authority (Brox 1975; 1978). Typically it is assumed that this author is one of Peter's disciples who was a member of the Petrine circle in Rome (Elliott 1980; 2000, 124–30) or a Roman Christian in general (Horrell 2002) who used Peter's teaching and pastoral advice to address a later generation. In antiquity it was a common practice for students of philosophers and religious teachers to write in their teachers' names, using what they had learned from them. The existence of the *Apocalypse of Peter* and the *Gospel of Peter* from the mid- to late second century illustrates the propensity to use Peter's name for pseudonymous works.

There are several indicators that 1 Peter is pseudonymous. One indicator is its elegant Greek and rhetoric. The Greek is of a higher quality than Koine (the common Greek) but is by no means the highest quality Greek. The rhetoric is studied, indicating that the author possesses an education at the secondary level, where rhetoric was the mainstay of the curriculum (Achtemeier 1996, 2–4). The quality of the Greek and rhetoric do not appear to be the work of a Galilean fisherman whose native tongue was Aramaic and who, along with John, was regarded by the religious authorities in Jerusalem as an "uneducated" and "ordinary" man (Acts 4:13). However, an amanuensis (scribal secretary) could have composed the letter at the dictation of Peter, a common practice for the apostle Paul (1 Cor. 1:1; 16:21; 2 Cor. 1:1; Gal. 6:11; Phil. 1:1; 1 Thess. 1:1; 2 Thess. 3:17), and the Greek style and rhetoric could be ascribed to the amanuensis. In addition, Peter had spent nearly three decades preaching to Greek-speaking audiences, which surely improved his skill in Greek. A second indicator of pseudonymity is the author's use of the Septuagint (Greek translation of the OT, usually abbreviated LXX, roman numerals for seventy) as his Scripture. Peter would have been familiar with the Hebrew text or Aramaic Targums of the OT (Aramaic paraphrases and commentary), but after working with the Greeks for almost thirty years, Peter likely also developed a familiarity with the LXX.

A third indicator of pseudonymity is the limited personal references (2:11; 5:1, 12) and the absence of any personal recollections of time spent with Jesus that go beyond well-known Gospel tradition (e.g., 2:18–25). However, personal reference is not natural in exhortation, nor is personal recollection common in any of the Letters of the NT. A fourth indicator of pseudonymity is the reference to "Babylon" (5:13), which suggests that 1 Peter was written after 70. "Babylon" as a designation for Rome is not attested in documents before Rome's destruction of Jerusalem and the temple in 66–70, as Babylon did in 586 BCE, but is frequent in Jewish and Christian literature after that time. However, the association of Babylon and Rome would have suggested itself to the Jews and Jewish Christians long before the destruction of Jerusalem because both nations were idolatrous, were immoral, and persecuted the people of God.

A fifth indicator of pseudonymity is the limited intensity of the persecution being experienced by the recipients of 1 Peter. Christians were persecuted by the Roman emperors Nero (60s) and Domitian (90s), but there was little persecution between their reigns in the 70s and 80s. Although the letter refers to a "fiery ordeal" (4:12), most of the abuse of Christians referred to is verbal (2:12, 15, 23; 3:9, 16; 4:4, 14). Thus a date in the 70s and 80s is indicated. However, there was also little persecution of Christians before 64, when Peter himself could have been writing. A sixth indicator of pseudonymity is the apocalyptic tone of 1 Peter (1:1–9; 4:7, 12–19), explained by the destruction of Jerusalem in 70 being interpreted as a precursor of Christ's return, but there was also plenty of apocalyptic fervor during Peter's lifetime.

I do not find these and other arguments for the pseudonymous authorship of 1 Peter convincing and consider the author to be the apostle Peter.

Date of Composition

External and internal evidence is inconclusive for determining the date of 1 Peter. Regarding the former, the author of 2 Peter (3:1; ca. 80–90) knows of 1 Peter. *First Clement* (80–140) has numerous affinities with 1 Peter, possibly either from knowing it or sharing tradition found at Rome (Elliott 2000, 138–40). Polycarp's *Letter to the Philippians* (100–140) has verbal affinities with 1 Peter (cf. *Phil.* 1.3 par. 1 Pet. 1:8; *Phil.* 2.1 par. 1 Pet. 1:13, 21; *Phil.* 8.1 par. 1 Pet. 2:22, 24). Eusebius notes that Polycarp used 1 Peter (*Hist. eccl.* 4.14.9), as did Papias around 140 (3.39.17). Irenaeus is the first-known author to explicitly cite 1 Peter by name around 180 (*Haer.* 4.9.2 and 5.7.2 cite 1 Pet. 1:8; *Haer.* 4.16.5 cites 1 Pet. 2:16). More specifically, tradition indicates that Peter suffered martyrdom in Rome at the hands of the emperor Nero around 64–68 (*Hist. eccl.* 2.25.5), which sets a latest possible date for Peter's authorship of this letter (see Aland 1960; Bauckham 1992).

Regarding internal evidence, the letter's positive view of the government (2:13–17; cf. Rom. 13:1–7) would have been difficult to maintain after Nero's persecution of Christians in 64–68. However, honoring the government is a hallmark of early Christian ethics and has theological underpinnings in God's providence, which transcends periodic persecution (*1 Clem.* 61.1–2; Tertullian, *Apol.* 30.1, 4; 32.1, 3; 33.1–2). Some have argued for a date after 70 because the letter refers to Rome metaphorically as "Babylon" (5:13), which also destroyed Jerusalem and the temple. As just discussed under authorship, the connection of Rome with Babylon would have suggested itself long before 70 due to the idolatrous and immoral nature of Rome. The persecution mentioned in the letter is more verbal than physical (2:12, 15, 23; 3:9, 16; 4:4, 14), but verbal persecution was common throughout the first century.

In summary, internal evidence does not provide a range of possible dates, and external evidence gives us a range of 80–180, with the earlier date being more likely due to the reference to 1 Peter in 2 Peter. In conjunction with my position that the apostle Peter wrote this letter and the verbal nature of the persecution, I am assigning 1 Peter to the quiet period before the Neronian persecution of 64–68, in which tradition says Peter was martyred (*1 Clem.* 5.4; Eusebius, *Hist. eccl.* 2.25.5). This date fits the verbal nature of the persecution and gives time for the letter to gain enough notoriety to be referred to by the author of 2 Peter (3:1) in 80–90.

Place of Composition

Many places have been proposed as the location for the composition of 1 Peter, including Antioch of Syria and Asia Minor. However, the author refers to his location as "Babylon" (5:13), a nickname for Rome. A mid-second-century tradition of Clement of Alexandria, cited by Eusebius and mentioned above

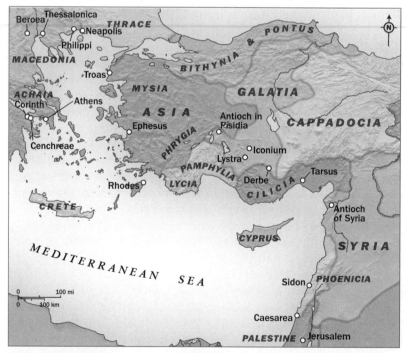

Figure 1. Map of the eastern Mediterranean region. This map shows the Roman provinces of Pontus, Galatia, Cappadocia, Asia, and Bithynia and their key cities, to which 1 Peter is addressed.

under authorship, supports Rome as the place of writing (*Hist. eccl.* 2.15.2). Also, as many commentators have noted, the letter shares many theological terms with other writings associated with Rome, including Romans, Mark, Hebrews, *1 Clement*, and the *Shepherd of Hermas* (R. Brown and Meier 1983, 134–39, 166–76).

Recipients

The recipients of 1 Peter are introduced as "the chosen resident foreigners of the Diaspora in Pontus, Galatia, Cappadocia, Asia, and Bithynia" (1:1). They are Christians in these Roman provinces in Asia Minor (now Turkey) covering approximately 129,000 square miles (for more on Christianity in Asia Minor, see S. Johnson 1971; 1975). The provinces are listed in the order in which letters were delivered by the mail couriers working for the emperor and rich merchants, and likely the route Silvanus used to deliver copies of the letter (5:12; Hort 1898, 167–84). A ship sailing from Rome to this region would likely stop at Pontus, which begins the list, and the carrier could depart back to Rome from Nicomedia in Bithynia (Elliott 2000, 317). The recipients were evangelized by Christian preachers (1:10–12), including Paul, whose ministry overlapped this region.

Are the recipients Jews or gentiles? The exile is a key motif in the letter. The readers are called "resident foreigners" (1:1) and "aliens and resident foreigners" where they live (2:11), and they are told to "conduct yourselves in fear during the time of your exile" (1:17). The word "Diaspora" (1:1) builds on the imagery of the Jewish people scattered throughout the ancient world since the Babylonian captivity (586 BCE). Peter identifies his own churches at Rome as being in "Babylon" (5:13), the name of the empire that sent the Jews into exile, and describes those outside the community as gentiles (2:12; 4:3). The exilic perspective of the letter—coupled with the heavy use of the OT for quotations, allusions, and historical references (see "Sources" below)—seems to indicate that the recipients are Jewish Christians. Further support comes from Paul's observation that Peter's mission was to the Jews (Gal. 2:7–8) and the church fathers' assumptions that the recipients were Jewish Christians (Eusebius, *Hist. eccl.* 3.1.2 [citing vol. 3 of Origen's commentary on Genesis]; 3.4.2).

Such indications are misleading because the recipients are probably gentiles. The exile motif can describe Christians metaphorically as those who are in the world but whose real citizenship is in heaven (cf. James 1:1). The recipients' sinful lifestyle before conversion characterizes a gentile background (1:14, 18, 21; 2:25; 4:3–4). Their assumed familiarity with the OT can be attributed to instruction following conversion. While the recipients are described as Jews, they are also described as once not being God's people (2:9–10). The recipients are gentile Christians described as Jews because they are God's new people. For contrast, all non-Christians are called "gentiles" (2:12; 4:3).

The social and economic status of the recipients is indicated in part by the household code (2:18–3:7). Some wives adorn themselves with gold ornaments and fine clothing, indicating considerable wealth (3:3–4). Some recipients are slaves (2:18–25). The word for "slave" is not the generic one (*doulos*), but one denoting a higher and more educated slave of larger households of some means (*oiketēs*). When Pliny the Younger as governor of Bithynia wrote Trajan around 112, he describes the Christians of this region as being from all levels of society, citizens and noncitizens. He also states that the Christian movement there has spread from city to countryside (*Ep.* 10.96). Thus the recipients are likely to be gentiles from all levels of society in urban areas of Asia Minor.

In recent years, it has been proposed that the designations "resident foreigners" (1:1) and "aliens and resident foreigners" (2:11) refer literally to the recipients as politically, socially, and legally dispossessed foreigners living outside their native lands (Elliott 1990, 21–49; 2000, 94, 101–3). However, this understanding assumes that Christianity had not made inroads into the resident population, but inroads are likely because Peter is trying to help the recipients assuage their neighbors with their good behavior (2:12–17; 3:13–17), neighbors who are surprised by the recipients' radical change in behavior (4:1–6). This dynamic implies long-standing relationships and considerable interaction. The metaphor of Christians as resident foreigners and the associated metaphor of the exile-Diaspora are rooted primarily in the stories of the social and political realities of Abraham and Israel respectively, not in the social and political situation of the first-century Roman Empire. Here in 1 Peter, these metaphors describe spiritual realities.

Occasion and Purpose

The recipients of the letter are suffering (1:6–7; 2:19–23; 3:13–17; 4:19; 5:9–10). The persecution is due to the remarkable difference that conversion to Christianity made in their lives and the negative response of their neighbors (4:4). The recipients could no longer participate in drunken parties or the worship of idols in a temple as a part of their social and business practices. This withdrawal made their neighbors angry, for it is an implicit condemnation of these activities and those participating in them. The very designation of the recipients as "resident foreigners" (1:1) and "aliens and resident foreigners" (2:11), as well as their time on earth being described as exile (1:17), indicates estrangement from neighbors and the larger world as the recipients behave in ways befitting their membership in the family and household of God (1:2–5, 14, 17, 23; 2:2; 4:17; 5:9).

This withdrawal left the recipients vulnerable to charges of being evil (2:12) and perhaps even criminal (cf. 2:13–17). They could be accused of being anti-social, which was considered to be a threat to the social fabric and a possible offense to the gods that could bring their judgment on the entire community. The Jews of that time were also subject to such slander and suspicion (cf. Josephus, *Ag. Ap.* 2.89–96; Tacitus, *Hist.* 5.5.1; Diodorus Siculus, *Hist.* 34.1–2).

The origin and nature of the persecution is a matter of debate. Was it verbal only, or did it also have a physical aspect? Was it unofficial or official? Local or more general? (For an overview, see Achtemeier 1996, 23–36.) Commentators often assume that this persecution was mainly verbal. Verbal abuse is indicated in some verses (2:12, 15; 3:16; 4:4), particularly abuse for the name of Christ (4:14, 16). However, physical abuse is also indicated by the description of the recipients as suffering a variety of trials (1:6); being subject to harm, suffering, and fear (3:13–17); undergoing a fiery ordeal (4:12); needing exhortation to look to Christ's example of enduring abuse and suffering (2:23; cf. 3:18); and hearing the commandment not to return evil and abuse (3:9).

The persecution is sometimes understood as official and more empire-wide. The persecution is partly for the name of Christ, which may imply an official charge (4:14, 16). The exhortation to make a defense to anyone needing an account of Christian hope may be an official response to accusations in a lawcourt (3:15). In addition, other Christians "in all the world" are suffering similarly (5:9). Commentators have tied this persecution to the reigns of the emperors Nero (54–68), Domitian (81–96), and Trajan (98–117). Under Nero, however, persecution of Christians was limited to Rome. Under Domitian the persecution was localized and sporadic, but did include Asia Minor (Rev. 2–3). Under Trajan there was no official empire-wide persecution or official policy on how to deal with Christians (Pliny, *Ep.* 10.96–97). Thus there was no official empire-wide persecution of Christians in the time frame in which 1 Peter may have been written. The first such persecution was under Decius (249–251) in 250.

It is possible that the persecution is local, as experienced also by others in the empire (5:9). It may have been official, as local magistrates created policies meant to maintain the public order, the *coercitio*. However, based on the facts that it is short-lived (1:6; 5:10) and the recipients can mitigate it with their behavior (2:13–17; 3:13–17), the persecution is likely unofficial (for more on the situation, see Molthagen 1995).

In light of the situation, the letter is written to encourage the recipients (5:12) and give their suffering theological purpose as a vital part of the Christian life, especially as a testing from God (4:12, 19) and an imitation of Christ (2:21–23; 3:18). It stresses that good conduct is the best way to quell verbal and physical abuse instigated by hostile gentile neighbors and authorities (2:12–17; 3:13–17), as well as an outworking of their new holy nature as obedient children of God (1:14–16). The recipients are to be respectful of authority (2:13–17) and not retaliate for suffering (3:9). This applies to slaves with non-Christian masters and to wives with non-Christian husbands (2:18–3:6), who are in more vulnerable positions in society and more likely to suffer. Here is even an evangelistic tone: motivating the exhortation to good works is the desire for the conversion of neighbors who may be curious enough to respect the recipients and inquire about the faith (2:12; 3:15).

Genre

First Peter is primarily a letter, having all the requisite parts of a letter as adapted by early Christianity: a prescript identifying the sender and recipients with theological elaboration (1:1–2); a blessing taking the place of a standard thanksgiving (1:3–12); a body (1:13–5:11) with an opening (1:13–2:10), middle (2:11–4:11), and closing (4:12–5:11); and a postscript with restatement of the purpose of writing, greetings, and a blessing (5:12–14). There were many types of letters within Judaism and the Greco-Roman world (Malherbe 1988; Stowers 1986), and 1 Peter is a paraenetic, or hortatory, letter designed to teach and call an audience to a course of action (Stowers 1986, 96–97; T. Martin 1992, 81–134).

First Peter is also a circular letter sent to many recipients, and more specifically, a Diaspora letter sent to "Israel." A Diaspora letter was used in Judaism for formal communication from Jerusalem to the Jewish communities in exile in Babylon (Jer. 29:1–23), Assyria (*2 Bar.* 78–87), Egypt (2 Macc. 1:1–10a; 1:10b–2:18), and elsewhere. The Diaspora letter is adapted to meet the need to correspond with Christians around the Roman Empire. The Epistle of James (1:1; cf. Acts 8:1) and the letter of the Jerusalem Council (Acts 15:23–29) are also Christian adaptations of the Diaspora letter.

Structure, Rhetoric, and Integrity

The epistolary structure outlined above is a good place to start for structural analysis. Two occurrences of the direct address "Beloved" (*agapētoi* in 2:11 and 4:12) divide the body of 1 Peter into three parts: 1:13–2:10; 2:11–4:11; and 4:12–5:11. Along with the letter prescript (1:1–2) and thanksgiving (1:3–12), the first section of 1:14–2:10 defines the recipients as God's people, based on the salvation that Christ has made possible. It begins and ends with a reference to the audience as a chosen people (1:2; 2:9), forming an *inclusio*, or bookends, defining the section. The second section, 2:11–4:11, develops the responsibilities of Christians to themselves and others as they live in the world as aliens and resident foreigners. The third section, 4:12–5:11, further counsels the recipients on the nature of Christian behavior in a hostile environment and within their own community. The references to "chosen" people in the prescript (1:2) and the postscript (5:13) provide an *inclusio* for the entire letter (for discussion of structure, see Combrink 1975; Antoniotti 1985; Talbert 1986a).

With these considerations noted, the outline for 1 Peter used in this commentary is as follows:

From our perspective, 1 Peter does not exhibit a clear sequential development within these sections, but its original hearers would have observed a careful rhetorical structure. The recipients were living in an oral culture, where less than 10 percent of the audience could read, so the letter is structured to help them understand and retain its content as it was read aloud and to persuade them of its truth. Repetition in many forms plays a key role. Topics are

---

An Outline of 1 Peter

God's provision for salvation, and Christians' status before God (1:1–2:10)

The letter prescript: Establishing authority, identity, and goodwill (1:1–2)

Thanksgiving for God's gift of salvation (1:3–12)

The blessing of God rooted in God's mercy (1:3–5)

The joy of the salvation experienced and to be experienced (1:6–9)

The past anticipation and the present experience of salvation now revealed (1:10–12)

The call and motivation to holiness (1:13–21)

The call to holiness (1:13–16)

The motivation to holiness (1:17–21)

Born anew by the word of God for mutual love (1:22–25)

Growing into salvation (2:1–3)

Christ as the living stone, and Christians as the spiritual house and God's people (2:4–10)

Living honorably among the gentiles (2:11–4:11)

Introduction to the main theme (2:11–12)

The household code (2:13–3:7)

The relationship of Christians to the civil authorities (2:13–17)

The relationship of slaves to masters (2:18–25)

The relationship between wives and husbands (3:1–7)

Practicing mutual love and peace with all (3:8–12)

Doing good rather than evil amid suffering, after Christ's example (3:13–22)

Doing good rather than evil amid suffering (3:13–17)

Christ's suffering brings victory over the powers (3:18–22)

Living in the Spirit and doing the will of God (4:1–6)

The need for mutual responsibility in light of the end (4:7–11)

Exhortations on faithful suffering among the gentiles, and conclusion (4:12–5:14)

Suffering faithfully among the gentiles (4:12–19)

Concluding exhortations (5:1–11)

Appeal to elders and the young (5:1–5)

Summarizing exhortations (5:6–11)

Epistolary postscript (5:12–14)

---

introduced, then reintroduced in a different form and elaborated, often in relation to other topics. This allows the recipients to hear topics several times without their becoming obvious or mundane, to make connections between the topics, and to come to a fuller understanding of the overall message. This repetition is also accentuated with a careful use of style (for the rhetoric of 1 Peter, see Thurén 1990; 1995; B. Campbell 1998; Elliott 2000, 64–68).

The integrity of the letter has been questioned because the doxology in 4:11 seems to signal the end of a letter. It has been suggested that 1:1–4:11 was the first letter and that 4:12–5:11 was a later letter added to the first. The shift from verbal abuse in 1:1–4:11, in which suffering is a possibility (as indicated by the future participle in 3:13 and the optative mood in 3:14, 17), to a "fiery ordeal," introduced as a reality (as indicated by the present tense in 4:12, 19) and placed within the context of God's impending judgment (4:12–19), is understood to indicate that 4:12–5:11 is from a later time, when the possibility of suffering has become a reality. Then the postscript of 5:12–14 is viewed as part of the first or the second letter. In other words, 1 Peter is a composite letter (Perdelwitz 1911).

However, doxologies can be found anywhere in the body of early Christian letters where the author thinks it is rhetorically effective, especially where God is praised (Rom. 1:25; 9:5; 11:36; Gal. 1:5; Eph. 3:21; 1 Tim. 1:17; Rev. 1:6), as is the case in 1 Pet. 4:11. Also, 4:12–5:11 provides repetition and amplification of many of the topics of 2:11–4:11, as would be expected in classical oral and written works, indicating that this section was part of the letter originally. From another perspective, the fiery ordeal of 4:12–5:11 is already mentioned in 1:6–7, further indicating that the letter was originally unified.

It has also been proposed that since 1:3–4:11 does not seem to apply to any particular situation and refers to spiritual rebirth (1:3, 23; 2:2) and baptism (3:21), it is a baptismal homily placed within the original letter of 1 Peter constituted by 1:1–2 and 4:12–5:14 (Perdelwitz 1911). Sometimes all of 1 Peter is viewed as a baptismal liturgy with the additions of the prescript (1:1–2) and postscript (5:12–14; Cross 1954; for a history, see Elliott 2000, 7–12). However, references to new birth are not necessarily tied to baptism every time they appear. Baptismal themes in the letter are subordinate to the discussion of living in the world as aliens amid suffering rather than being the main theme, as would be expected in a baptismal liturgy or homily. The liturgical elements are easily attributed to the use of early Christian tradition in the original composition of the letter.

Sources

A variety of sources are used in the composition of this letter, including the OT and Jewish tradition, Gospel tradition, and hymns and creeds.

The Old Testament (Septuagint) and Jewish Tradition

The only source 1 Peter explicitly cites is the Septuagint (LXX). The letter frequently alludes to or quotes from the LXX, either weaving the words into its arguments without signaling a formal quotation or explicitly quoting the LXX. It primarily uses the Psalms, Proverbs, and Isaiah (for a detailed list, see Elliott 2000, 12–17). The letter makes specific reference to characters in the OT including angels (1:12), Noah (3:20, from Gen. 6–8), Sarah and Abraham (3:6, from Gen. 18:12), and the prophets (1:10–12). It makes use of key events from the life of Israel including the exile (1:1; 2:11; 5:13) and the Dispersion (1:1). The OT and Jewish tradition supply nearly all the imagery of the letter, and the church understood as Israel is a governing metaphor (Chevallier 1978; Brox 1981). Just as Israel was once in exile in Babylon, the recipients now are exiles on earth (1:1, 17; 2:11). The author's location is nicknamed "Babylon," and thus he is a "fellow exile" like the recipients (5:13). The recipients are gentiles themselves but are now understood to be God's chosen people among the gentiles (2:12).

The interpretation of the OT is christological. The prophets of Israel spoke of the grace that has come through the sufferings and glorification of Christ (1:10–12). Thus, for example, the "word of our God" that abides forever (Isa. 40:6–9) is the gospel of Jesus Christ (1:24–25); "a tested" and "precious cornerstone" laid in Zion (Isa. 28:16) and the sinless Suffering Servant with "no deceit in his mouth" (Isa. 53:5–12) are Christ (2:6, 22–25).

The letter also draws on tradition in works once considered authoritative within Judaism and early Christianity but no longer thus regarded. For example, the tradition about Noah and the spirits in prison in 3:18–22 is elaborated in *1 Enoch* (Dalton 1989, 165–71).

Early Christian Tradition

First Peter relies on early Christian tradition devised to facilitate preaching the gospel; tradition on such central subjects as Christ's redemptive sufferings, resurrection, and exaltation; baptism; exhortation to love and good works; and the second coming of Christ in judgment. This tradition was encapsulated in exhortation, kerygmatic formulas, liturgies, hymns and creeds, and catechetical instruction (1:18–21; 2:21–25; 3:18–22; Best 1970; Elliott 2000, 20–40).

More specifically, the letter draws on the Gospel tradition of the sayings of Jesus (for a detailed list, see Achtemeier 1996, 10n97). There is an interest in the commandment of Jesus to "love your enemies," the subject of the center section of 1 Peter in 2:11–4:11 (e.g., 2:12, 15, 17, 18–20, 23; 3:1–2, 9, 10–12, 15–16; 4:1), and in forms of Jesus's sayings found in the Sermon on the Mount (Matt. 5:10 par. 1 Pet. 3:14; Matt. 5:11//Luke 6:22 par. 1 Pet. 4:14a; Matt. 5:16 par. 1 Pet. 2:12; Luke 6:28 par. 1 Pet. 3:9). There is no literary dependence on Q, the sayings of Jesus in written form used by Matthew and Luke.

Due to similarities of vocabulary, there is a question whether the author knew Paul's Letters, especially Romans, and if 1 Peter is pseudonymous, whether the author knew Paul's Letters known as the Pseudo-Paulines, especially Ephesians (for a detailed list of similar passages, see Foster 1913, 411–532; Achtemeier 1996, 15–19; Elliott 2000, 20–30, 37–40). There is no conclusive evidence that 1 Peter uses any of Paul's Letters or those known as the Pseudo-Paulines. Similarities with these letters are due to the use of shared oral and written Christian tradition. Interesting parallels between 1 Peter and Romans (sent to Rome) and Hebrews (written from Rome) suggest a common milieu in Roman Christianity, of which the author was a part and within which he wrote 1 Peter.

Theology

Many of the theological points of 1 Peter are practical. They are intended to address the problem that the recipients are having with suffering at the hands of others by providing a model of suffering in Jesus Christ and a perspective on suffering offered by the broad purposes of God for their lives and the world (Bechtler 1998; for the theology of 1 Peter, see R. Martin 1994; Van Rensburg 2005; Dryden 2006; J. Green 2007, 187–288).

Doctrine of God

The theology of 1 Peter is God-centered. God is presented as the Creator, Redeemer, Father, and Judge. God is the Creator of all things (4:19), who foreknows everything that happens in the divine redemptive plan (1:2). Thus Christ can be described as "chosen before the foundation of the world, but . . . revealed in the last of the ages for your sake" (1:20). The recipients of the letter can understand their suffering in the context of God's will (4:19). God is the Father of both Jesus Christ and all Christians (1:2–5, 17). The most important aspect of God's relationship to Jesus is not the eternal Father-and-Son relationship in heaven, but the historical fact that God has raised Jesus from the dead, which results in extending the relationship of parent and child experienced by the Father and Son to include all Christians (1:3–5, 21; 3:22). God is the judge of believer and unbeliever alike (1:17; 2:23; 4:5, 17). Judgment begins with God's household (4:17) and proceeds on the basis of deeds (1:17).

Christology and Soteriology

The Christology centers on Christ's future revelation and his salvific work. Regarding Christ's revelation, Christ is currently not visible (1:8), having gone to heaven (3:22). However, the Christian hope is that he will be revealed as one who is somehow already present. The revelation of Christ on the last day (1:7, 13) means that the revelation of salvation (1:5), grace (1:13), and glory

(4:13; 5:1; cf. 5:4) will be fully experienced, fulfilling the promise that Christians will share in Christ's glory to be revealed (4:14; 5:1). Elsewhere, the NT speaks of Christ's future "revelation" (*apokalypsis*; 1 Cor. 1:7; 2 Thess. 1:7; cf. Luke 17:30).

Regarding Christ's salvific work, the basis of salvation is "the sufferings of Christ and the glory to follow" (1:11). These sufferings are described in 2:21–25, and the glory in 1:21 and 3:18–22. Salvation is achieved by the suffering and death of Christ, his resurrection, and his ascension to heaven. Christ was not a mere passive victim but an active sin-bearer (1:18–21; 2:21–25; 3:18): "He offered up our sins in his body on the cross, in order that dying to sins we might live in righteousness; by his bruise you have been healed" (2:24).

This salvation is presented in a variety of images. There is the more traditional sacrificial image, drawn from the temple cult, of Christ as the sacrifice for sin (3:18); Christ as the Suffering Servant of Isaiah, who suffered for the people of God (2:21–23, quoting Isa. 53:7, 9b); Christ as the Shepherd, to whom the Christians as errant sheep return (2:25); and Christ as the rich patron, who buys the freedom of a slave at a temple, that is, by manumission (1:18–19). This latter image is mixed with priestly and sacrificial language so that "financing" is made through the sacrificial blood of Christ.

It is by the resurrection of Jesus that God in great mercy is able to give Christians a new birth, a living hope, and an inheritance (1:3–4). The purpose of the resurrection is that a Christian's faith and hope might be placed in God instead of pursuing the futile ways inherited from previous generations (1:18, 21). It is because Christ was raised that baptism saves, and baptism is associated with embracing the new life in Christ (3:21). Baptism is associated not with the death of the old life but rather with embracing the new life. In contrast, Paul associates baptism with the death of the old life as well as walking in newness of life (Rom. 6:4; cf. Col. 2:11–12; 3:1).

The ascension of Christ (3:19, 22) is like the description found elsewhere in the NT (John 3:13; 6:62; 20:17; Acts 2:33; 5:31; Eph. 4:8–10). The letter's unique emphasis, in reliance on Jewish tradition, is that in going to heaven, Jesus announced his victory over the angelic forces that had fathered children with human women and created the evil generation that disobeyed in the time of Noah—angels that were subsequently punished by imprisonment until the last day (3:18–22; cf. Gen. 6:4). (For more on Christology, see Richard 1986.)

Ethics and Salvation

The ethics of the letter are governed by the motif of *imitatio Christi*, the imitation of Christ. The path of Christ that led from suffering to resurrection to heaven to glorification is the path that God intends for Christians to follow as well (2:21). The suffering of the disciples of Christ is part of the redemptive plan of God (4:19), and the purpose of such imitation is the glory and blessing to be enjoyed in heaven, where Christ now resides (1:7; 3:9, 18;

5:10). The imitation/discipleship motif invites comparison with the Gospel tradition, including the first indications that suffering and death are part of discipleship (Mark 8:34–38//Matt. 16:24–28//Luke 9:23–27). The motif also appears in certain Johannine traditions associated with Peter, such as Jesus's telling Peter "Where I am going, you cannot follow me now; but you will follow afterward" (John 13:36) and his last words to Peter in the entire Gospel of John, "Follow me!" (21:19, 22).

The proper response of Christians to redemption is to do the will of God (4:1–2). This response is summed up by the concept of "doing good" (*agathopoiein*: 2:12, 15, 20; 3:6, 13, 17; 4:19). Doing good is to do the will of God, especially in situations where one suffers for it (3:17; 4:19), as a way to leave the accusations of non-Christians hollow and perhaps even lead to their conversion (2:12). More specifically, doing good is to fulfill the spirit of Jesus's command to love one's enemies. This understanding is implicit in the letter's emphasis on humility, gentleness, and nonretaliation as the proper response to those who oppress the community (2:12, 15–17, 18–25; 3:8–17). The ethical ideal is also expressed as "keep your conscience clear" (3:16) or "live for righteousness" (2:24). The negative of this ethical ideal can be expressed as "do not sin" (2:1, 11, 24; 3:10; 4:1–2).

Pneumatology

The Holy Spirit is the power by which Christians are set apart from the world as God's chosen people and sanctified (1:2). The Spirit is central to the church's being built into the spiritual house and a holy priesthood offering spiritual sacrifices (2:5). The Holy Spirit is the power by which the proclamation of the Christian message takes place (1:12) and rests on Christians when they are under persecution (4:14). The spirit is used in contrast to flesh as an indicator of God's power to raise the dead (3:18; 4:6).

Eschatology

The day of visitation (2:12) is "the last time" (1:5), when salvation is revealed; it is the end of all things (4:7), when all people—living and dead—are judged by God (1:17; 4:5, 17), Jesus Christ is revealed in his glory (1:7, 13; 4:13; 5:1), and those who were faithful to him will receive their unfading crown (5:4; see Parker 1994).

P A R T   1

1 Peter 1:1–2:10

God's Provision for Salvation,
and Christians' Status before God

Part 1 of 1 Peter describes God's provision of salvation through the death and resurrection of Christ and the new status of Christians before God. It contains

---

1 Peter 1:1–2:10 in Context

▶ **God's provision for salvation, and Christians' status before God (1:1–2:10)**

    The letter prescript: Establishing authority, identity, and goodwill (1:1–2)

    Thanksgiving for God's gift of salvation (1:3–12)

    The call and motivation to holiness (1:13–21)

    Born anew by the word of God for mutual love (1:22–25)

    Growing into salvation (2:1–3)

    Christ as the living stone, and Christians as the spiritual house and God's people (2:4–10)

Living honorably among the gentiles (2:11–4:11)

Exhortations on faithful suffering among the gentiles, and conclusion (4:12–5:14)

---

a letter prescript establishing the authority of the writer and creating goodwill with the recipients (1:1–2); a thanksgiving for God's gift of salvation (1:3–12); a call to be holy as children born anew by the word and growing into salvation (1:13–2:3); and a portrayal of Christians as the spiritual house of God built on Christ, the living stone (2:4–10).

1 Peter 1:1–2

The Letter Prescript: Establishing Authority, Identity, and Goodwill

Introductory Matters

Verses 1–2 are the letter prescript with its three standard parts: the superscription (identifying the sender), the adscription (naming the recipients), and the salutation (Aune 2003, 166–67). The long list of recipients indicates that 1 Peter is a circular letter, meant to be delivered to more than one location. The wording of the prescript identifies 1 Peter more specifically as a Diaspora letter, a letter type with a long tradition in Judaism. Diaspora letters represent themselves as written from Jerusalem to the Jewish Dispersion, or Diaspora, communities in Babylon, Assyria, and Egypt (see "Genre" in the introduction). First Peter is slightly different: although using the Jewish Diaspora metaphor, it is being sent to gentile Christians (see "Recipients" in the introduction).

The three parts of the letter prescript are expanded for theological purposes, as they typically are in the letters of the NT. In the superscription, Peter is designated as an apostle of Jesus Christ. In the adscription, the recipients are described by using a trinitarian formula that defines them as a chosen people and outlines their responsibilities as such. The salutation, which usually was a wish for good health, is replaced with a blessing.

The prescript also introduces topics that will be developed in the body of the letter, including being chosen in the foreknowledge of God, as developed in 1:3–12; the sanctification of the Spirit, as elaborated in 1:13–17; and Christ's redemptive work and the need for obedience, as expanded in 1:18–25. The topic of exile introduced here is the underlying metaphor of the entire letter

(1:3–4:11), introducing the first two of the three main parts of the letter (1:3–2:10; 2:11–4:11).

Tracing the Train of Thought

1:1. The superscription of verse 1a invokes the authority of an apostle: **Peter, an apostle of Jesus Christ.** "Peter" (*petros*), or "rock," is the Greek equivalent of Peter's Aramaic name, "Cephas." It was the name given to Peter either at his call (John 1:42), at the appointing of the Twelve for preaching and casting out demons (Mark 3:16; Luke 6:14), or at his confession at Caesarea Philippi (Matt. 16:18). "Apostle" designates someone sent with the authority and message of a more powerful sender (*TDNT* 1:407–46). As an apostle of Jesus Christ, Peter has been sent by Jesus Christ and bears his authority and message, an authority now borne by 1 Peter.

> **1 Peter 1:1–2 in the Rhetorical Flow**
>
> God's provision for salvation, and Christians' status before God (1:1–2:10)
>
> ▶ The letter prescript: Establishing authority, identity, and goodwill (1:1–2)

The letter's adscription (vv. 1b–2a) is addressed **to the chosen** (*eklektoi*), which typically refers to the nation of Israel as a chosen people (Deut. 4:37; 7:6–8; 10:15; 14:2; 1 Chron. 16:13; Ps. 105:6; Isa. 65:9, 15, 22) or, in apocalyptic literature, means the faithful within an unfaithful Israel, who will be vindicated on the last day (*1 En.* 1.1, 8; 39.6–7; 48.1; 58.1–4). Here the reference is to the church as God's chosen people, a prominent topic in the letter, being particularly associated with sanctification and holiness (1:2, 15–16; 2:9).

The chosen are also **resident foreigners** (*parepidēmoi*), people residing temporarily in a foreign place (1:1b). The term is used in the LXX of Abraham's living among the Hittites (Gen. 23:4) and in the NT of Abraham and his descendants, the people of God, as foreigners and exiles on earth (Heb. 11:13). The recipients are resident foreigners, not because of race or nationality, but because, like Abraham, they are chosen by God to live among those not chosen (Chin 1991). The second section of the letter begins by calling the recipients "aliens and resident foreigners" (*parepidēmoi*, 2:11), which indicates how important this metaphor is for their identity. Some interpreters propose that "resident foreigners" refers to the recipients as official political resident foreigners in Asia, but this is unlikely (see "Recipients" in the introduction).

The recipients are resident foreigners **of the Diaspora** (1:1b). Literally, the Diaspora refers to all Jews living as resident foreigners outside Palestine since the deportation to Babylon in 586 BCE. Jews living in the Diaspora were not typically granted citizenship where they lived and were classified as resident foreigners. "Diaspora" is used metaphorically for Christians as a group scattered in the world (T. Martin 1992, 144–61), as is the synonym in 2:11 (*paroikos*) and terminology of exile in 1:17 (*paroikia*). Metaphorically, all Christians are in this Diaspora, including the author's church in Rome, as the reference to Rome as "Babylon" indicates (5:13).

The recipients are scattered **in Pontus, Galatia, Cappadocia, Asia, and Bithynia** (1:1b). These all are Roman provinces in Asia Minor north of the Taurus mountain range, in what today is Turkey. The provinces may be listed in the order in which the messenger, Silvanus (5:12), would deliver the letter (Hemer 1978).

1:2. The recipients are characterized in rich theological terms that describe the origin and nature of the Christian life. They are chosen **according to the foreknowledge of God the Father.** God chose the recipients according to God's foreknowledge (*prognōsis*). This is more than knowing ahead of time: it involves choice according to purpose and plan. It is being called by God to God's purposes, including the call to be holy (1:15), to be God's people (2:9), to follow Christ's example (2:21), to be nonretaliatory (3:9), and to experience the eternal glory in Christ (5:10). Christ himself was "chosen [*proginōskō*] before the foundation of the world" in God's plan to provide his blood as the ransom for those chosen and called (1:20; cf. Acts 2:23).

In the choice of the Christian and Christ, God has acted as "Father." God is the Father of Jesus (1:3) and of all Christians (1:17) as they are reborn (1:3, 23) to be God's children (1:14) and brothers and sisters (5:9, 12–13) forming a family, or household, of God (4:17; 5:9). God has provided redemption through the Son and chooses many sons and daughters to participate in that redemption (Rom. 8:28–30).

As those chosen in the plan of God, the means by which this choice becomes effective is **through the sanctifying of the Spirit** (1:2a; subjective genitive; cf. 1 Cor. 6:11), an important topic in 1 Peter (1:15–16, 19, 22; 2:5, 9; 3:5, 15). This sanctifying of the chosen by the Spirit has two purposes: **for obedience and sprinkling of the blood of Jesus Christ** (1:2a). The first purpose, being obedient (*hypakoē*), refers specifically to conversion from paganism to living according to the holy nature of God (1:14–16) and, more generally, to obeying the truth (1:22; cf. Rom. 1:5; 10:16; 16:26; 1 Thess. 2:13–14).

The second purpose, the sprinkling of the blood of Jesus Christ, refers to entering the covenant that his blood inaugurates. The Jewish sacrificial system provides the imagery here, specifically Num. 19, where the ashes from the burning of a red heifer are mixed with water and sprinkled on those who became unclean by contact or association with a corpse, in order to purify them (cf. *Barn.* 8). Another influence may be Exod. 24:3–8, where Moses offers burnt and peace offerings to God and throws half the oxen blood on the altar and half on the people, as the blood of the covenant into which they were entering. Hebrews uses this passage to argue that Christ's blood inaugurates a new covenant (9:15–22; 12:24; cf. 10:29). In 1 Peter the text from Exodus is further in the background than it is in Hebrews, but the understanding is the same. The choice of God and the sanctification of the Spirit are intended to

21

create a new covenant people through the redemptive death of Jesus Christ in the shedding of his blood. The reference here to the sprinkling with Jesus's blood introduces the broad topic of the redemptive work of Christ that runs throughout the letter (1:18–21; 2:21–25; 3:18–22; 4:1).

Recently it has been proposed that obedience and sprinkling of the blood are not the *purpose* of the choice of God and the sanctification of the Holy Spirit but the *cause* and should be translated "because of the obedience and sprinkling of the blood of Jesus Christ" (Agnew 1983; Elliott 2000, 319–20). However, this translation makes the choice of God and the sanctification of the Holy Spirit dependent on an individual's obedience and sprinkling with blood, when theologically it is the other way around.

The letter prescript ends with a standard Christian salutation or blessing, **May grace and peace be multiplied to you** (1:2b). The grace is that which the prophets prophesied (1:10–12) and will be revealed in its complete measure when Jesus is revealed at the consummation (1:13; cf. 1:5, 7). It is all the benefits that Christians receive by the mercy of God (1:2, 10, 13; 3:7; 4:10; 5:5, 10, 12). Peace is a reality in the lives of those who have experienced God's grace (3:11; 5:14).

Theological Issues

To be in exile in the world is to be in the world, but not of the world. It is to establish values and goals for individual and corporate life that are conformed to the values and goals of God. Unfortunately this metaphor of exile does not resonate with many contemporary Christians. Often Christians naively assume that societal values are Christian, but clearly many societal values are not, particularly those based on the pursuit of material wealth, power, fame, and pleasure. Our culture has recently and rightly been labeled "post-Christian," and the metaphor of "exile" may more clearly resonate with faithful Christians whose values increasingly differ from those of the unredeemed. The purpose of being chosen by God is for obedience through the sanctifying work of the Spirit, obedience being one way the grace and peace of God are multiplied.

The triad of the Father, Son, and Spirit in 1 Peter is unique in the opening of a NT book (cf. Rom. 1:1–6). While a fully developed doctrine of the Trinity is not found here, this triad is shown to act jointly in the lives of Christians: God chooses Christians, the Spirit sanctifies them, and the blood of Jesus Christ atones for their sin. It is a threefold, coordinated effort of a loving God. This coordinated effort is the grace of God and, in conjunction with obedience, leads to peace and a life that is whole. It is a life with the problems that afflict all humankind, and perhaps more issues due to a Christian witness, as the rest of 1 Peter makes clear. However, it is a life in which no affliction can squelch the grace and peace of God.

1 Peter 1:3–12

Thanksgiving for God's Gift of Salvation

Introductory Matters

A thanksgiving typically follows the letter prescript (using "be thankful," *eucharisteō*: Rom. 1:8–15; 1 Cor. 1:4–9; Phil. 1:3–11; Col. 1:3–14; 1 Thess. 1:2–10; 2 Thess. 1:3–4; Philem. 4–7). Sometimes a blessing of God and the reasons God is worthy of praise follow (using "blessed," *eulogētos*: 2 Cor. 1:3–7; Eph. 1:3–23), as 1 Peter does here. Some understand this latter blessing to be a declaration that God is worthy of praise rather than an actual blessing of God—and the grammar can support this reading—but praise is more apropos and typical of letter thanksgivings. The thanksgiving/blessing also introduces topics to be developed in the letter (Schubert 1939), and here it introduces suffering and hope (Kendall 1986).

This blessing is one long and complex sentence. The prepositions followed by relative pronouns in verses 6 and 10 break the sentence into three parts, which guide the outline below.

> **1 Peter 1:3–12
> in the Rhetorical Flow**
>
> **God's provision for salvation, and Christians' status before God (1:1–2:10)**
>
> > The letter prescript: Establishing authority, identity, and goodwill (1:1–2)
> >
> > ▶ Thanksgiving for God's gift of salvation (1:3–12)
> >
> > > The blessing of God rooted in God's mercy (1:3–5)
> > >
> > > The joy of the salvation experienced and to be experienced (1:6–9)
> > >
> > > The past anticipation and the present experience of salvation now revealed (1:10–12)

Tracing the Train of Thought

The Blessing of God Rooted in God's Mercy (1:3–5)

1:3. The thanksgiving opens with a standard blessing characteristic of other early Christian works (2 Cor. 1:3; Eph. 1:3): **Blessed is the God and Father of our Lord Jesus Christ.** This could be translated "blessed be" (optative), but "blessed is" is preferred here as introducing God's benefactions (Elliott 2000, 330). God is defined in relation to Jesus Christ. God is God of Jesus Christ, the one who has sent, resurrected, and glorified Jesus in God's redemptive plan. God is also the Father of Jesus Christ, developing the family metaphor so prevalent in the letter (1:2, 14, 17, 23; 2:2).

The blessing of God is grounded in God's mercy: **By his great mercy he has given us a new birth** (1:3b). It is out of the mercy of God the Father that Christians have been born as God's children and can bless him (1:23; 2:2). A new birth (*anagennaō*) continues the family metaphor of God as Father and is synonymous with being sanctified by the Spirit and sprinkled with the blood of Christ (1:2; cf. 1:23; John 1:13; 3:3, 7; Titus 3:5; James 1:18; 1 John 2:29; 3:9; 4:7; 5:1, 4, 18).

The benefits for Christians given a new birth follow, each introduced with the preposition "into" (*eis*): a living hope (v. 3), an inheritance (v. 4), and salvation (v. 5). The first benefit of a new birth is **into a living hope through the resurrection of Jesus Christ from the dead** (1:3b). This hope is living because it is based on Christ's resurrection, the means by which God has made believers to be children through the new birth and the means by which baptism has its salvific power (3:21). The resurrection of Jesus secures eternal life and a living hope for all Christians (Rom. 6:4). By raising Jesus from the dead, God's intention to likewise raise Christians is demonstrated, and thus our hope is in God (1:21; 3:15; cf. 3:5; Cothenet 1980–81).

1:4. A second benefit of a new birth is to be brought **into an inheritance that is imperishable, undefiled, and unfading.** "Inheritance" (*klēronomia*) is a word used in the LXX for Israel's inheritance of the land of Canaan and a life of peace and prosperity (Jer. 2:7; Lam. 5:2; Jdt. 8:22; 2 Macc. 2:17). The affirmation that Christians have an inheritance is common in the NT (Rom. 8:14–17; Gal. 4:7; Eph. 1:14) but does not refer to physical land and kingdom as in the OT. Rather, the inheritance is the kingdom of God (Matt. 25:34; 1 Cor. 6:9–10; 15:50; Gal. 5:21; James 2:5) and its synonym, eternal life (Matt. 19:29; Mark 10:17; Luke 10:25; 18:18; Titus 3:7).

The Christian inheritance is described with three adjectives for incorruptible. Imperishable (*aphthartos*) is freedom from the possibility of corruption and decay, undefiled (*amiantos*) is being free from uncleanness or moral impurity, and unfading (*amarantos*) is being immune from losing a pristine quality through the wear and tear of time. Later, the recipients are described as ransomed from their futile ways, not with perishable things (*phthartos*) but with the faultless (*amōmos*) blood of Jesus (1:18–19), for an inheritance of life and blessing (3:7, 9).

The recipients are told that this inheritance is **kept in heaven for you** (1:4b; cf. Matt. 5:12; 6:19–20; Luke 12:33). Only an inheritance in heaven is safe from corruption and decay. The passive participle of the verb "kept" (*tēreō*) refers to God as the one preserving and guarding the inheritance; keeping is another aspect of God's mercy (1:3).

1:5. Christians are described as **those being guarded by God's power through faith** (1:5a). As the inheritance is kept by God (v. 4), the inheritors themselves are guarded by God through their continued faith (v. 5). Faith brings God's guarding power into Christians' lives (cf. 5:10). Faith is the total dependence upon and trust in God for salvation and resurrection (1:9, 21) and during times of trial (1:7; 5:9). Such trust is based on God's resurrection of Christ from his suffering to glorification (1:4, 21; 3:18–22). The reasons the recipients need to be guarded are the trials from their neighbors (3:13–4:6; 4:12–19) and the devil (5:8–9) that test their faith (1:6–7).

God's guard over the Christian is the third benefit of God's mercy, **for a salvation ready to be revealed in the last time** (1:5b). Salvation in 1 Peter is both present and future but expressed as mainly future. It has been made available through the suffering and death of Christ (1:2, 10–12, 17–22), can be presently experienced (1:9; 3:21), and needs to be revealed in its fullness (1:5, 9–10; 2:2). Salvation is a reality and will be fully experienced the moment that Christ and his glory are revealed (1:7, 13; 4:13; 5:1, 4), a revelation that is near, with the coming of the end of the ages and its accompanying judgment (1:20; 4:5–7, 17–18). This is the Christian hope (1:13, 21; 3:15).

The Joy of the Salvation Experienced and to Be Experienced (1:6–9)

1:6–7. The joy that Christians will have when their salvation is fully experienced is now described. **In this you rejoice** (1:6a) is a reference to the recipients as rejoicing in the salvation that will be revealed at the coming of Christ (1:5) and more broadly to the three mercies of God outlined in verses 3–5 (Elliott 2000, 338–39). The verb form (*agalliasthe*) can be translated as "rejoice" (present imperative) or "you rejoice" (present indicative; cf. 1:8). The latter translation is preferred because the author is not commanding the recipients to rejoice but is only observing their current rejoicing in God's mercies.

Some interpreters understand the rejoicing in this section to be future rejoicing in the salvation coming in the last time. "In this" (*en hō*) is understood as the time of the coming of Christ (v. 5), and the present tense of rejoicing is understood to have a future reference because confident assertions about the future can be written in the present tense (Michaels 1988, 27–28). However, this letter is written to help the recipients find joy and hope in their present situation of suffering, not in the future with the coming of Christ (cf. 4:13), and it does so by referring back to the mercies of God that can be celebrated in the present (vv. 3–5). Also, finding joy amid current suffering was a Christian (James 1:2–4) and Jewish topic (*2 Bar.* 52.6–7; *Sib. Or.* 5.269–70) and one to be immediately discussed here.

The recipients are told that rejoicing in the mercies and salvation of God continues, even **though now for a little while you must be distressed by diverse trials** (1:6b). The distress (*lypeō*) refers to the persecution that they are experiencing at the hands of their neighbors for being Christian. The distress is diverse because it involves their social, religious, and political lives, including exclusion from the social life of the community and trade guilds and the business opportunities they offer (see "Occasion and Purpose" in the introduction). The distress is for a little while because the coming of Jesus to reveal salvation is near (1:5; 5:9–10).

The word "must" (*dei*) in "must be distressed" frequently refers to God's will for the suffering of Christ (Mark 8:31 par.; Luke 17:25; 24:7, 26; John 3:14; 12:34; Acts 17:3) and of Christians (Acts 14:22). In this letter Christian suffering is well within the parameters of God's will (3:17; 4:19). Distress does not preclude rejoicing when it is viewed in the light of God's will. The recipients are informed that they are suffering trials **so that the genuineness of your faith** may be tested (1:7a). Their faithfulness in their relationship to God as their new Father, who has given them great mercies (1:3–5, 21), and to Jesus Christ (1:8–9; 2:6–7) is proved by trial (cf. 4:12). When persecuted by neighbors, the recipients can deny their faith and return to their gentile ways or continue in genuine faith.

Faith is described as **more valuable than gold that, though destructible, is tested by fire** (1:7b). This is a traditional comparison of the testing of faith and the refinement of gold and silver (Ps. 66:10; Prov. 17:3; 27:21; Zech. 13:9; Mal. 3:2–3; Sir. 2:5; Wis. 3:4–6). The recipients' faith is more precious than gold because gold is perishable and less precious than Christ's blood (1:18–19). Faith, and the inheritance and salvation that accompany it, are eternal (1:4–5). If gold is tested by fire, how much more will the more valuable commodity of indestructible faith be tested. This connection of suffering, testing, and joy is common in Jewish and Christian texts (4:12–13; Selwyn 1947, 439–58; Nauck 1955; Thomas 1968; Villiers 1975).

The desired outcome of the testing of the recipients' faith is that it **may be found for praise, glory, and honor at the revelation of Jesus Christ** (1:7c). Hopefully, after the suffering and the testing of the recipients, God will find their faith to be worthy of praise, glory, and honor at the revelation of Jesus Christ at the end of time (1:13; 4:13; 5:4). These rewards are part of the salvation revealed at the last time, for which Christians wait (1:5, 9–10). Praise is the admiration and approval of God. Glory is the splendor of God (4:11), conferred by grace on the Son (1:11, 21; 4:13) and on those God loves (1:7; 4:14; 5:1, 4, 10). Honor was a coveted commodity in the ancient world. It was the respect due to one's position in society, and here it is God's respect for Christians (cf. 2:6). Within the family metaphor that began this section (1:2–3), these are gifts from a father to his faithful children within his household (1:3); faithful children were also expected to give gifts to their father.

1:8. The recipients receive high praise for their stance toward Jesus Christ: **While not seeing him, you love him; while not seeing him now, you believe in him and rejoice with inexpressible and glorious joy.** While in the midst of suffering, testing, and waiting for their salvation to be revealed by Jesus Christ (v. 7), and while not seeing him now, surprisingly the recipients still love and believe in him—and even rejoice (cf. James 1:2)! Believing in God, Jesus, and the salvation to be revealed as superior to actually seeing and experiencing them now is a common theme in the NT (John 20:29; 2 Cor. 4:17–18; 5:6–7; Heb. 11:1–3; cf. 1 Cor. 2:9). Rejoicing is also part of both the present Christian life concurrent with loving and believing in Christ (1:6; 4:13) and the future, when he is revealed (4:13). It is not limited to the future, as some commentators claim (Michaels 1988, 34–35). Being inexpressible and glorious implies that this rejoicing is in part enabled by God, who will provide the salvation (1:5, 9; Achtemeier 1996, 103–4).

1:9. While enduring in their love for and faith in Christ amid their suffering and testing, the recipients are reminded that they rejoice **because you are receiving the outcome of faith, the salvation of your souls.** The recipients can rejoice now because they are already experiencing the salvation to be fully revealed with Christ on the last day (1:5, 7; cf. 2:2). The outcome (*telos*) of faith is the salvation of souls already in process. The soul (*psychē*) is not the soul in distinction from the body, to be rescued from imprisonment in the body at death, as in much Greek thought, but a person's essence or self-identity, as in OT thought. This innermost self is saved from suffering and death in a new birth for an imperishable inheritance (1:3–4; cf. 5:4). Eschatological reward awaiting those who love God is an important topic in NT theology (1 Cor. 2:9; 2 Cor. 5:10; Eph. 6:8; 2 Tim. 4:8; Heb. 10:35).

The Past Anticipation and the Present Experience of Salvation Now Revealed (1:10–12)

1:10–11. Verses 10–12 affirm that the prophets and angels anticipated and longed to witness the salvation that the recipients enjoy (vv. 5, 9, 12; Calloud 1980). They begin, **Concerning this salvation, the prophets who prophesied of the grace intended for you searched and carefully inquired** (1:10; cf. Matt. 13:17). Some interpreters understand the reference here to be early Christian prophets (Selwyn 1947, 134, 259–68; Warden 1989; Rigato 1990), but since the prophecy here has preceded Christ's incarnation (v. 11) and the prophets did not experience this salvation (v. 12), this is not possible. Rather, most interpreters understand the prophets to be those from ancient Israel who besought God about the nature of the grace about which they were prophesying. Grace is virtually synonymous with salvation (1:5, 9, 13), being all that God gives to bring about redemption (1:2, 13; 3:7; 4:10; 5:5, 10, 12), and is fully experienced at the time when Jesus Christ and the salvation he brings are revealed (1:13).

These prophets were **inquiring what kind of person or what kind of time the Spirit of Christ within them was indicating** (1:11a). Through the Spirit of Christ the prophets prophesied about Christ, but they did not know the nature of Christ or the historical circumstances in which he would be manifested. In prophetic and apocalyptic literature we see the tradition of the prophets' asking when their prophecies would be fulfilled (Dan. 12:5–13; 2 Esd. [*4 Ezra*] 4:33–5:13).

The phrase "Spirit of Christ," which describes the spirit at work in the prophets, does not designate Christian-era prophets rather than prophets of the OT, as some suggest (see 1:10 above). No distinction can be made between the Holy Spirit and Christ before his incarnation. Even after the incarnation, Paul in Romans interchanges "Spirit of God," "Spirit of Christ," and "Christ" (8:9–11), and similar interchange is found elsewhere (Acts 16:7; Gal. 4:6; Phil. 1:19). By the second century, it was a common understanding that OT prophets were inspired by Christ to prophesy about him (*Barn.* 5.6; *2 Clem.* 17.4; Ign. *Magn.* 8.2; 9.2; Justin, *1 Apol.* 31–53; Irenaeus, *Haer.* 4.20.4).

The prophets were inquiring about the nature of the Christ and the timing of his appearance **while they were witnessing beforehand to the sufferings of Christ and the glory to follow** (1:11b). In this summary of messianic prophecies, the suffering and glory of Christ are inseparable, as they are in Jesus's postresurrection pronouncement to his disciples that the OT messianic prophecy of suffering and glory had been fulfilled (Luke 24:25–27). Suffering was essential to Christ's mission on earth, and his current glory is to be revealed in the future (4:13; 5:1). The suffering of the Messiah and his eventual glorification are not an explicit OT concept but are implied in Isa. 52:13–53:12 and in 1 Pet. 2:21–25 (cf. Heb. 2:9–10).

"Glory" (*doxai*) is plural and difficult to translate, but the plural is meant to show that the glories of Christ surpass his sufferings. Glory certainly includes Christ's resurrection (1:3, 21; 3:22), his announcement of victory to the imprisoned spirits during his ascension (3:18–21), his enthronement at the right hand of God (3:22), and the revelation of salvation and his glory to the world at his return (1:7, 13; 4:13; 5:1).

1:12. It is affirmed about the prophets that **it was revealed to them that they were not an intermediary of these matters for themselves, but for you** (1:12a). "Revealed" (*apokalyptō*) is a theological passive and indicates that God or the Spirit of Christ (v. 11) revealed to the prophets that they were intermediaries for the recipients of this letter. The idea that the OT prophets and the OT in general ministered and spoke for later Christian believers, even more than for the original audiences, is common in Paul's Epistles (Rom. 4:23–25; 15:4; 1 Cor. 9:9–10; 10:11). The new element here is that the prophets actually knew through revelation that their prophecies pertained to a time beyond their own.

The recipients are told that the prophets were intermediaries of matters **that have now been announced to you by those who proclaimed the gospel to you through the Holy Spirit sent from heaven** (1:12b). The preaching of the prophets about the suffering and glorification of Christ was the content of the gospel that the recipients heard from the apostles and evangelists who came to them (1:25). These proclaimers of the gospel came by means of the Holy Spirit sent by God (or Christ; 3:22). In the NT, either God (John 14:16, 26; Gal. 4:6) or Jesus (John 15:26; 16:7; Acts 2:33) sends the Spirit.

This proclamation is described as **matters that angels desire to investigate!** (1:12c). The idea that certain heavenly mysteries are hidden even from angels who dwell in heaven is found in Jewish apocalyptic literature (e.g. *1 En.* 16.3; *2 En.* 24.3), the NT (Mark 13:32; Eph. 3:10), and early Christian literature (*Ep. Apos.* 19). The angels are curious about the salvation now revealed and are longing to investigate it closely. The implication is that the recipients of the letter are in a very privileged position indeed—better than that of prophets and angels!

Theological Issues

The activity of God, working in mercy and power, is central to this section. Through God's mercy, Christians are born again and given the assured hope of a permanent inheritance kept in heaven by God. In the meantime, as we wait for that inheritance and the fullness of the salvation that is ours, God guards us through God's power.

This rebirth and inheritance are founded on the mercy of God as expressed in God's resurrection of Jesus from the dead. Jesus's resurrection is the means by which we too can be born again from the power of sin and death. While awaiting the full experience of our salvation and receiving our inheritance, our continued faith and trust in God is the means by which God's power to guard us becomes effective in our lives.

Suffering and rejoicing are natural companions in our Christian life. Suffering tests our faith, but when this testing is complete, God gives us praise, glory, and honor when Christ returns to reveal our full salvation. This promise, this wonder that will one day be ours as a gift of God's grace, gives breath to our rejoicing, which cannot be squelched by life's struggles.

Better yet, this salvation is ours in part now. We receive it the day we accept God's offer of grace in Jesus Christ and will fully receive it on the day of Christ's return. This experience of salvation allows us to love and believe in Christ even though we cannot see him now and to rejoice with great joy without having to wait until this salvation is fully revealed.

This salvation is not something new but has been part of the redemptive plan of God from the beginning. The prophets of Israel prophesied about it, as did the apostles who founded the church. It was planned and executed by God for the benefit of the recipients of the letter and all Christians. It is what motivates our rejoicing and blessing of God.

1 Peter 1:13–21

The Call and Motivation to Holiness

Introductory Matters

First Peter 1:13–2:10 concerns personal and corporate holiness as required by the eschatological hope of salvation spelled out in the epistolary prescript and thanksgiving in 1:1–12. The ethics required by this eschatological hope as rooted in the personal and corporate holiness of the faith community are detailed in 2:11–4:11.

This discussion of holiness commences in 1:13–21 with a call to holiness (vv. 13–16) and motivation to respond to the call to holiness (vv. 17–21). This section begins and ends with references to hope, forming an *inclusio* (1:13, 21), demonstrating that hope is the basis for instruction in holiness. This "living hope" is grounded in the resurrection of Christ (1:3) and defined as an "inheritance" (1:4), "salvation" (1:5, 9, 10), and "praise, glory, and honor at the revelation of Jesus Christ" (1:7). The living hope is the reason and motivation for the recipients' ethical walk (Cothenet 1980–81). (For a thorough discussion of 1:13–25, see Prasad 2000.)

> **1 Peter 1:13–21 in the Rhetorical Flow**
>
> **God's provision for salvation, and Christians' status before God (1:1–2:10)**
>
> > The letter prescript: Establishing authority, identity, and goodwill (1:1–2)
> >
> > Thanksgiving for God's gift of salvation (1:3–12)
> >
> > ▶ **The call and motivation to holiness (1:13–21)**
> >
> > > The call to holiness (1:13–16)
> > >
> > > The motivation to holiness (1:17–21)

31

Tracing the Train of Thought

The Call to Holiness (1:13–16)

Five exhortations on holiness that should characterize the recipients' current lives as God's children now contrast the desires that characterized their pre-Christian lives. The same contrast occurs with different wording in the exhortation opening the second section of the letter (2:11–12), indicating the importance of the ethical life.

1:13. The conjunction **therefore** (*dio*) bases the exhortations to follow on the mercies of God just described in the thanksgiving of 1:3–12. The first exhortation is **prepare your mind for work** (1:13a). The literal reading is "bind up the waist of your mind," referring metaphorically to tucking the hem of a garment under the belt worn at the waist, to facilitate physical labor. It would be comparable to our expression "roll up your sleeves." A similar expression is "gird up your loins" (Exod. 12:11; Job 38:3; 40:7; Nah. 2:1) and describes the preparation of Christians for the second coming of Christ (Luke 12:35). "Your" is plural and "mind" is singular, which acts to call the recipients to work as a corporate body rather than rallying each member to his or her own individual effort (cf. Phil. 1:27; 2:2). The second exhortation, **be self-controlled** (*nēphō*; 1:13b), is a virtue associated with the first exhortation because self-control certainly requires work and determination. It is also a virtue necessary for keeping prayers unhindered while awaiting the end (4:7) and keeping alert to the wiles of the devil while suffering (5:8).

The third exhortation is **hope completely in grace being brought to you at the revelation of Jesus Christ** (1:13c). It begins with the adverb "completely" (*teleiōs*), which grammatically can go with either the second or third exhortation: "be completely self-controlled" or "hope completely." Adverbs ending in *-ōs* usually follow the word they modify, which would indicate the former possibility. However, theologically, hope can be fully placed only in the grace of God, which is imperishable and protected by God in heaven (1:4–5). Also, the grace being hoped for is "brought" (*pherō*), a theological passive indicating that God brings it. Thus the second alternative is preferred: "completely" applies to the hope fully secure in the grace guarded and brought by God when God fully reveals Jesus Christ (1:7; 4:13; 5:4).

The subjects of these exhortations are related. Hope in the grace to be revealed at Christ's appearance motivates work and self-control. This grace is already experienced in part by the recipients (4:10; 5:12) in their faith and salvation, which brings them current joy (1:8–9) and provides a foundation for hope in salvation's eventual fulfillment when Christ returns. The recipients have been born into a living hope (1:3) and are now exhorted to conform their behavior accordingly.

1:14–16. The fourth and fifth exhortations are employed in a contrast to better define the nature of the ethical life that Christian hope requires. The contrast begins by establishing the status of the recipients **as obedient children** (1:14a). The recipients are children because they have been born anew (1:3, 23; 2:2) and can call God their Father (1:17). They are obedient because they have accepted the gospel as proclaimed to them (1:8–9, 12). Obedience to God in conformity with Christ's example is a main topic of the letter (1:2, 14–17, 22; 2:1, 8, 11–20; 3:1–6, 13–17; 4:1–6, 13–19; 5:1–11).

The negative exhortation in the contrast is **Do not be shaped by the desires of your previous ignorance** (1:14b). These desires or passions (*epithymiai*) are not just sexual desires but all kinds of self-seeking—whether for personal pleasure, greater power, or more wealth—such as characterize the life of the unredeemed (4:2–3; Mark 4:19; Rom. 1:24; Eph. 4:22; 1 Thess. 4:5). The recipients indulged in these desires when they were in ignorance (*agnoia*), which is not a lack of knowledge per se but ignorance of what is right in religion and morality. It is rebellion against God, common to all those who do not have God's law (Wis. 13:1; 14:22; 15:11) or have not accepted the gospel and become obedient (2:15; Acts 3:17; 17:30–31; Eph. 4:18; cf. Gal. 4:8–10). The recipients are to remain obedient to their new Father rather than revert to being children of ignorance and rebellion (4:2–3).

The positive exhortation of the contrast is **Rather, as the one who called you is holy, be yourselves holy in everything you do** (1:15). God "called" (*kaleō*) the recipients: as a person in authority, God chooses others for a designated status and work (BDAG 503). "Called" refers to Christians as those summoned to salvation, discipleship, and witness (Rom. 1:1–6; Gal. 1:15). God as Father has chosen the recipients as children (1:2–3) and called them from darkness to light (2:9). God is holy and wholly separate from evil (Isa. 1:4; 40:25), and Christians should be holy as well (2:5, 9). As chosen by God, they are being sanctified by the Spirit for obedience (1:2). In the repetition of this contrast of 1:14–15 in 2:11–12, "holy" is replaced by the synonymous phrase "good works." Being holy in conduct is doing what is right, especially when suffering (2:12–15, 20; 3:9–17; 4:15–19).

A quotation of Lev. 19:2 LXX supports the exhortation to holy conduct: **As it is written, "Be holy because I am holy"** (1:16; cf. Lev. 11:44–45; 19:2; 20:7–8, 26). The quotation comes from the Holiness Code (Lev. 17–26), which admonishes Israel to live differently from its gentile neighbors, as here Peter admonishes the new holy people (cf. 2:9).

The Motivation to Holiness (1:17–21)

This section provides factors that motivate the recipients to heed the call to holiness. It refines the topics of hope in God and the need to conduct life according to that hope as it is defined in 1:13–16.

1:17. A premise and conclusion begin the section. The premise is **If you call upon a Father who judges impartially according to the work of each** (1:17a). God as Father continues the family metaphor (1:2–3, 14) and is expected in a patriarchal culture, where the father is the supreme authority in the family. The God that the recipients call Father in prayer (cf. Matt. 6:9//Luke 11:2) is the final judge of every human being (cf. 2:12, 23; 4:5; Rom. 14:10–12; 1 Cor. 3:10–15; 2 Cor. 5:10–11). Judaism and early Christianity understood that God's judgment is impartial (*aprosōpolēmptōs*; Deut. 10:17–18; 2 Chron. 19:7; Acts 10:34; Rom. 2:11). The judicial system of that day was rife with bribes and judgments that favored the rich. The more status and wealth a person had, the more likely the verdict was to go in that person's favor. Rather than status and bribes, God's judgment is according to works (Ps. 62:12; Prov. 24:12; 1 Cor. 3:10–15; Rom. 2:1–11; 2 Cor. 5:10; Rev. 20:12; 22:12).

The conclusion to this premise is **then conduct yourself in fear** (1:17b). Because God judges impartially based on works, the recipients are advised to conduct their lives with a fear or reverence toward God until the grace they hope for is fully realized (1:13, 21; cf. 2:17). Fear (*phobos*) is not terror, for God is a loving Father, but is a healthy respect of God's sovereignty as the Creator and Judge (4:17, 19). God will judge their holy conduct, the works that Christians prepare their minds to perform (1:13, 15).

Continuing the exile metaphor from 1:1, the recipients are told to fear God **during the time of your exile** (1:17c). They are children currently in exile from their Father but must conduct themselves in ways that honor their Father, with whom they will one day be united and by whom they will be judged. This exile is a time in which they might conform to the desires of their preconversion ignorance (1:14; cf. 2:11), so conduct must be carefully guarded. Although it has been argued that exile (*paroikia*) is a social/political designation for foreigners living for an extended time in a foreign land (Elliott 1990, 37–49; 2000, 366–69), here exile is actually a spiritual designation for Christians away from their heavenly home (see "Recipients" in the introduction).

1:18–19. The work of God for the redemption through Jesus Christ is now given in 1:18–21 as the motivation for living in reverent fear of God. We begin with the phrase **You know** (*eidotes*; 1:18a), reminding the recipients what they know from tradition, which is a typical way in the NT to provide the basis for a preceding imperative (1 Cor. 15:58; Eph. 6:8, 9; Col. 3:24; 4:1; James 3:1). Here the recipients' knowledge of the work of God for redemption provides the basis for all the imperatives of 1:13–17 involving their obedience.

Reminding them of their tradition, the recipients are told **You were ransomed** (*elytrōthēte*; 1:18b). This theological passive indicates that God does the ransoming. The same verb is used in the LXX to describe God's ransom or redemption of Israel from bondage and slavery in Egypt and Babylon (Exod. 6:6; 15:13; Deut. 7:8; 9:26; 15:15; 24:18; Isa. 44:22–23; 51:11; 52:3) and in the NT for Jesus's redeeming humanity from sin and bondage (Luke 24:21; Titus 2:14) in which he is a ransom (*lytron*) for many

Manumission of Slaves

A third party can buy a slave from his or her master, and that slave becomes a slave of the third party. Or the third party can buy the freedom of a slave and become a patron of the newly freed slave, who is now a client of the patron for life. In the NT these images are often intertwined. Christ's death paid the purchase price to free all people from slavery to sin so that God is now their patron and they his clients, and/or God is now the Master and they the slaves (Rom. 6:16–22; 1 Cor. 6:19–20; 7:22–24; Gal. 5:1; Col. 4:1; Lyall 1984, 38–46). Romans is illustrative: "For just as you once presented your members as slaves to impurity and to greater and greater iniquity, so now present your members as slaves to righteousness for sanctification" (6:19b).

(Mark 10:45//Matt. 20:28; cf. Mark 14:24). The verb describes the manumission of slaves (BDAG 606).

The recipients are told that the ransom God has provided is to free them **from the empty living inherited from your forebears** (1:18c). Living (*anastrophē*) is a way of life, including attitudes, values, commitments, and goals. The recipients' former living is characterized as empty, fruitless, or useless (*mataia*), a common Jewish and Christian characterization of pagan life (Jer. 2:5 LXX; Acts 14:15; Rom. 1:21; Eph. 4:17), discussed in more detail in 4:1–4. This empty way of life was inherited from forebears (*patroparadotos*). Ordinarily in this culture, living according to the ways of the ancestors would be wise counsel, but here this way of living is empty because it does not know God (1:14) and is guided by the desires of flesh (2:11; 4:2–4). This empty living contrasts with the holy living (*anastrophē*) that characterizes the recipients' lives as children obeying a new Father (1:15) and living (*anastrophē*) in reverent fear of God the Judge (1:17), that is, living according to the ways inherited from their new Father (1:3–4, 14, 17).

God paid this ransom from empty living **not with perishable things like silver or gold** (1:18c), which would normally be used for a sacral manumission, **but with the precious blood of Christ** (1:19a). God used the blood of Christ as the price to ransom the recipients because it has redemptive power (1:2; Rom. 3:21–26; Eph. 1:7; Heb. 9:11–14; Rev. 1:5; 1 Clem 7.4). Christ is **like an unblemished and spotless lamb** (1:19b), thus worthy of sacrifice to God; this is a general image drawn from the sacrificial cult of Israel, where only perfect animals could be sacrificed (Exod. 29:1; Lev. 22:17–25; Num. 28–29).

The imagery in verses 18–19 is drawn from the sacrificial system of Israel in general and possibly from specific OT texts. One possibility is Isa. 52:3 LXX: "You were sold for nothing, and you will be redeemed without money."

Whereas in Isaiah redemption is without money, here the price of redemption is with blood. The other possibility is the Passover lamb, described as "perfect" in Exod. 12:5 LXX and clearly tied to Jesus and his redemptive death in the Johannine (John 1:29, 36; 19:36) and Pauline (1 Cor. 5:7) traditions. The Passover celebrates God's liberation of Israel from slavery and here is celebrated as God's ransoming Christians from empty living.

1:20. Elaborating the nature of Christ's sacrifice, it is affirmed that **He was chosen before the foundation of the world, but was revealed in the last of the ages for your sake.** As the theological passives indicate, Christ was "chosen" (*proginōskō*) by God long before the creation of the world (John 17:24) and is now "revealed" (*phaneroō*) by God at the end of the world, the last of the ages, in accord with God's purposes. These purposes are indicated by prophets sent beforehand with the message of salvation and the suffering and death of Christ (1:10–12). According to Judaism and early Christianity, God has a plan for salvation that underlies world history (Matt. 13:35; 25:34). The plan is a mystery that was announced and is now revealed in Christ (Rom. 16:25–26; 1 Cor. 2:7–13; Eph. 3:3–11; Col. 1:26; 2 Tim. 1:9–10; Titus 1:2–3; Ign. *Magn.* 6.1; *2 Clem.* 14.2; *Herm. Sim.* 12.2–3).

In God's plan the revelation of Christ was in the last of the ages, a phrase that assumes that world history is a succession of specific ages (2 Esd. [*4 Ezra*] 12:9; *2 Bar.* 13.3). The last age is inaugurated by Jesus's life and ministry (Acts 2:16–21; 1 Cor. 10:11; Heb. 1:2; 9:26). The revelation of the Messiah in the last age is part of Jewish apocalyptic expectation that the messiah is waiting in heaven to be revealed when it is appropriate in the plan of God (*1 En.* 48.6; 62.7; 2 Esd. [*4 Ezra*] 12:32; 13:52). The last of the ages is to be followed by the consummation of all things, when salvation is revealed in full (1:5, 13), God brings judgment (4:5–6, 17), and Christians are rewarded (1:7)—and the end is near (4:7, 17).

1:21. Having just described the work that Christ has fulfilled in the plan of God (1:18–20), the recipients are informed what this means for their spiritual lives: **Through him you have faith in God, who raised him from the dead and gave him glory, so that your faith and hope are in God.** The work of God in Christ, which culminates in his resurrection and glorification, is the basis for the recipients' faith and hope in God for their own salvation, resurrection, and glorification (1:3–5; 3:18, 21–22). "In God" begins and ends the sentence in Greek to emphasize that God is the basis for this faith and hope.

That God has raised Jesus from the dead is taught elsewhere in the NT (Acts 2:32; 3:15; 4:10; 13:30; Rom. 4:24; 8:11; 10:9; 1 Cor. 6:14; 15:15; 2 Cor. 4:14; Gal. 1:1; Eph. 1:20; Col. 2:12; 1 Thess. 1:10), as is God's glorification of Jesus, usually expressed as exalting Jesus to God's right hand (Acts 2:33; 5:31; Rom. 8:34; Eph. 1:20; Col. 3:1; Heb. 1:3; 8:1; 10:12; 12:2). Yet the formulaic combination of resurrection and glorification found here is unique in the NT (cf. Acts 3:13, 15).

Theological Issues

The hope in the grace that Jesus Christ will bring when he returns motivates Christians to have a mind that is ready to work and to be self-controlled. We want to be obedient children of God who, knowing better than to fall back into the ignorance of our former lives, seek to be holy like our new Father. Striving for holiness is presented in corporate terms. This holiness is to be exhibited in all aspects of our lives as we conduct all our interactions with good works and reverence, not selfish desires. We imitate our Father and live in such a way that the family resemblance is clear. The "you" here is plural—the entire community of faith needs to be striving together for holiness (vv. 15–16). Sanctification and obedience (1:2) can be fully developed only in community.

As we strive for holiness, we are commanded to live in reverent fear of God, who is the Judge. Too often we rely on the phrase "once saved, always saved" as a justification for indulging in our favorite sins, but God judges both Christians and non-Christians for the way they live (4:17). A loving Father might have to discipline and shame us on the day of judgment if we are not living in reverent fear.

A dynamic contrast hinted at in the thanksgiving (1:4) is made explicit here and runs throughout the remainder of the letter: what is empty and perishable versus what is precious and imperishable. God ransoms us from empty and futile living, which is the plight of those without God, and instead provides the precious blood of Christ (1:19), which brings an inheritance that is imperishable, undefiled, and unfading (1:4). We are born anew through the imperishable seed of the living and enduring word of God (1:23), a word that endures forever (1:25). We are called to "a living stone," which is precious in God's sight (2:4, 6–7), and our reward is a crown of glory that never fades (5:4).

We live in the tension between our initial experience of salvation and the ultimate experience of it at death or Christ's return. We need to remember the great lengths that God took to bring us salvation: even before creating the world, God was planning to ransom us from empty living, with its destructive desires (1:14, 18). This plan is now revealed in the last of the ages. Through the knowledge that God raised Jesus from the dead and glorified him, we can firmly set our faith and hope in God.

1 Peter 1:22–25

Born Anew by the Word of God for Mutual Love

Introductory Matters

Based on the assumption that the recipients are obedient to the truth and are born again by the word of God, they are exhorted to mutual love (1:22). As born-again children of God, they are to love the rest of the family (1:3, 14, 17). This new birth is through the imperishable seed, the word of God that endures forever, as affirmed in Isa. 40:6–8 and announced to the recipients here (1:23–25).

Tracing the Train of Thought

1:22. The positive assumption, **having purified your souls by obedience to the truth** (1:22a), continues the association of purification and obedience found in the letter prescript, where the Spirit sanctifies Christians for obedience to Jesus and for sprinkling with his blood (1:2). Obedience to the truth is accepting the gospel, the word of God, and its truth (1:12) in contrast to continuing to live in what is false (James 4:8; 1 John 3:3)—like the desires of their previous ignorance (1:14) and empty living inherited from the

---

> ### 1 Peter 1:22–25 in the Rhetorical Flow
>
> **God's provision for salvation, and Christians' status before God (1:1–2:10)**
>
> > The letter prescript: Establishing authority, identity, and goodwill (1:1–2)
> >
> > Thanksgiving for God's gift of salvation (1:3–12)
> >
> > The call and motivation to holiness (1:13–21)
> >
> > ▶ Born anew by the word of God for mutual love (1:22–25)

38

Love of Family

The love of family members by blood was an important virtue in the world of the recipients (Malina 1993, 117–48). Plutarch's discussion of the love between brothers is illustrative: "Now, as regards parents, brotherly love is of such sort that to love one's brother is forthwith a proof of love for both mother and father; and again, as regards children, for them there is no lesson and example comparable to brotherly love on their father's part" (Plutarch, *De fraterno amore*, in *Mor.* 480F). Love of family members has been applied more broadly here (1:22) and elsewhere to the members of the household of God (Mark 3:35//Matt. 12:50//Luke 8:21).

forebearers (1:18). It is being holy in conduct as God is holy (1:15–16) and rejecting vices (2:1).

A word of caution: The recipients were purified by their obedient acceptance of the living word preached to them (1:12, 23–25), not by obedience that followed conversion as they worked to be holy like God (1:15; contra Achtemeier 1996, 136–37). Their obedience led to conversion and purification by the Spirit. To make this point clearer, some scribes added "through the Spirit" to this phrase in the ancient manuscripts.

This purification by the Spirit has a very positive consequence: **so that you have genuine mutual love** (1:22b). Having been purified by the Spirit by accepting the gospel, the recipients are now able to genuinely love others. Mutual love is the reason why their souls have been purified. Being purified is part of being born into a new family (1:2–3, 14, 23), and love of the family members is expected (2:17).

In light of the assumption that the recipients were purified for obedience to the truth so they can have genuine mutual love, the recipients are encouraged to **eagerly love one another from the heart** (1:22c; cf. 2:17; 3:8; 4:8). This mutual love is to be expressed eagerly or constantly (*ektenōs*) from the heart, not just when convenient or easy (4:8). Mutual love is a common topic in the teaching and moral exhortation in the NT (Rom. 12:9–10; 13:8; Gal. 5:14; 1 Thess. 4:9–10; Heb. 13:1; 1 John 2:10; 3:10–11, 14, 23; 4:7, 11–12, 20–21). Some manuscripts read "pure heart" here, a reading that elaborates the sense of the verse but does not change its meaning.

1:23. The recipients are reminded that **You have been born again, not from perishable seed, but from imperishable seed through the living and abiding word of God**. The thanksgiving introduced the new birth (*anagennaō*) as a gift of God's mercy through the resurrection of Jesus Christ from the dead to a living hope (1:3). The recipients have been ransomed from empty living not with perishable things but with the precious blood of Christ (1:18–19). These topics are now combined, retaining the contrast between the perishable and the imperishable.

As in the parable of the sower, the seed is the word (*logos*) of God (Mark 4:14// Luke 8:11). All that is from human procreation is transitory (cf. 1:18), in contrast to the dynamic and permanent nature of the word of God, which is the power of God, bringing life and salvation into the world through the proclamation of Jesus Christ (John 6:63, 68; 1 Cor. 1:18; Phil. 2:16; Heb. 4:12; cf. 1 John 3:9).

The translation here can be either "living word of God" or "word of the living God." Some interpreters prefer the latter because the "living God" is used in the OT and NT to contrast God with the lifeless idols of paganism (Acts 14:15; 1 Thess. 1:9; Heb. 9:14). However, since idolatry is not the focus here, the following quotation from Isa. 40:6–8 emphasizes the enduring nature of the word of God, and early Christian tradition describes the word of God as living and abiding (Heb. 4:12; 1 John 1:1; 2:14), the former translation is preferred (contra Michaels 1988, 76–77).

1:24–25a. A quote of Isa. 40:6–8 LXX further supports the point that the word of God is living and abiding (using *rhēma*, a synonym for *logos*, which appears in v. 23): **For, "All flesh is as grass and all its glory as a flower of the grass; the grass withers and the flower falls, but the word of the Lord abides forever."** The quotation continues the contrast between the perishable and imperishable that is so central to the rhetoric of this letter (1:7, 18–19, 23), here contrasting the living and abiding word of God with humanity as perishable seed, analogous to perishable plant life (cf. Mark 13:31//Matt. 24:35//Luke 21:33). The image of humanity as transitory as grass or a flower that withers is common in the OT (Job 14:1–2; 15:30; Ps. 102:11; Isa. 51:12; Jer. 12:4). The glory of the flesh, the accomplishments of Roman and Greek culture and humanity in general, fades in contrast to the permanent word of God. The faithful are born anew by God's word and will one day experience glory from God (1:7; 4:13; 5:1, 4), a glory that Christ now enjoys (1:11, 21).

1:25b. In 1:25a the quotation of Isa. 40:6–8 LXX substitutes "Lord" (*kyrios*) for "God" (*theos*). In light of 1:10–12, where the OT prophets prophesied about the sufferings and glory of Christ, it may be assumed here that Isaiah prophesied about the word of the Lord as proclaimed in the gospel to the recipients. This assumption is supported by the identification of the word (*rhēma*): **This word is the gospel preached to you.** The word of God as embodied in and proclaimed by Jesus Christ and now proclaimed as the gospel is the enduring truth that has purified the recipients and enabled their new birth (1:22–23), as anticipated by Isaiah (Schutter 1989, 124–29). The recipients enjoy a salvation that is part of the long plan of God (1:10–12, 20).

Theological Issues

Being purified and born anew is effected through obedience to the truth and the living and permanent word of God. It is not in the glory of the flesh, with its perishable inheritance (cf. 1:4), desires of ignorance (1:14), or inherited empty living (1:18). This new status before God, this new reality of the new birth, allows Christians to love one another. It is in the creation of a new family of God in which God is Father, Jesus is his Son, and we are God's children (1:2–3, 14, 17) that we can love others as family members (2:17; 3:8; 4:8). This mutual love is surely understood by the recipients as "nurturing the bonds of affection, being generous and unstinting in the material and emotional support of fellow believers, being respectful of those in authority, avoiding familial strife, maintaining the solidarity of the household, offering hospitality, and conduct in the public arena that will bring honor to both the family and its heavenly father" (Elliott 2000, 385; cf. Elliott 1990, 165–266; Richard 2004).

1 Peter 2:1–3

Growing into Salvation

Introductory Matters

The conjunction "therefore" (*oun*) that opens this section is used elsewhere to introduce an imperative based on what has already been said (4:1, 7; 5:1, 6). Here it indicates that the commandments to follow are a direct consequence of having purified souls and being born again (1:22–25) and more broadly of everything discussed since the letter began.

Tracing the Train of Thought

2:1. Based on their new status as purified and born again by the living and abiding word of God, for the purpose of holiness and genuine mutual love (1:16, 22–25), the recipients are exhorted: **Therefore rid yourselves of all ill will, all deceit, pretenses, jealousies, and all slanders.** This is a call to the recipients to conform their behavior to the spiritual reality that they have left the desires and empty living that once characterized their lives (1:14, 18; cf. 2:11), here described with a vice list (cf. 4:3, 15).

> **1 Peter 2:1–3 in the Rhetorical Flow**
>
> God's provision for salvation, and Christians' status before God (1:1–2:10)
>
> > The letter prescript: Establishing authority, identity, and goodwill (1:1–2)
> >
> > Thanksgiving for God's gift of salvation (1:3–12)
> >
> > The call and motivation to holiness (1:13–21)
> >
> > Born anew by the word of God for mutual love (1:22–25)
> >
> > ▶ Growing into salvation (2:1–3)

Virtue-and-Vice Lists

The virtue-and-vice lists are literary forms common in Greco-Roman, Jewish, and Christian moral instruction. They originated in Stoic ethical teaching and reflect the moral conventions of the Hellenistic world. They were used for a variety of purposes, including instruction, exhortation, polemic, and apology. Plutarch's remarks about wealth are illustrative: "But money cannot buy peace of mind, greatness of spirit, serenity, confidence, and self-sufficiency" (*On the Love of Wealth*, in *Mor.* 523D). Within the NT, virtue-and-vice lists are adapted to the needs of the rhetorical situations addressed (e.g., Gal. 5:19–23; 2 Pet. 1:5–7; Aune 2003, 89–91).

The main verb in this vice list, "rid" (*apotithēmi*), is metaphorical and suggests "taking off" clothing (other clothing metaphors: 1:13; 4:1; 5:5). The verb is used for ridding oneself of sin (Eph. 4:22; Heb. 12:1–2), often in lists of vices (Rom. 13:12–13; Eph. 4:25–32; Col. 3:8; James 1:21). In early baptismal liturgies, the candidates removed their old clothing before baptism and put on new clothing afterward to symbolize their cleansing.

The list begins with the two general vices of ill will, or wickedness (*kakia*), and deceit (*dolos*). Ill will is something contrary to social and religious conventions. Deceit is the opposite of obedience to the truth (1:22) and the "deceitless" (*adolos*) spiritual milk (2:2). Christ is later upheld as a model of one without deceit (*dolos*, 2:22). These general vices cover many unethical behaviors and are later used together in regard to speech (3:9–12).

To these two general vices are added the three more specific ones of pretenses (*hypokrisis*) and jealousies (*phthonos*), which are forms of deceit, and slander (*katalalia*), which is a form of ill will. Pretenses are hypocrisy, the opposite of genuine (*anypokritos*) mutual love (1:22). Jealousies are envy of the success or possessions of others. It was one of the primary vices of that culture, in which goods were in limited supply and those who had more were envied (Malina 1993, 90–116). Slander is insulting others to inflict emotional or social harm. This was common in the culture, where competition for honor played such an important role. One way to aggressively move forward in society was to slander others who ranked above you.

It is uncertain if these vices merely illustrate behavior that is not compatible with mutual love or are a problem for the recipients, but there is some indication of the latter. The first vice of ill will appears throughout the letter in exhortation not to do evil or return evil (2:12, 14–16; 3:9–13, 17; 4:15). The recipients are victims of slander by their non-Christian neighbors and may have been tempted to respond in kind rather than to leave such slander

Honor Challenges

Honor challenges are prevalent throughout the NT. Of particular note are the attempts of the Sanhedrin to trap Jesus in theological debate and lessen his honor in the eyes of the crowds. A fine example is Mark 11:27–33. Members of the Sanhedrin challenge Jesus's honor by demanding that he reveal by whose authority he conducts his ministry, particularly in cleansing the temple. Jesus knows they will reject his answer of relying on God's authority, so he counterchallenges their honor by demanding that they answer his question before he answers theirs: "Did the baptism of John come from heaven, or was it of human origin?" They can neither affirm divine origin without showing their hypocrisy in not having believed John nor affirm human origin without alienating the crowd, who revere John. Either way they lose honor, so their opting to answer "We do not know" shows that the honor they receive for being teachers is not warranted if they cannot answer a simple question. In the end, Jesus actually gains honor for baffling his challengers!

without foundation (2:12, 15; 3:13, 16). Christ's example of nonretaliation is upheld for all the recipients (2:20–23).

2:2–3. The negative exhortation, to be rid of five vices that impede genuine mutual love, is followed by a positive one, with an accompanying purpose and reason. The exhortation is **Like a newborn baby, long for the pure spiritual milk** (2:2a). The metaphor of being born anew (1:3, 23) and then of childhood in the Christian family (1:14) continues but with the more specific image of a newborn baby's longing for the mother's milk and the physical and moral growth that follows (Francis 1980; Tite 2009). The predominance of this metaphor does not mean that the recipients are all new Christians, for it is not the age of the Christians in Christ that is the point of the comparison but their desire for growth as Christians. As a baby desires the mother's milk, so the Christian should long for spiritual milk. The proper longing or deep desire (*epipotheō*) is for Christ and spiritual milk, not the desires (*epithymiai*) that have controlled the recipients in the past (1:14; 2:11; 4:2–3). Within the metaphor is the image of Christians suckling at the breast of Christ, one of the few feminine images of the Godhead in the Bible (cf. *Odes Sol.* 8.13–16; 19.1–4; 35.5).

But what is pure spiritual milk? Elsewhere in the NT milk is a metaphor for elementary teaching given to new converts, to be followed by more mature teaching (1 Cor. 3:2; Heb. 5:12–14), but this cannot be the meaning here because the milk is something to be desired by all Christians always. Looking more closely at the adjectives, "pure" (*adolos*) means "without deceit" (cf. 2:1), and "spiritual" (*logikon*) can also be translated "rational" or "belonging to verbal communication," the latter of which pervades the context (1:23–2:1;

McCartney 1991). Thus this milk is partially a corrective for the vice of deceit and involves verbal communication.

In light of this, many identify this milk as the word of God (Selwyn 1947, 154; Achtemeier 1996, 146–47; Elliott 2000, 400–401). The word (*logos*) of God was effective in the recipients' being born anew (1:23), and the word (*rhēma*) is the gospel that the community has heard (1:25; cf. 1:12). However, this milk has to do with the recipients' experience of the risen Lord. They have tasted that the Lord is loving (2:3). The focus is not on the means by which the Christians have come to rebirth (the word of God) but on the Lord they have found (the Word). Longing for milk is to actively seek a relationship with Christ based on a beneficence and love already experienced.

The purpose of drinking the spiritual milk is expressed not as spiritual maturity, as might be expected, but as **that by it you may grow into salvation** (2:2b; cf. James 1:18, 21). Salvation is present at baptism (3:21) yet is a process to be experienced fully when Jesus returns in the last times (1:5, 7, 9, 13; 4:18). The recipients are to be active in the process of their salvation by seeking Christ. They are a family of newborns (1:3, 23) who will grow up in the family of God into salvation together as brothers and sisters (1:3, 14). The reason for the exhortation to long for pure spiritual milk is given in an allusion to Ps. 34:8 (33:9 LXX): **for you have tasted that the Lord is loving** (2:3; Jobes 2002). The recipients have tasted the love and beneficence of the Lord (Heb. 6:4–5) and are encouraged to experience it more fully.

Theological Issues

The vices of our old lives are incompatible with our new, born-again lives (1:23; 2:1). The desires of former ignorance (1:14) and the empty ways of our ancestors (1:18) are replaced by a call to holiness (1:15–16) and genuine mutual love from the heart (1:22). Ill will, deceit, and all related vices that are self-serving and that harm others should no longer be entertained. Simply trying not to be jealous, envious, and slanderous will not successfully eliminate these vices from our lives, for then the source of strength remains our frail selves. The most effective means for overcoming vices is seeking the close relationship with Christ that we have and continue to experience. It is seeking the love and beneficence that he offers us at salvation and continues to demonstrate. With that focus, vices will diminish as we share the love we experience from Christ with others, grow in holiness, and prepare for the full experience of our salvation.

1 Peter 2:4–10

Christ as the Living Stone, and Christians as the Spiritual House and God's People

Introductory Matters

This section contrasts the fate of those who come to the living stone and those who reject it. The main topics are introduced in verses 4–5 and then developed by using OT quotations from the LXX (vv. 6–10). The topic of the living stone introduced in verse 4 is developed in verses 4–8, with quotations from the LXX in verses 6–8 all containing the word "stone" (Isa. 28:16; Ps. 117:22 [118:22]; Isa. 8:14; see Snodgrass 1977; Minear 1982; Elliott 1966, 26–33; Wagner 2008, 91–98). The topic of the people of God introduced in verse 5 is developed in verses 9–10, with the adaptation of several texts from the LXX containing references to mercy and the people of God (Exod. 19:5–6; Isa. 43:20–21; Hosea 1:6–7, 9; 2:1 [1:10]; 2:25 [2:23]).

1 Peter 2:4–10 in the Rhetorical Flow

God's provision for salvation, and Christians' status before God (1:1–2:10)

  The letter prescript: Establishing authority, identity, and goodwill (1:1–2)

  Thanksgiving for God's gift of salvation (1:3–12)

  The call and motivation to holiness (1:13–21)

  Born anew by the word of God for mutual love (1:22–25)

  Growing into salvation (2:1–3)

  ▶ Christ as the living stone, and Christians as the spiritual house and God's people (2:4–10)

It has been established that the recipients have been born anew and should long for the Lord, whom they have found to be loving and beneficent; now their new identity is further established. In line with the OT imagery that pervades the entire letter, the recipients are given an essentially Jewish identity as God's people and as a priesthood to God (Achtemeier 1989, 222–31).

Tracing the Train of Thought

2:4. With the opening exhortation, **Come to him, a living stone** (2:4a), the metaphor shifts dramatically from Christ as a wet nurse in 2:2–3 to Christ as a stone. Stone (*lithos*) is not natural rock but dressed stone used in a building, as it is with the stone language in the LXX quotations of Isa. 28:16 (in v. 6); Ps. 117:22 [118:22] (v. 7); and Isa. 8:14 (vv. 7–8). The stone image was used in early Christology as a reference to the Messiah, often using these same texts (Acts 4:8–12; Rom. 9:30–33; Eph. 2:19–22; *Barn.* 6.2–4; *Gos. Thom.* 66).

"Living stone" is a contradiction. In the OT, idols are presented as lifeless "gods of wood and stone" that are the works of human hands, in contrast to the living God, who created all things (Deut. 4:28; 28:36, 64; 29:17; 2 Kings 19:18; Isa. 37:19; Jer. 3:9; Ezek. 20:32). To call Christ a "living stone" is to say that he is a true rather than a false god and, in light of the messianic connotations of stone, a living messiah. Christ is living because of his resurrection—a fact that provides Christians with a living hope (1:3, 21; 3:18)—and he is the central subject of the living word of God (1:23).

On the one hand, in spite of being a true God and living Messiah, Christ was **rejected by human beings** (2:4b). The verb "rejected" (*apodokimazō*) is drawn from Ps. 117:22 LXX [118:22] and anticipates the quotation of this psalm to follow in verse 7. Those who rejected Christ are not the Jews or their religious leaders, as in the Gospels and Acts, which cite this psalm (Mark 12:10–12// Matt. 21:42–46//Luke 20:17–19; Acts 4:8–12), but humanity in general. The perfect tense of the verb implies that humans not only rejected Christ at his crucifixion but have also continued to reject him to the time of writing of the letter (and, of course, to this moment!).

On the other hand, Christ was rejected by humans **but chosen by and precious to God** (2:4c). The adjectives "chosen" (*eklektos*) and "precious" (*entimos*) are drawn from Isa. 28:16 LXX and anticipate its quotation to follow in verse 6. This description of the stone, especially in light of the use of this description in verses 6–7 in connection with the cornerstone, implies that it is dressed and valuable for building. Jesus was chosen by God before the foundation of the world (1:20) to be a dressed stone, useful in the redemptive building described here in 2:4–10. Some interpreters translate the word "precious" (*entimos*) with its other prevalent meaning, "honored" (Elliott 2000, 410–11), but the focus of 2:4–8 is not honor and shame but usefulness for building.

Figure 2. Ruins of the ancient Temple of Concordia in Agrigento, Sicily. Peter describes believers as a spiritual house and holy priesthood.

2:5. The building metaphor persists in the description of the recipients: **and you yourselves, like living stones, are being built** (2:5a). The recipients are living stones, participating in the life made possible by the resurrection of Jesus Christ from the dead (1:3, 21; 3:7, 18). Although the verb "build" (*oikodomeisthe*) can also be a present middle imperative ("build yourselves"), it should be understood as a present passive indicative ("being built"). It is God who builds a temple with Christians, lays the cornerstone of Jesus Christ (v. 6), and establishes the holy priesthood that functions as this spiritual house (vv. 5, 9).

The recipients are also **like a spiritual house** (2:5b). This translation takes "spiritual house" as an appositive to "living stones," not as the object of building, which would yield the translation "built into a spiritual house" (NRSV). The translation here more accurately reflects the case of spiritual house (nominative, not accusative). In any case, a spiritual house (*oikos pneumatikos*) is a community of believers where the Spirit of God dwells. It is the Spirit who sanctifies the believers (1:2) and rests upon them (4:14).

Tying this verse closely with 2:9 and 4:17, "spiritual house" (*oikos pneumatikos*) has recently been understood as the household of God (Elliott 1990, 167–70, 200–237; 2000, 415–18). However, the language and the context pertain to the sacrificial system, so "spiritual house" is best understood as a temple (Best 1969, 282; Achtemeier 1996, 158–59). In the LXX, "house" (*oikos*) can refer to the Jerusalem temple (2 Chron. 36:23; Ps. 69:9; Isa. 56:7), and the related verb "build" (*oikodemeō*) to the building of the temple (2 Sam. 7:5–6; 1 Kings 8:27; Isa. 66:1). In the NT, "house" can also designate the temple of God (John 2:16; Acts 7:47–50). The references to priesthood and sacrifices to follow in this verse, and the designation of the community as a priesthood in verse 9, further support understanding "spiritual house" as a temple. Christians are often described as a new temple (*naos*; 1 Cor. 3:16–17; 6:19; 2 Cor. 6:16; Eph. 2:19–22; Rev. 3:12; 11:1), as are their contemporaries, the Essenes, at Qumran (1QS 5.5–7; 8.1–10; 9.3–6; 4QFlor 1.1–7; Gärtner 1965, 16–46).

We need to be cautious about making too great a distinction between house and temple here. Christians are also called a "house" or "household" (*oikos*) of God (1 Tim. 3:15; Heb. 3:6), and there is the natural blending of the concepts of house and temple with regard to God, since God's house would be a temple (Heb. 10:21; 1QS 5.5–7; 8.4–10). For example, in Eph. 2:19–22 we find the metaphor of the *household* (*oikeios*, v. 19) of God built on Christ the cornerstone and growing into a holy *temple* (*naos*, v. 21) where God dwells.

Being built into a spiritual house, the recipients are transformed **to be a holy priesthood, to offer spiritual sacrifices acceptable to God** (2:5c). Israel was also a holy priesthood (Isa. 61:6). This verse is an allusion to Exod. 19:6, where God makes a covenant with Israel on Mount Sinai that Israel should be "a priestly kingdom and a holy nation." As a holy priesthood, the recipients offer spiritual sacrifices (*pneumatikai thysiai*; cf. 2:9). In the OT the metaphor of sacrifice was used for prayer, thanksgiving, and a repentant heart (Pss. 50:13–14, 23; 51:17; 141:2; cf. 69:30–31; Isa. 1:11–17), and in Jewish tradition sacrifice can refer to pure hearts, love, and good works (Hosea 6:6; Sir. 35:1–5; 2 En. 45.3; 4QFlor 1.6–7). Spiritual sacrifices are the worship and daily conduct of the community, including holy conduct (1:15–16), good works (3:6, 10–13), mutual love (1:22), and righteousness (2:24). Such worship and good deeds are acceptable to God **through Jesus Christ** (2:5d), who is the intermediary between God and humanity (1:3, 21; 3:21; 4:11) and central to God's redemptive work (2:4, 6–8).

2:6. A quotation of Isa. 28:16 provides a reason to come to the living stone and be living stones in a spiritual house: **For it says in Scripture, "Behold, I am placing a stone in Zion, a chosen and precious cornerstone, and whoever believes in him absolutely will not be put to shame."** The quotation is not used to prove that God is building the Christians into a spiritual house (v. 5), but rather to demonstrate that this transformation is true and based on a promise of God. The quotation varies from both the Hebrew and Greek texts of Isaiah, particularly in the addition of "in him" (*en autō*). This addition shifts the focus from God's work to Christ himself as the object of belief (an addition Paul also makes when using this verse in Rom. 9:32–33; 10:11), demonstrating that the relationship between the living stone (Christ) and the living stones (the Christians) is faith (cf. Eph. 2:20).

This promise of not being put to shame rests on the recipients' relationship with Christ, who is a chosen and precious cornerstone in God's sight. "Chosen" (*eklektos*) refers literally to a dressed stone that is the right size and strength to serve as a cornerstone of a building and is thus very precious (*entimon*) in the building project. Of course, metaphorically it refers to Christ as chosen by God and thus precious as the cornerstone of a spiritual house (v. 5). The verb "put to shame" (*kataischynō*) is in the form of a passive subjunctive, which in the LXX refers to God's shaming opponents and the unfaithful (Ps. 118:31, 78, 116 [119:31, 78, 116]; Isa. 47:3; Jer. 23:40; Ezek. 16; 23). The quotation's double negative affirms that God will absolutely never shame those with faith in Christ. The recipients can be assured that however they are shamed by their neighbors for association with the rejected Stone (v. 7), they will not be shamed by God.

2:7–8. An OT quotation from Ps. 117:22 LXX [118:22] and an allusion to Isa. 8:14 about stones contrast those who believe in Christ with those who reject him; it is introduced with **Therefore the honor belongs to you who believe** (2:7a). The previous verse affirms that those who believe in Christ will not be put to shame, while this verse affirms the positive, that the recipients are honored. This honor is described in verses 9–10 and is part of the praise, glory, and honor to accompany the coming of Christ, which completes salvation (1:7, 21).

Psalm 117:22 LXX [118:22] provides a contrast with believers: **but to those who do not believe, "A stone that the builders rejected has become the head of the corner"** (2:7b). Elsewhere in the NT this verse describes the Jewish leaders who rejected Jesus (Mark 12:10–11//Matt. 21:42//Luke 20:17; Acts 4:11), but here it refers more broadly to anyone who rejects Christ the living stone (v. 4), particularly those persecuting the recipients (2:12; 3:8–20; 4:1–6). Though Christ may have been rejected by some, God has made him the cornerstone, the most important stone in a building, from which all further measurements are made and materials are placed (v. 6; see Siegert 2004).

An allusion to Isa. 8:14 (the LXX is quite different) amplifies the fate of unbelievers (cf. Rom. 9:33). The stone in Zion is **"A stone that causes people to stumble, a rock that makes them fall"** (2:8a). A stone (*lithos*) is a dressed stone used for building, and a rock (*petra*) is a rough stone in its natural state. Thus the allusion can refer to Christ as the dressed cornerstone, as in the wider context (vv. 4–7), as well as a stone one can simply trip over. In its context in Isaiah, this verse refers to God's becoming a stumbling block to Israel, but here Christ is the stumbling block for all unbelievers.

The application of the quotation and allusion in verses 7–8a is now given: **Those disobeying the word stumble** (2:8b). "Disobeying" (*apeitheō*) is "not believing" (v. 7), and the "word" (*logos*) is the good news proclaimed (1:25).

The "word" can be understood as the object of "disobey," as translated here, or of the previous verb, "stumble" (*proskoptō*), with the resultant translation "those disobeying stumble on the word." The former is preferred because it conforms to this letter's use of this verb "disobey" with an object referring to unbelievers ("disobey the word" in 3:1 and disobey the gospel in 4:17), and the use of the complementary topic of obedience with an object (obey Jesus Christ in 1:2 and obedience to the truth in 1:22). Disobeying the word is the specific issue (v. 4, 7), not disobedience itself.

Those disobeying the word stumble (*proskomma*). By rejecting the word that was preached to them, the unbelievers have not been born anew (1:23–25) and have not come to the living stone to be built into a spiritual house. In fact, they are tripping over its very cornerstone (2:4–7). Unbelievers stumble by disobeying the word **as they were consigned to do** (2:8c). In God's plan unbelievers are consigned to stumble as much as those who believe are consigned to be honored (1:7, 21; 2:6). This does not refer to predestination, as though God has predetermined that some will be believers and others unbelievers. Rather, the reality is that all those who disobey the word will stumble. The disobedience is their own choice.

2:9. In contrast to the stumbling unbelievers (vv. 7–8), the believing recipients are described by four honorific titles originally applied to Israel as the covenant people of God. These are drawn from Exod. 19:6 (in the context of making the covenant at Sinai) and from Isa. 43:20–21 (in the context of the renewal of this covenant). The description begins **But you are a chosen people** (*genos eklekton*; 2:9a). This title comes from Isa. 43:20 and reiterates the topic of election applied to Christians (1:2) and Christ (2:4, 6). The Christians are also a **royal priesthood** (*basileion hierateuma*; 2:9b), a title coming from Exod. 19:6 and recalling the topic of Christians as a holy priesthood (2:5). Christians are also a **holy people** (*ethnos hagion*; 2:9c), a title coming from Exod. 19:6. People (*ethnos*) are those who share kinship and culture, here the shared experience of being chosen by God. The title reminds Christians that they need to be holy as God is holy (1:15–16) and that they are a holy priesthood (2:5). Finally, Christians are also **God's own possession** (*laos eis peripoiēsin*; 2:9d), a title from Isa. 43:21 and perhaps Exod. 19:5. This title could be translated "a people for saving" and refer to the future aspect of salvation in 1 Peter (1:5; 2:2; Michaels 1988, 109–10), but such a translation does not conform with the other three as titles applied to Israel and also describing Christians' current status before God.

The recipients are told that the purpose of their new status as reflected in these four titles is **that you may declare the manifestations of power of the one who called you out of darkness into his awesome light** (2:9e). The first half of the purpose relies in part on Isa. 43:21, in which Israel's purpose as a people of God is to declare God's praise. The verb "declare" (*exangellō*) is used in the LXX for proclaiming the praises and works of God in worship

(Pss. 9:15 [9:14]; 70:15 [71:15]; 72:28 [73:28]; 78:13 [79:13]; 106:22 [107:22]; 118:13, 62 [119:13, 62]). This suggests that worship is a partial explanation of "spiritual sacrifices" mentioned in 2:5 and that "declaring" is equivalent to "glorifying God" (2:12; 4:11, 14, 16).

One of the manifestations of God's power (*aretē*) is God's calling the recipients out of darkness into the light. The calling (*kaleō*) is another aspect of being elect (1:15; 5:10). Calling can be either to final salvation, as here, or to a certain pattern of behavior that should accompany a calling from God (2:21; 3:9). Thus declaration of God's power, while primarily by word and worship, should also be understood as being done by deeds that glorify God (2:12) and influence the broader community (2:11–5:11). The darkness is the ignorance and empty living in which the recipients wallowed during their former lives (1:14, 18), which is defined in the next verse as not knowing God's mercy (2:10). The passing from darkness to light is conversion from paganism to Christianity (Acts 26:18; 2 Cor. 4:6; 6:14; Eph. 5:8; Col. 1:12–13; *1 Clem.* 36.2; 59.2; *Barn.* 14.5–7).

2:10. This section ends with a reworking of Hosea LXX to complete this description of the recipients' new status as the people of God: **Once you were not a people, but now you are God's people; once you had not received mercy, but now you have received mercy.** It uses the names of Hosea's second and third children—"Not-shown-mercy" and "Not-my-people"—who symbolize Israel's relationship with God (Hosea 1:6, 9). Israel eventually received mercy and received the name "Children of the living God" (Hosea 2:1 [1:10]) and "My People" (2:25 [2:23]). Once the recipients were not a people and without mercy. Now they are God's people, God's own possession (v. 9) with mercy.

Theological Issues

Having decided to embrace Jesus Christ (2:4) by obeying the proclamation of the word (1:25; cf. 2:8) and bringing the power of God into our lives to birth us anew (1:23), we Christians become God's own people. All the titles of honor once attributed to Israel are ours (2:9–10). We are living stones of a spiritual temple, established on Jesus Christ as cornerstone (2:4–5), a holy priesthood offering spiritual sacrifices to God through our prayer, praise, worship, and the activities of our daily lives (2:5, 9).

The priesthood of the community is for the purpose of proclaiming God's mighty acts in Jesus Christ, bringing us out of darkness into the light (2:9; cf. 1:25). Every aspect of our lives should both praise him and witness to the world that has yet to accept him (2:11–4:11). All our God-given honor and mercies motivate our evangelism (2:9) of those who reject and stumble over Christ (2:4, 7–8) as they choose to remain in the desires of their ignorance (1:14) and the empty living of their ancestors (1:18). Our challenge is to help those in darkness see the wisdom of our choice through proclamation and the outworking of our spiritual sacrifices in everyday life.

The status of the church as a spiritual house and holy priesthood offering spiritual sacrifices was understood by the Reformers to justify the priesthood of all believers. They understood it to teach that anyone can be the leader of their own spiritual fellowship. However, this passage does not speak to church order or to the role of priests and hierarchy, nor does it support the position that anyone can be the leader of their own spiritual fellowship. The reference is to the church as a whole and each individual believer in it working out the worship of God in daily life. Leadership roles are for the church to define within this larger priesthood that all share (see Schweizer 1992; 2000).

1 Peter 2:11–4:11

Living Honorably among the Gentiles

Part 1 of 1 Peter describes God's provision for salvation in the death and resurrection of Christ, as well as the new status of Christians before God (1:1–2:10). Part 2 outlines the Christian life in relation to the world (2:11–4:11). Part 2 begins with "Beloved, I appeal. . . ." The verb for appeal (*parakaleō*)

---

1 Peter 2:11–4:11 in Context

God's provision for salvation, and Christians' status before God (1:1–2:10)

▶ **Living honorably among the gentiles (2:11–4:11)**

   Introduction to the main theme (2:11–12)

   The household code (2:13–3:7)

   Practicing mutual love and peace with all (3:8–12)

Doing good rather than evil amid suffering, after Christ's example (3:13–22)

Living in the Spirit and doing the will of God (4:1–6)

The need for mutual responsibility in light of the end (4:7–11)

Exhortations on faithful suffering among the gentiles, and conclusion (4:12–5:14)

---

with a noun in the vocative (e.g., "brothers," *adelphoi*) often marks a new section of a letter (Rom. 12:1; 15:30; 16:17; 1 Cor. 1:10; 1 Thess. 4:1, 10b; 5:14) as does "beloved" (*agapētoi*) by itself (Heb. 6:9; 2 Pet. 3:1, 8, 14, 17; 1 John 2:7; 3:2, 21; 4:1, 7, 11; Jude 3, 17, 20). The address "beloved" and the reference to glorifying God in 2:11–12 and 4:11–12 form an *inclusio* to frame part 2 as 2:11–4:11 (Achtemeier 1996, 169–70).

1 Peter 2:11–12

Introduction to the Main Theme

Introductory Matters

These two verses introduce the second part of 1 Peter, 2:11–4:11, focusing on its main theme: conduct among the gentiles that will not give them any reason to persecute Christians, with the hope that they will eventually glorify God. It starts with an appeal, a common beginning for moral exhortation, as follows here.

Tracing the Train of Thought

2:11. The appeal begins with the direct address **Beloved** (*agapētoi*), which reminds the recipients that they are now loved by God as God's children (1:14, 17, 23; 2:2) and by one another in mutual love (1:22; 2:17; 3:8; 4:8). The basis of the appeal is not the personal authority of Peter but the recipients' current status: **I appeal to you as aliens and resident foreigners** (2:11a). An alien (*paroikos*) is someone living as a resident outside the country of their birth and enjoying some of the same rights and privileges as a full citizen (cf. "exile," *paroikia*, 1:17), while a resident foreigner (*parepidēmos*) is someone passing through a country without intending to become a

> ┌─────────────────────────────┐
> │ **1 Peter 2:11–12** |
> │ **in the Rhetorical Flow** |
> │ |
> │ **God's provision for** |
> │ **salvation, and Chris-** |
> │ **tians' status before** |
> │ **God (1:1–2:10)** |
> │ |
> │ **Living honorably** |
> │ **among the gentiles** |
> │ **(2:11–4:11)** |
> │ |
> │ ►**Introduction to the** |
> │ **main theme (2:11–12)** |
> └─────────────────────────────┘

permanent resident. Some of the recipients may have fallen into these two categories (Elliott 2000, 481–83).

However, it is primarily the recipients' new spiritual status that makes them aliens and resident foreigners in their own land (cf. Eph. 2:19). They are children of their Father in heaven (1:14, 17), and their inheritance is in his heavenly household (1:4). It is the recipients' status as God's people (2:9–10) that makes them aliens and resident foreigners on earth (1:1; for full discussion, see Feldmeier 1992). The actual legal and social status of his community as displaced people or migrant workers is not the subject (contra Elliott 1990, 30; 2000, 457–62, 476–83) but rather the status of Christians in the world in terms reminiscent of God's people in Egypt and Canaan (Lev. 25:23; Wis. 19:10; Chin 1991). The pairing of alien and resident foreigner (*paroikos kai parepidēmos*) is used in the LXX to describe Abraham in Canaan (Gen. 23:4) and David metaphorically in his earthly existence (Ps. 38:13 [39:12]). In the NT, the coupling of "strangers and resident foreigners" (*xenoi kai parepidēmoi*) refers to Abel, Enoch, Noah, Abraham, and Sarah as people of God seeking their heavenly homeland (Heb. 11:13–16 AT).

The appeal is **to refrain from the desires of the flesh** (2:11b). This appeal reiterates the topic of not being conformed to the desires (*epithymiai*) the recipients pursued when they were living in ignorance of the gospel (1:14); those desires are to be replaced by living according to God's will (4:2). "Flesh" (*sarx*) in 1 Peter is always associated with being apart from God (1:24; 3:18; 4:1–2), and the adjectival form here (*sarkikos*) carries the same negative connotation. It is whatever turns focus away from the mutual love of God and neighbor toward the self (cf. Rom. 7:14–20; 8:1–8; Gal. 5:16–21).

These desires belong to the darkness from which the recipients have been called (2:9), physical impulses **that are conducting a battle against the soul** (2:11c; cf. Rom. 7:14–20; Gal. 5:16–21). The soul (*psychē*) is not the immaterial part of a person in distinction from the flesh or body but a person's life that survives death. It is not an entity contained within the body but the essence of a person's life that endures. The outcome of faith is the salvation of the soul (1:9), and the obedience to the truth purifies the soul (1:22). The battle with desires can jeopardize this new status, as indicated by God's watch and guard of the soul (2:25; 4:19). The desires of the flesh battling the soul is a metaphor common to early Christianity (Rom. 7:23; 2 Cor. 10:3–6; Gal. 5:17; James 4:1; Pol. *Phil.* 5.3, quoting Gal. 5:17) as well as Greco-Roman philosophical discussion of morality (Seneca, *Ep.* 124.3; Dio Chrysostom, *Or.* 5.16).

2:12. The appeal to the recipients continues as **Maintain your good conduct among the gentiles** (2:12a). "Gentiles" does not refer to non-Jews as in postexilic Jewish tradition (Isa. 24–27; Ezek. 38–39; Zech. 9–14) but to all unbelievers. It is a natural extension of the close association of Israel and

---

Resisting Bodily Desires

The battle within humanity of restraining the impulses and pleasures of the body to pursue disciplined goals of philosophy and religion is ages old. It is chronicled in the moral exhortations of Greece and Rome, Judaism, and Christianity alike. A prime example is plucked from Plato's *Phaedo*:

> *"And no one who has not been a philosopher and who is not wholly pure when he departs, is allowed to enter into the communion of the gods, but only the lover of knowledge. It is for this reason ... that those who truly love wisdom refrain from all bodily desires and resist them firmly and do not give themselves up to them.... They themselves believe that philosophy, with its deliverance and purification, must not be resisted, and so they turn and follow it whithersoever it leads."* (82C–D)

---

believers in the letter (2:9–10). The reference is to one's stance toward faith, not ethnicity. Thus far in the letter, conduct (*anastrophē*) has pertained to the practice of holiness (1:15, 17–18), but now it pertains more specifically to behavior that unbelieving neighbors will perceive as good and honorable (3:1–2, 16). The call to good conduct among the gentiles is common to Christian tradition, especially the Pauline tradition (1 Cor. 10:32; Col. 4:5; 1 Thess. 4:12; 1 Tim. 3:7; 6:1; Titus 2:5, 8; cf. 1 Tim. 5:14). What is meant by good conduct is outlined in 2:13–4:11.

The reason for the appeal to good conduct among the unconverted is **so that whenever they slander you as wrongdoers, they may observe your good works and glorify God** (2:12b). The accusations of the gentiles are not formal legal indictments but malicious gossip and slander provoked by the recipients' nonconformity to cultural expectations (2:23; 3:9, 16; 4:4, 14). Such nonconformity includes not attending the many events involving idolatry, such as business lunches in temples and local festivals honoring the gods. Wrongdoing can include breaking the law (2:14; 4:15), but there is nothing to indicate that lawbreaking is a problem for the recipients.

In contrast to slander for wrongdoing, the hope is that neighbors will observe the recipients' good works and glorify God. The verb "to observe" (*epopteuō*) is used in 3:2 of unbelieving husbands who observe their Christian wives' good behavior and convert. Conversion is implied here too, because after seeing the good deeds of the Christians, the gentiles glorify God, which is worship (4:16; cf. 4:14; Titus 2:7). The letter works to dissociate the recipients from any hint of wrongdoing and associate them with doing good, especially for the sake of evangelism (2:1, 14–16, 20; 3:6, 10–13, 17; 4:15, 19).

The hope is that the slanderers would be converted and glorify God **on the day of visitation** (2:12c), the day of consummation (Isa. 10:3–4; Wis. 3:7–8).

This may not be realistic, for some slanderers will be put to shame (3:16), but the expectation of a future time when gentiles will glorify God is consistent with the eschatology of Jesus (Matt. 8:11//Luke 13:28–29; Matt. 24:14; 25:31–46). The day of visitation is more than God's visitation of individual gentiles who recognize the good deeds of Christians, convert, and glorify God (contra Elliott 2000, 471).

Theological Issues

Christians are aliens and resident foreigners on the earth because we are now God's children and members of God's household (1:14, 17, 23; 2:2). We have been sanctified by the Spirit (1:2) and called to be holy like our new Father (1:15–16); we have purified our souls through obedience to the truth (1:22). Now we are a spiritual household and holy priesthood (2:5), a chosen people, royal priesthood, and holy people, who live in the light (2:9–10). We are no longer to conform to the desires of our former lives, which were in ignorance (1:14), and to the futile wisdom of the unredeemed (1:18), living in darkness (2:9–10). In this section, the introductory plea to refrain from the desires of the flesh brings together these previous descriptions of the reality of being a Christian to emphasize that as Christians we are holy and enlightened: living by the desires with which the flesh tempts us is no longer appropriate (4:1–3).

The perspective of the unredeemed does not align itself with the Father or acknowledge the final judgment (1:17). Such a perspective does not have grounding in anything permanent and enduring from which to evaluate itself or its choices and lifestyles. As Christians we now conduct our lives by the will of God as found in Scripture, often putting us at odds with the unredeemed. By not participating in many of their activities, whether we intend to or not, we subtly demonstrate that what they are doing is unacceptable to us and to the God we now call Father. Needing to acknowledge what they hold to be the truth, they lash out against us in hopes that their slander will show the false nature of Christian claims—or at least our weak adherence to them—and the truth of their own claims.

The strongest response to slander by unbelievers is consistent, honorable living. Good deeds are the way to undermine slander and demonstrate the truth claims of Christianity. This emphasis on lifestyle and deeds motivates daily living. Every action is a witness to the glory of God and has an evangelistic impact on the world. Our behavior is a witness to the God who has led us out of the darkness into the light. Older methods of evangelism like camp meetings and passing out tracts are no longer effective. Evangelism is rooted in the behavior of every believer, and those roots need to be reemphasized. This is especially true when we consider how many Christians are also guilty of the dishonorable behavior common to unbelievers around them, especially sins such as pornography, sex outside of marriage, shoplifting, gossip, and the like. We may have problems relating to this section of 1 Peter because often there is so little in our behavior to distinguish us from unbelievers that they would never think to slander us!

1 Peter 2:13–3:7

The Household Code

Introductory Matters

Part 2 of the letter, 2:11–4:11, specifies conduct to be exhibited among the gentiles that will not give them any reason to persecute Christians and may eventually lead them to glorify God. The largest portion of this discussion is 2:13–3:7, a *Haustafel*, "household duty code," which outlines the various obligations of the members of a household toward one another and civil authorities (Lips 1994). Such a code was widely adapted by early Christians for organizational and ethical instruction (Eph. 5:21–6:9; Col. 3:18–4:1; 1 Tim. 5:1–6:2; Titus 2:1–10).

As the previous thematic statement of 2:11–12 indicates, here the code functions apologetically. Living by the code is to live in a manner that will not create any further hostility with gentile society and silence the criticism of pagan neighbors, perhaps leading them to conversion. Having an apologetic intent and written from the perspective of faith, household codes in early Christianity deal with relationships a bit differently than in the broader Hellenistic world. Typically the relation of the household to its city is addressed, but here the relationship to authorities and the emperor is the focus (2:13–17) because slander can lead to legal claims that need to remain groundless. Usually masters are the only ones addressed, since slaves have no legal rights, but here only slaves are addressed (2:18–25). Ordinarily husbands receive the bulk of instruction since they rule the household, but here the wives are primarily addressed, especially those married to non-Christian husbands (3:1–7). Slaves and wives were vulnerable and likely to suffer for

Household Codes (*Haustafeln*)

As early as Aristotle, the ancient Greeks assumed that the basic building block of a stable society was the extended family, where societal values were nurtured—values like honor and shame, obedience to authority, gender roles, and wisdom. Household codes were devised to help ensure stability in society, outlining the duties of each member of an extended household and duties of the family to the city-state (Aristotle, *Pol.* 1.1253b.1–14). Within the household, relationships were defined in terms of the male head of the house and all his dependents. The man was the supreme authority in relations with his wife, children, and slaves. The codes also outlined the relationship of the household to the government. In 1 Peter we see an approach that seeks to be a part of the world and lessen tensions with it by adapting what was useful from it (Balch 1981; 1988; Achtemeier 1996, 52–55). A real question for interpretation is how to free the gospel from the framework of the household code (Aageson 2004).

their Christian faith (Achtemeier 1996, 191–92), for conversion to a god other than that of one's master or husband would dishonor him and subject oneself to persecution. All these changes to the household code stress the relationship of Christians to non-Christians, with the topic of obedience being central (2:13, 18; 3:1, 5).

Tracing the Train of Thought

The Relationship of Christians to the Civil Authorities (2:13–17)

This opening section of the household code pertains to Christians' obeying civil authorities, a common emphasis in Greco-Roman tradition (Légasse 1988) and early Christian teaching, rooted in part in two commandments of Jesus: "Love your enemies and pray for those who persecute you" (Matt. 5:44//Luke 6:27, 35) and "Give to the emperor the things that are the emperor's, and to God the things that are God's" (Mark 12:17//Matt. 22:21//Luke 20:25; cf. Matt. 17:24–27; see also Rom. 13:1–7; 1 Tim. 2:1–3; Titus 3:1). The Apostolic Fathers continue this emphasis with instructions to pray for governing

1 Peter 2:13–3:7 in the Rhetorical Flow

God's provision for salvation, and Christians' status before God (1:1–2:10)

Living honorably among the gentiles (2:11–4:11)

    Introduction to the main theme (2:11–12)

▶ The household code (2:13–3:7)

    The relationship of Christians to the civil authorities (2:13–17)

    The relationship of slaves to masters (2:18–25)

    The relationship between wives and husbands (3:1–7)

authorities because God has instituted them (*1 Clem.* 60.4–61.2; Polycarp, *Phil.* 12.3; *Mart. Pol.* 10.2).

2.13–14. The first exhortation is to **Be subordinate to every human authority** (2:13a). To be "subordinate" (*hypotassō*) is to give the deference or honor to others that is appropriate to their higher place in society, but it is not blind submission or obedience. "Authority" (*ktisis*) could also be translated "something created" or, more rarely, "humans as created beings" (BDAG 572–73) to yield the translation "human being" (Michaels 1988, 124; Achtemeier 1996, 182–83; Elliott 2000, 489). This translation does comply with the focus on all people in the passage (v. 17) but works only if the verb "be subordinate" (*hypotassō*) is weakened to simply mean "consider." Being subordinate to every human being would be nonsensical in the hierarchical society of that day, where superiors were not subordinate to those with lesser status.

"Authority" is better translated as "human-established authority" (Senior 2003, 68), to contrast the authority of God as judge in the preceding verse and give the verb "be subordinate" its full and natural force in household codes (Eph. 5:21, 22, 24; Titus 2:5, 9; 3:1; cf. Col. 3:18, 20, 22). This translation also conforms to the context, in which Jesus is the role model of one who was subordinate to human authorities but not to every human (2:21–25).

The motivation for subordination to human authority is **for the sake of the Lord**, which can refer to Christ (1:3; 2:3; 3:15) or God, with the context strongly indicating the latter (2:12, 15, 16, 17). Subordination to human authorities is motivated by trying to convince unbelievers to honor God (2:12), doing good as God's will (2:15), and acknowledging God as judge (1:17; 2:12, 17).

These authorities are to be obeyed **whether the emperor having controlling power or governors as those sent by him for punishment of wrongdoers and recognition of those doing good** (2:13b–14). "Emperor" (*basileus*) is literally "king" and was used to refer to the emperor as the highest authority. Classifying the emperor as a "human authority" is probably a subtle polemic against the growing tendency in Asia Minor at this time to regard the emperor as divine. Also, the preceding motivation, "for the sake of the Lord," reminds the recipients who is the true divine authority. The question of lordship had to be balanced with a concern not to appear unpatriotic—a common accusation against Christians.

The subordination to the emperor extends to his appointed provincial governors or other appointees. Here civil government is understood to exist to punish those who are wrongdoers (*kakopoioi*) and praise those who do good (*agathopoioi*; cf. Rom. 13:1–7; Lysias, *Or.* 31.30; Xenophon, *Cyr.* 1.6.20; Diodorus Siculus, *Hist.* 1.70.6; Dio Chrysostom, *Or.* 39.2; Pliny, *Pan.* 70.7; Josephus, *J.W.* 6.134). Doing good is not simply obeying the laws of the state but also obeying the will of God (2:15) and displaying good works that will influence gentiles to come to God (2:12).

Figure 3. A marble bust of the Roman Emperor Nero.

Photos.com

2:15. A reason for the commandment to submit to authority is now provided: **For it is God's will that by doing good you silence the ignorance of foolish people.** Doing good works to silence slanderers (v. 12) is the will of God. It assumes that what are good works in God's sight, especially in obeying the civil authorities, will be considered good works by society at large and will refute any false charges made against Christians. This assumption can be made because Christian and Greco-Roman moral codes overlapped. However, this strategy will not always work, since Christian conduct also differs from social norms on many scores (3:14, 17; 4:3–4). These good works are not necessarily large civic projects but acts of daily beneficence (cf. Winter 1988). The goal of silencing the ignorant helps confirm that the recipients primarily suffer from slander (2:12; 3:9, 16; 4:4). "Ignorance" (*agnōsia*) on the part of the slanderers is not a lack of knowledge per se but a lack of religious experience or discernment (BDAG 14), like the ignorance (*agnoia*) of the Christians themselves before their conversion (1:14).

2:16. Further exhortation helps to ensure that no charges of wrongdoing have any basis in fact: **As free people also obey, not exercising your freedom as a cover for doing evil but as slaves of God.** This verse does not have its own main verb but is probably governed by the imperative "obey" (*hypotagēte*) in verse 13. Such freedom is not social or political freedom but freedom in Christ from the ignorance (1:14) or darkness (2:9) of human existence before conversion. It is a freedom that may be falsely construed as freedom from social and political obligations as well, a problem Paul also faced (1 Cor. 8:1–13; 10:23–11:1; Gal. 5:13). Also, this freedom should not be exercised to conform to social and political demands at odds with Christian faith, especially just to avoid persecution (Achtemeier 1996, 186). Christians are free from all that has bound them in the past and should not be returning to evil behavior (2:1), for they are slaves to God and freely committed to obedience (cf. Rom. 6:18, 22).

2:17. A series of four commands follows, the first and fourth regarding outsiders and the second and third regarding the community of faith. The first, **Honor everyone**, reflects the Greco-Roman value of honor based on social class but also the Christian value that everyone is a creation of God, has the possibility of redemption, and is thus worthy of honor regardless of social standing (Rom. 12:10). The second command, **Love the fellowship of believers**, has familial connotations. All people are to be given their honor as humans, yet fellow Christians, brothers and sisters in Christ (1:14, 17), are to be loved (1:22; 3:8; 4:8). The commandment to love neighbors (and God) is rooted in the sayings of Jesus (Mark 12:28–34//Matt. 22:34–40//Luke 10:25–28). The third command, **Fear God**, refers to awe and reverence elicited by God's holy being and role as judge (1:17). This fear manifests itself in praise and glorification of God (2:9; 4:16), humility before God (5:6), and trust in God (5:7). Fearing God is contrasted with the last command, **Honor the emperor**, a contrast found in Prov. 24:21 as "Fear the LORD and the king." While God is to be feared as the ultimate judge, the emperor deserves only honor (cf. Matt. 10:28; Matt. 22:21//Mark 12:17//Luke 20:25; Rom. 13:1–7). This structure may be part of a subtle polemic against any claim to divinity for the emperor.

The Relationship of Slaves to Masters (2:18–25)

This section is the part of the household code describing the relationship between masters and slaves (cf. Col. 3:22–4:1; Eph. 6:5–9). It provides a specific instance of being subordinate to every human authority (2:13), as does the next instance of the relationship between wives and husbands (3:1–7). The section is structured in two parts. First is an exhortation to slaves to be subject to both kind and harsh masters, with rationale and amplification (vv. 18–20). Second is Christ's example of unjust suffering, which provides a model for the slaves as well as the rest of the recipients (vv. 21–25).

Greco-Roman Slavery

In ancient Greco-Roman culture, many people were legally owned as property by others. Slavery was located in the context of the extended household, where the father, as paterfamilias, exercised total legal control over enslaved members of his household. The quality of daily life for slaves depended on the quality of the paterfamilias, including workload, corporal punishment, and sexual misuse. Slaves were the basic labor force of the imperial economy. We must not impose our knowledge of slavery as practiced in the New World in the seventeenth through nineteenth centuries. Ancient slavery differed in that racial factors played no role, education was greatly encouraged, many slaves held highly responsible roles, and most urban and domestic slaves would anticipate being emancipated by the age of thirty (Carrez 1980; Bradley 1984; 1994).

Figure 4. An ancient Roman fresco depicting slaves.

This section uses the Jesus tradition to support the exhortation, especially Jesus's moral teaching about loving enemies (vv. 19–20; cf. Luke 6:32–35) and his own example of innocent suffering and nonretaliatory ethics (vv. 21–25). This section reworks Isa. 53:4–12 LXX, understanding Christ as the Suffering Servant and providing a paradigm for Christians persecuted by those in authority. It has been postulated that verses 21–25 rely on an early Christian hymn based on Isa. 53 (Boismard 1961, 111–32), but Peter's own use of Isa. 53 is more likely (Osborne 1983, 381–87; Michaels 1988, 136–37; Achtemeier 1996, 192–93).

2:18. The section begins with the exhortation, **Slaves, be subject to your masters with all fear, not only those who are good and kind but also those who are unscrupulous.** Masters could be nurturing or cruel, including inflicting physical and sexual abuse. With fear, Christian slaves are to be subject to their masters regardless of their master's quality. The word "fear" or "respect" (*phobos*) is reserved for God (1:17; 2:17), so fear of God motivates obedience to masters, not fear of the masters themselves (BDAG 1062). Further support for this interpretation is the consciousness of God in the next verse (cf. 2:15) and other household codes in which fear of God is a motivation for slaves to obey their masters (Col. 3:22; cf. Eph. 6:5). Such fearful obedience would not give non-Christians basis for any accusations against a slave (2:12).

2:19. The rationale for the commandment for slaves to be subject to their masters is **For people receive grace, if, being aware of God, they endure afflictions while suffering unjustly** (2:19a). The general nature of the rationale indicates that the instruction to slaves is applicable to all the recipients. On the basis of similar usage of grace (*charis*) in Luke (1:30; 2:52; 6:32–34) and early Christian works (*Did.* 1.3; *2 Clem.* 13.4; Ign. *Pol.* 2.1), grace is sometimes translated as "favor" (Achtemeier 1996, 196) or "credit" (NRSV; cf. Elliott 2000, 518) with God both here and in the next verse. However, it is more naturally understood as grace extended by God to those who please God (BDAG 1079 [2b]), as it is elsewhere in the letter (1:2, 10, 13; 2:20; 4:10; 5:10, 12; Goppelt 1993, 199–201; Senior 2003, 75).

The possibility of God's grace provides a motivation for unjust suffering and comes from **being aware of God** (2:19b), that is, keeping in mind the will and purposes of God, which include obedience to an unjust master (2:15; 3:17; 4:1–2, 19). Awareness of God in daily decisions regarding obedience is an aspect of fearing God as judge (1:17; 2:17–18). God's grace comes from slaves' being aware of God's will as **they endure afflictions while suffering unjustly** (2:19c). Suffering for obedience includes beatings (2:20) and other suffering, as expected of all faithful Christians in the world (1:6). The theme of unjust suffering is introduced here, exemplified by Christ (2:21–23; 3:18; 4:1), and expected in the lives of all believers (3:14, 17; 4:19; 5:9–10).

2:20. The rationale of verse 19 is amplified in verse 20 more specifically in relation to the slaves: **For what glory is there if you do wrong, are beaten for it, and endure it patiently? But if you do good, suffer for it, and endure it patiently, you have grace before God's judgment.** There is no glory for those who endure suffering for doing wrong, but there is glory and grace in God's judgment for those who endure unjust suffering for doing good. Slaves may need to suffer for doing good, like all Christians (3:14, 17; 4:12–16, 19), because good is defined by God's will (2:15; 3:17; 4:19) and may not be to the liking of an unbelieving master. This passage indicates the harsh treatment that slaves endured. Masters could severely beat them, to the point of crippling and death (Elliott 2000, 521). The verb "beaten" (*kolaphizō*) used here describes Jesus's beating at the crucifixion (Mark 14:65//Matt. 26:67), a suffering about to be described in verses 21–25. This verse is part of the instruction to all the recipients to do good rather than evil (2:11–17; 3:10–12; 4:14–16).

On a technical note, while *kleos* is generally translated as "glory" (BDAG 547), at the beginning of this verse many commentators translate it as "favor" or "credit" with God or neighbors—a translation that corresponds to their translation of *charis* ("grace") as "favor" or "credit" in verse 19 and this verse (NRSV; Elliott 2000, 520). However, "glory" in this letter and early Christian literature is a reward from God, not "credit" granted by God (1:6–7, 11; 5:10; *1 Clem.* 5.6; 54.3; Goppelt 1993, 196; Senior 2003, 75).

The slaves suffering unjustly for doing good also have grace (*charis*) before God's judgment. Here *charis* is often translated "God's favor, approval, or credit," as in verse 19, "You have God's approval" (NRSV). Based on the theology of 1 Peter, however, *charis* in verse 20 should be translated as "grace," as in the previous verse (Senior 2003, 75). This translation is further justified not only by the earlier part of the verse, where God gives glory, but also by the preposition "before" (*para*) in the phrase "before God," which can mean "before God's judgment" (BDAG 757 [B2]). The slave who suffers unjustly for doing right will receive grace at God's judgment—a strong motive for obedience. This same mix of topics (suffering, grace, and glory) is found in 5:10 and further supports this interpretation.

2:21. Verses 21–25 further exhort the slaves to obedience by upholding Christ as an example of someone suffering and enduring unjust punishment for doing what is right (2:21–23), as well as emphasizing the redemptive value of his suffering and death (2:24–25). The focus is more general, to include all Christians (Achtemeier 1993) and is based in part on Isa. 53 (Langkammer 1987; Elliott 2000, 540–50).

The exhortation begins with **for to this you have been called** (2:21a), reminding the recipients of their call by God to holiness and light (1:15; 2:9; cf. 3:9; 5:10), a calling that results in suffering for doing good as just outlined (vv. 18–20). Now follows a christological reason for suffering for God's calling: **because Christ also suffered for you, leaving for you an example, in order that you should follow in his footsteps** (2:21b). This suffering is not primarily Christ's redemptive suffering for sins (as in 3:18), for the NT does not speak of Christ's suffering *for* (*hyper*) anyone ("dying for," yes). Rather, the reference is primarily to Christ's suffering for doing good, which provides a moral example (*hypogrammos*) that Christians can follow as they too suffer for doing good (3:16; 4:1–2, 13–14).

2:22–23. Christ's example of unjust suffering is now described using Isa. 53, beginning with a quotation of Isa. 53:9b LXX: **He did not commit sin, nor was deceit found in his mouth** (2:22). This quotation is slightly modified, with the word "sin" (*hamartia*) substituted for the synonym "lawlessness" (*anomia*), a change emphasizing that Christ was sinless (2 Cor. 5:21; Heb. 4:15; 7:26; 1 John 3:5; cf. John 8:46). Christ also provides an example of one not speaking deceit, which is to be a virtue of the recipients as well (2:1; 3:10).

The thought of Isa. 53:7 now amplifies Christ's verbal purity: **When he was verbally abused, he did not verbally abuse in return** (2:23a). The recipients are primarily suffering verbal abuse (2:12, 15; 3:16; 4:4, 14), and the hope is that they will not return that abuse (2:1; 3:9; cf. 3:16). While Jesus was verbally abused throughout his ministry, the focus here is on the passion week. The Gospel tradition emphasizes the verbal abuse Jesus suffered and his silence

---

Martyrs' Last Words

The threats that martyrs issue against their oppressors are often motivated by the confidence the martyrs have in their deity, cause, or beliefs. When about to suffer martyrdom at the hands of Antiochus, the sons of Eleazar are portrayed as saying,

> *"Put us to the test, then, tyrant; and if you take our lives for the sake of our religion, do not think you can harm us with your torments. By our suffering and endurance we shall obtain the prize of virtue and shall be with God, on whose account we suffer. But you, because of our foul murder, will suffer at the hand of divine justice the everlasting torment by fire you deserve."* (4 Macc. 9.7–9, trans. H. Anderson, OTP 2:554)

---

before his accusers at his trial (Mark 14:61//Matt. 26:62–63; Mark 15:1–5// Matt. 27:11–14; Luke 23:9; John 19:9–10), before the soldiers (Mark 15:16–20// Matt. 27:27–31//Luke 23:11; John 19:1–3), and passersby who mocked him during his crucifixion (Mark 15:29–32//Matt. 27:39–44//Luke 23:35–38).

Now the thought moves from verbal to physical abuse: **When he was suffering, he did not threaten, but he gave himself over to the one who judges justly** (2:23b). The reference is unclear. It could mean that Jesus silently gave the judgment of his tormentors to God, the ultimate judge (1:17; 4:5, 17–18), without threatening the vengeance of God on them, as martyrs were known to do (4 Macc. 9:5–9; *Mart. Pol.* 11.2; Michaels 1988, 146–47). But the more likely meaning is that Jesus gave himself or his cause over to God (Luke 23:46). Later, those suffering for God's will are instructed to entrust themselves to God for judgment (4:19). Either way, Jesus's action is in league with his ethic of nonretaliation (Matt. 5:38–42//Luke 6:27–30) and provides a model for those suffering unjustly.

2:24–25. These verses highlight the value of Christ's unjust suffering for redemption, beginning with a combination of Isa. 53:4 and 53:11–12: **He offered up our sins in his body on the cross, in order that, having died to sins, we might live in righteousness** (2:24a). The reason for Christ's unjust suffering is so that Christians can die to sin and live in righteousness, that is, have a dramatic break with the sinful behavior of their pagan past (1:14, 22–23; 2:11; 4:2). Dying to sin is not an end in itself but the prerequisite to living in righteousness, which is good works (2:15, 20; 3:6, 11, 17; 4:19). The contrast between sin/righteousness and death/life is characteristic of Paul's argument in Romans (5:12–21; 6:1–14, 23; 8:10).

A quotation of Isa. 53:5b further affirms the move from dying to sin onward to life in righteousness: **by his bruise you have been healed** (2:24b). "Bruise" refers to bruising from blows and is singular, connoting all of Christ's suffering and death (metonymy). The focus is on the healing that Christ's vicarious

Figure 5. An artistic representation of the crucifixion of Jesus Christ.

Photos.com

death has provided and not on his death itself. That healing in part is the restoration of fellowship with God (v. 25).

Next follows the reason why Christ bore our sins and healed us, as well as a definition of what that healing entails. The reason is partly based on Isa. 53:5b–6 and Ezek. 34 (cf. Isa. 6:10): **For you were straying like sheep, but now have been returned to the Shepherd and Guardian of your souls** (2:25). The imagery here is commonly applied to Israel as straying sheep without a shepherd, without faithful leadership (Num. 27:16–17; Isa. 13:14; Jer. 23:1–8; Ezek. 34; Zech. 10:3; 13:7), and is here applied to initial conversion. The recipients in their pre-Christian lives were like lost sheep and have been returned by God (cf. 1:14, 18; 2:9, 22–23) to their shepherd. Some mistranslate the passive form of the verb "returned" (*epistrephō*) as active, as if disobedient Christians return to God (NRSV), but God calls the Christians (v. 21), and the verb "return" is typically used of the conversion of gentiles (Acts 14:15; 15:19; 26:18, 20; Elliott 2000, 538).

Although the OT refers to God as shepherd (Ps. 23; Isa. 40:11; Ezek. 34:5–6, 15–16), the NT does not. Here it is Christ (cf. 5:4, with Christ as "chief shepherd" [*archipoimēn*]), as elsewhere in the NT and early Christian tradition, who fulfills the shepherd role through his resurrection from the dead (Mark 14:27–28//Matt. 26:31–32; John 10:11–17; Heb. 13:20; *1 Clem.* 59.3). The other title, "Guardian" (*episkopos*), can refer to God or Christ. It refers to God in the OT (Job 20:29 LXX), and in the context of 1 Peter, it is God who protects his people for their salvation (1:5). Yet in the immediate context it is most naturally a second reference to Christ and an aspect of his role as a shepherd. "Shepherd and Guardian" then forms a hendiadys, the two terms expressing a single thought. Besides, if God is the one returning the congregation to the Guardian, it makes little sense that he is the Guardian. "Souls" (*psychai*) are not souls in contrast to bodies. Rather, it is people's essence or self-identity, always in some connection with salvation and obedience after salvation (1:9, 22; 2:11; 3:20; 4:19).

The Relationship of Husband and Wife

In the Greco-Roman world, the wife, as well as the entire household, was expected to adopt the religion and customs of the male head of the household (Plutarch, *Mor.* 140D; Dionysius of Halicarnassus, *Ant. rom.* 2.25.1–2). A wife who became Christian was already considered highly insubordinate and subject to everything from ridicule to expulsion from the home (Balch 1974, 240–46). This was a problem that Paul experienced in Corinth and for which he advocated divorce if peace could not be created in the relationship (1 Cor. 7:12–16). Women's subordination was rooted in the Hellenistic world's understanding that they are by nature inferior to men physically, intellectually, and morally. They are inferior in strength, reasoning, and judgment; subject to emotion; and easily enticed to immorality. Thus a woman needs the instruction of her husband (Hesiod, *Op.* 695–705; Xenophon, *Oec.* 3.11–14; 7.4–8; Plutarch, *Mor.* 145C–D; Achtemeier 1996, 206–7; Elliott 2000, 554–55). In Judaism, the inferior status of the woman was traced to Gen. 2–3, her formation from the rib of the man, and her failed engagement with the serpent, which led to subjugation by law (Gen. 3:16). (For further study, see Achtemeier 1996, 206–7; Elliott 2000, 555–57.)

The Relationship between Wives and Husbands (3:1–7)

This section is the final portion of the household code, which began at 2:13, and concerns the relationship between wives and husbands (cf. Col. 3:18–19; Eph. 5:22–33; Titus 2:3–5). Typically such codes address only husbands because they had the greater authority in the relationship. Here the code departs considerably from tradition, mainly addressing the wives. This direct and disproportionate address to wives is consistent with the letter's emphasis on the one most likely to be oppressed in a relationship, like the slaves just addressed. The details of the relationship here are best understood culturally as a Christian wife and a non-Christian husband.

3:1. This section begins with the commandment **In turn, wives be subject to your husbands** (3:1a). Wives (*gynaikes*) and husbands (*andres*) can also be understood as women and men in general. However, the adjective "own" (*idioi*), as in "own man," and the following example of the married couple Abraham and Sarah (v. 6) indicate a marriage relationship. The adverb "in turn" (*homoiōs*) ties this exhortation to the relationship of slaves to masters (2:18–25) and more remotely to the recipients' relationship to civil authorities (2:13–17). The adverb typically means "similarly" or "likewise" (BDAG 707–8), so although it may appear that wives are to be submissive to their husbands as slaves to masters, the point is more broadly to be subject to those in authority. The verb "be subject" (*hypotassō*) is a participle, to be understood as an imperative like other participles in 1 Peter (1:14b; 2:1, 18; 3:7, 9; 4:8, 10). The verb is commonly used in other household codes to define the role of wives to their husbands (Eph. 5:21–22, 24; Col. 3:18; Titus 2:5; cf. 1 Cor. 14:34). Being subject clearly involves dress, adornment, and good works, as indicated in this context (vv. 1–6) and Greco-Roman culture. The wife is not always to be subject to her husband—only in those things in conformity with Christian faith (cf. 2:15).

The reason given to wives for being submissive is **so that if any are disobeying the word, they may be won over without a word by the behavior of their wives** (3:1b). In this letter dis-

Figure 6. An ancient mosaic of a Roman woman.

obeying (*apeitheō*) refers to the unconverted (2:7–8; 4:17). Apparently some of the husbands were in that group and may even have been among those slandering the Christians (2:12, 15; 3:9, 16). These husbands disobey the word (*logos*), that is, the gospel (1:23; 2:8; cf. 1:25), and the wives' behavior might win them over. "Win" (*kerdainō*) means "to convert" and is used in missionary contexts in the NT, where it is equivalent to salvation (1 Cor. 9:19–22). The letter understands behavior to be a strong tool of evangelism (2:12), as did Paul (1 Cor. 7:12–16), and strong enough to be effective without words. This is not to exclude verbal witness but to emphasize that actions are a witness as well. The point is made with a clever play on words: whereas the unbelieving husbands disobey the word, they can be won by their wives' behavior without a word!

3:2. The wives are told that conversion of unbelieving husbands occurs after **having observed your reverent, pure conduct**. Reverent (*en phobō*) is fear before God as judge (1:17; 2:17, 18), not fear of husbands (as in v. 6; Eph. 5:33), and such fear keeps conduct pure. This description of the wife's behavior corresponds to descriptions of the ideal wife (Pliny, *Ep.* 4.19) and faithful Christians (1:14–16, 22; 2:4–10; 3:15). By this kind of behavior the wife assures her husband that she is virtuous, even though she cannot join him in worshiping his gods, and may lead him to seek out his wife's God (cf. 2:12). Paul gives similar instruction for a Christian wife with a non-Christian husband (1 Cor. 7:12–16).

3:3–4. Verses 3–4 illustrate the reverent, pure conduct of Christian wives that works to convert their non-Christian husbands, using a contrast between the outward appearance and inward nature. They begin, **Do not let your adornment be the outward braiding of hair and putting on of gold jewelry or fine apparel** (3:3). In Jewish and Greco-Roman traditions, people expected women to be modest in dress and adornment (Phintys the Neo-Pythagorean, *Concerning the Temperance of a Woman* 153.15–28; Juvenal, *Sat.* 3.180–81; 6.457–63, 495–511). Overindulgence in either was considered immodest and sexually provocative (*T. Reu.* 5.1–5; Philo, *Virt.* 39–40; *Sacr.* 21; Balch 1981, 101–2) and could lead to the woman and her husband being dishonored for such extravagance (Batten 2009).

> Clothes, bathing, anointing, dressing the hair, and . . . decoration from gold and jewels. For whatever of a sumptuous nature is employed by women in eating and drinking, in garments and trinkets, renders them disposed to be guilty of every crime, and to be unjust both to their husband's bed and to every other person. . . . The beauty . . . produced by prudence and not by these particulars pleases women that are wellborn. (Perictione, *On the Harmony of a Woman*, 143.10–14, 26–28, in Balch 1974, 103–4)

Women are not prohibited from wearing better clothing or jewelry, but the letter promotes dress suitable for a wife, especially one trying to assure her husband that she still honors him while seeking to convert him.

The presence of this instruction indicates that some women in these churches have the luxury goods to dress in the manner described (Beare 1970, 155; Achtemeier 1996, 212). It is not just a foil for moral instruction (contra Elliott 2000, 564; Michaels 1988, 172), for good rhetoric typically has relevance to the audience addressed. Also, braiding of hair was part of women's devotion to Isis and Artemis of Ephesus, but there is no indication that this instruction is aimed at trying to ensure that Christian women will not be confused with the devotees of these goddesses (Balch 1981, 101–2). Rather, the braiding of hair had become very elaborate, with gold chains, strings of pearls, and gemstones woven into it (cf. Ovid, *Ars* 3.136–38; Elliott 2000, 562–64).

The other half of the contrast is **Rather, let your adornment be the hidden person of the heart** (3:4a). The heart (*kardia*) is the seat of thought, emotion, and disposition (1:22; 3:15). The "hidden person of the heart" reminds us of Paul's distinction between the outward and the inner person (2 Cor. 4:16; cf. Rom. 7:22; Eph. 3:16), but here the reference is to the transformation of the inner self at conversion, which is not visible to others except through actions. The heart is where emphasis should be placed in assuring and converting a husband.

This inner emphasis should be accompanied **with the incorruptible quality of a humble and quiet spirit** (3:4b). Humility is a virtue required of wives (*1 Clem.* 21.7) and all Christians (Matt. 5:5; 11:29; Gal. 5:23; Eph. 4:2; Col. 3:12; Titus 3:2; 1 Pet. 3:16; 5:5–6). The virtue of a quiet spirit, remaining steady in the daily ups and downs of life, is to characterize women (1 Tim. 2:11, 13) as well as all Christians (1 Thess. 4:11; 2 Thess. 3:12; 1 Tim. 2:2). This combination of a humble and quiet spirit was common in early Christian instruction (*1 Clem.* 13.4; *Barn.* 19.4; *Herm. Mand.* 5.2.3; 11.8), and similar attributes describe the perfect wife in Jewish (Prov. 31:10–31; Sir. 26:1–4, 13–18) and Greco-Roman instruction (Plutarch, *Mor.* 144E). These virtues are incorruptible (*aphthartos*), outlasting mortality. Since Christians have an incorruptible inheritance (1:4), being ransomed not with perishable things (1:7, 18), but reborn with imperishable seed (1:23), Christian women need to exhibit virtues that are incorruptible and suited to their new status before God.

Such an imperishable, inward, humble, and quiet spirit is that **which is valuable in God's opinion** (3:4c). Typically the word "valuable" or "expensive" (*polytelēs*) is used in criticisms of the extravagance of wealthy women's dress (Musonius Rufus, *Or.* 40.17–20; Plutarch, *Mor.* 141E; 1 Tim. 2:9; cf. Mark 14:3), but here it is used to form a strong statement of what is truly valuable in God's sight. God sees beyond the outward appearance to the heart, where true value is found (1 Sam. 16:7; Wis. 1:6; Rev. 2:23).

3:5. An example further supports the exhortation to wives to be subject to husbands and to nurture a humble and quiet spirit: **For so once the holy wives, those hoping in God, were adorning themselves while subjecting themselves to their husbands.** The article before "holy wives" indicates a specific group, probably the wives of Israel's patriarchs, as the following example of Sarah indicates. These wives include Sarah (Abraham), Rebecca (Isaac), and Leah and Rachel (Jacob). They adorned themselves with a humble and quiet spirit while being subject to their husbands, although their husbands were men of faith, unlike those of the wives here. The participle "subjecting" can be circumstantial ("while being subject") or instrumental ("by being subject"). The circumstantial understanding is preferred so that subjection accompanies adornment with a humble and quiet spirit, but is not restricted to it.

3:6. The more specific example of subjection of holy wives to their husbands is Sarah: **as Sarah obeyed Abraham, calling him lord** (3:6a). The reference is to Gen. 18:12 LXX: after God's promise to Abraham that he and Sarah would bear a son in their old age, Sarah laughs and says, "My lord is old." Calling one's husband "lord" (*kyrios*) is not common in the OT or in the ancient world, for it refers more specifically to a man's importance and position in the larger community. In its context, Sarah is mocking God's announcement, not exhibiting a humble and quiet spirit! Probably Gen. 12 and 20 are in mind, when Sarah is temporarily given to a foreign king as wife, that is, being obedient to a husband in a foreign land (Kiley 1987, 689–92; Van Rensburg 2004, 253), or the *Testament of Abraham*, where Sarah calls Abraham "lord" (recension A: 5.13; 6.2, 4–5, 8; 15.4) and is herself recognized as mother of the elect, as implied later in this verse (T. Martin 1999).

Now the application is made: **And you have become her children, doing good and not fearing anyone in terror** (3:6b). The wives being addressed have become children of Sarah, not through faith in Christ expressed in baptism (contra Michaels 1988, 166; cf. Gal. 4:31) but in modeling Sarah's behavior (Elliott 2000, 573). How being children of Sarah relates to the participles of being good and not fearing anyone is unclear. These participles can be understood conditionally, to imply that this new status occurs if wives do right; imperatively, as commanding wives to do good (Michaels 1988, 166–67; Forbes 2005); purposefully, to act like Sarah as children of Sarah (T. Martin 1999, 144; Senior 2003, 83); or descriptively, as characteristics of children of Sarah. The latter is the preferred understanding, reflected in my translation (Achtemeier 1996, 216).

The topic of doing good is prevalent in 1 Peter, especially in the face of power (2:14) and hostility (2:15, 20; 3:8–17; 4:19; cf. 2:12; 4:17). Here a source of hostility and terror is a non-Christian husband who does not tolerate his wife's having a different religion, even (or especially) when the wife is doing good in the eyes of her God. Thus the Christian woman married to a non-Christian husband is to be a model of how to act in an environment hostile to Christianity—with humility and doing good (T. Martin 1999; cf. Kiley 1987).

3:7. Now the exhortation turns to address the husbands. Unlike the advice to wives, it does not address Christian husbands married to non-Christian wives. This would be a rare situation, since the wife was expected to adopt her husband's religion (Balch 1981, 99). Now a Christian marriage is the focus, as the reference to sharing the grace of life and prayers indicates (contra Gross 1989): **In turn, husbands, live according to knowledge, as the wife is the weaker vessel** (3:7a). The use of the adverb "in turn" (*homoiōs*) here is a simple connective (cf. 3:1; 5:5) and does not imply that the husband is to be subject to his wife as she is to be subject to him (Elliott 2000, 574). "Live" (*synoikeō*) refers to marriage, both in its social and sexual aspects, and is "according to knowledge" (*gnōsis*). This knowledge is the opposite of the unbeliever's ignorance (*agnoia*, 1:14; *agnōsia*, 2:15) and is gained from becoming a believer. It is not mere "consideration," as sometimes translated (NRSV), but knowledge from conversion, which a husband needs in order to live properly with his wife as a fellow member of the household of God.

This description of the wife as the weaker vessel (*skeuos*; cf. 1 Thess. 4:4) reflects the assumption of the period that women were physically, intellectually, morally, and spiritually weaker than men (Plato, *Leg.* 6.781A; *Resp.* 5.455D–456A; *Let. Aris.* 250–51; Philo, *Ebr.* 55; Tacitus, *Ann.* 3.34). The author has just stressed women's spiritual strength and is about to stress their share of the gift of life, but women's physical weakness is also something husbands need to consider with their newfound Christian knowledge. A similar understanding of the need to treat wives kindly as the weaker sex is found in Hellenistic sources (Plutarch, *Mor.* 142E; Callicratidas, *On the Happiness of the Household* 106.1–10 as preserved in the *Anthology* of Joannes Stobaeus; Balch 1981, 56–57).

A husband's living according to knowledge with his wife is to be done while **paying honor to her as one also sharing the grace of life** (3:7b). Honoring a wife was a commonplace in the Greco-Roman world (Pseudo-Aristotle, *Oec.* 3.2–3; Plutarch, *Mor.* 144F), but here it is given a Christian motivation. The wife's share of God's grace (1:3–9) gives her a status worthy of honor. That honor (*timē*) is given to all Christians upon Christ's return (1:7) and given by Christians to Christ (2:7) and to everyone (2:17). Thus a husband's granting his wife honor is a practical expression of the honor that Christ will afford her and that the husband is obligated to give to all people and to Christ himself. Yet the husband's rule of his wife, common in Hellenistic exhortation to husbands, is not present here (Aristotle, *Pol.* 1.1259a; Tacitus *Ann.* 3.34; Elliott 2000, 574–75).

Grammatically, the reference to the woman as the weaker vessel can also be understood as the object of "honor" rather than "live." Theologically, this translation makes weakness the basis of honor, which is not typical in the Greco-Roman perspective and loses the radical shift the author is making in the household code—that a wife is honorable because of her new status in Christ (cf. 1 Cor. 12:22–25).

The exhortation to the husbands concludes with a reason and motivation: **so that your prayers may not be hindered** (3:7c). The implication is that since God does not listen to the prayers of the disobedient (cf. 3:12; 4:7; Isa. 1:10–17), the husbands need to obey to be able to pray effectively.

Theological Issues

Maintaining behavior that cannot be faulted by nonbelievers is as valuable today as it was then as an effective tool of evangelism (2:11–12). Christian freedom from the ignorance of the past means now being slaves of God and obeying God as Master (2:15–16). Central to this obedience is extending honor to all humans as a significant part of the evangelistic strategy, for those we honor are far more likely to seek us out.

There is the admonition to give the emperor and his appointees honor so that Christians are blameless before the state (2:13). It is not calling us to naively accept all that government officials are doing but to give them honor as those with authority while they hold office. Such honor is ultimately tempered in that God is the only one to be feared as the ultimate authority (2:17).

In the exhortation to slaves, why is slavery accepted and not condemned? For one thing, the response of Rome would have been catastrophic for early Christianity, since slavery was embedded in the culture. It also may not have entered Christians' minds to do so because slavery was not like the American system, in which there was little concern for the slave, although that could be the case then. Rather, owners often educated, trained, and paid the slaves, who looked forward to freedom at about age thirty to forty, depending on the amount the master had invested in them.

The exhortation to the slaves is meant to help them maneuver their dual positions within their master's household and the household of God. They accept the authority of their earthly masters to avoid punishment, but they endure punishment when they need to disobey their earthly masters to obey their heavenly Master, who is the final judge. Even so, unjust suffering is easier to bear, knowing that it has God's approval and, if endured with God's will and purposes in mind, receives God's glory and grace.

Christ provides the example of unjust suffering for the slaves and entire Christian community—a model of nonretaliation. He was verbally abused, yet did not respond in kind. He was physically abused, yet gave himself over to God and did not threaten God's vengeance. Christ also provides the reason why righteous living that leads to unjust suffering can be endured: his own suffering freed us from sin, healed us, and provided us with a guardian of our spiritual lives (1:18–20; 2:21–25; 3:18–22). Our dying to sin opens up the possibility of righteous living and the guidance of God as we live that righteousness out. God actually works in our conversion to turn us from sin to righteousness, and thus to our new Shepherd and Guardian, Jesus Christ.

A wife who has a pagan husband and has converted to Christianity is vulnerable because, by not abiding by the religion of her husband, she is impugning the husband's honor (in that culture) and is subject to his anger. Such wives should do nothing that could further dishonor their husbands, like bedecking themselves with jewels and fine clothes, which were considered provocative at that time. Adornment that is the transformation of the mind and the will to exhibit a humble and quiet spirit is what stands the best chance of evangelizing a husband and showing faithfulness to God. Today quality jewelry and clothing do not necessarily have the provocative connotations of that day and certainly are acceptable for Christian attire; yet clothing and jewelry that are too extravagant can hinder evangelism by their obvious self-indulgence. Husbands are to honor their wives because they too share in the gift of life and to do otherwise hinders their prayers.

This advice to wives and husbands was meant to ameliorate the specific problem of a Christian wife living with a non-Christian husband. The subjection of a wife to her husband is here enjoined, to lessen conflict over a radical change within an existing marriage. This counsel was given in a strongly patriarchal society and has a patriarchal bias. As such it is not necessarily applicable to modern Christian marriage nor a theological principle for marriage for all time. We are free to find principles applicable to marriage, such as the value of pure conduct, a gentle and quiet spirit, and honor in marriage. We are free to let the understanding of wives as sharing the grace of life (v. 7), and the broader vision of Christianity as one of mutuality (Gal. 3:28), transform the marriage relationship. The culture-bound nature of this passage can be transcended for mutuality in Christian marriage. We have already transcended the master-slave relationship in our culture over the past two hundred years (2:18–25).

1 Peter 3:8–12

Practicing Mutual Love and Peace with All

Introductory Matters

This section forms a conclusion of the household code that began in 2:13 and a transition to the discussion of suffering for doing good to follow in 3:13–4:6. This section concludes with an extensive quotation from Ps. 33:13–17a LXX (34:12–16a; cf. the use of Ps. 33:9 LXX [34:8] in 2:3) to further support the exhortation, underscoring the good behavior that is needed, both inside and outside the community. There are numerous similarities between the moral exhortation here and Rom. 12:9–18.

Tracing the Train of Thought

3:8. Five adjectives or virtues that should characterize all Christians are now listed with imperatival force: **Finally, everyone be like-minded, sympathetic, loving one another, compassionate, and humble.** "Like-minded" (*homophrōn*) is not to think alike but to be agreeable and sensitive to the concerns of others through mutual respect (cf. Rom. 12:16; 15:5; 1 Cor. 1:10; 2 Cor. 13:11; Phil. 2:2; 4:2). "Sympathetic" (*sympathēs*) is

1 Peter 3:8–12 in the Rhetorical Flow

God's provision for salvation, and Christians' status before God (1:1–2:10)

Living honorably among the gentiles (2:11–4:11)

Introduction to the main theme (2:11–12)

The household code (2:13–3:7)

▶ Practicing mutual love and peace with all (3:8–12)

sharing the full range of emotions and experiences, both positive and negative, with others (cf. Rom. 12:15; 1 Cor. 12:26). "Loving one another" (*philadel-phos*) denotes emotional bonding and commitment (cf. 1:22; 2:17; 4:8; Rom. 12:10; 1 Thess. 4:9; Heb. 13:1; 2 Pet. 1:7; *1 Clem.* 47.5; 48.1). "Compassionate" (*eusplanchnos*) is having tender feelings and concern for someone (Eph. 4.32). "Humble" (*tapeinophrōn*) was typically considered a weakness in Greco-Roman society, characterizing those who could not defend their social position and honor, but it was adapted by Christianity as a virtue (1 Pet. 5:5–6; Eph. 4:2; Phil. 2:3; Col. 2:18, 23; 3:12; Ign. *Eph.* 10.2; *Barn.* 19.3; *Herm. Mand.* 11.8) based on the teaching and example of Jesus (Matt. 11:29; 18:4; 23:12; Phil. 2:8).

3:9. An exhortation from early Christian tradition follows: **Do not repay evil for evil or insult for insult, but on the contrary, bless** (3:9a). It refers to all relationships but primarily between the recipients and outsiders who are slandering them (2:12, 15; 3:16; 4:4, 14). The recipients are called to employ the nonretaliatory ethic of Jesus (Matt. 5:38–42, 44; Luke 6:27–29; Rom. 12:14–21; 1 Cor. 4:12–13; 1 Thess. 5:15) and to imitate the unjust suffering of Christ's passion (2:21–23). However, rather than remain silent when abused as Jesus did in his unique situation, they are to bless their enemies, that is, offer a person the prospect of salvation. Blessing is like intercessory prayer except that it is directed to a person rather than to God. It facilitates the hope that enemies will be saved and glorify God on the day of judgment (2:12; Michaels 1988, 178).

Whether the next portion of the sentence points forward (bless in order to be blessed) or backward (bless because you are called to a blessing) is grammatically uncertain (see Achtemeier 1996, 224; Elliott 2000, 609–10). Rhetorically, it points backward, for a reason and a motivation for nonretaliation and blessing others when verbally abused is now given: **For to this you have been called, that you may obtain a blessing** (3:9b). The reason is that Christians are called to holy conduct and nonretaliation (1:15–16; 2:21–23), and the motivation is that they will receive a blessing, which is partially defined as an inheritance (1:4) and grace (1:13; 3:7). It is not that Christians earn a blessing by blessing others, but they are in jeopardy of losing their blessing if they do not live up to their calling and bless those persecuting them (Piper 1980; Achtemeier 1996, 224). A similar understanding of the Christian life as being called by God to current suffering and future blessing is found in 1:1–9.

3:10–12. The quotation of Ps. 33:13–17a LXX (34:12–16a) provides a warrant and amplifies the point of verse 9 that blessing others is necessary to receive God's blessing: **For "those that want to love life and to see good days, let them keep their tongue from evil and their lips from speaking deceit"** (3:10). Whereas the psalm speaks of life and good days on earth, in this new context life refers to salvation (v. 7) and good days to the unseen inheritance (1:4, 9; 3:9). Christians who want life and good days watch their speech, avoiding evil and deceit (2:1). Speech is the easiest way to return evil for evil (cf. v. 9), something to which Christ the exemplar did not resort (2:22).

In verse 11 the psalm continues with commandments that move the thought from speech to action, an inseparable combination in 1 Peter (2:1; 3:15b–16), and set the groundwork for the following discussion of doing good and evil (vv. 13–17). Those desiring life and good days **let them cease from evil and do good** (3:11a; cf. 2:11–12, 14–16, 19–20; 3:6, 17; 4:2–3, 15, 19), and **let them seek peace and pursue it** (3:11b). Peace, whether with everyone (Rom. 12:18; Heb. 12:14) or with fellow believers in particular (Mark 9:50; Rom. 14:19; 2 Cor. 13:11; 1 Thess. 5:13), is a major concern in early Christian ethics (Matt. 5:9; *2 Clem.* 10.2) and nicely summarizes the exhortation about relationships in the household code (2:13–3:7).

The justification for the commandments of verse 11 is now expressed as an inexact antithesis: **Because the eyes of the Lord are upon the righteous, and his ears are open to their prayers. The face of the Lord is against those doing evil** (3:12). Again, the effectiveness of prayer is tied to righteousness (3:7; cf. 4:7). Here "the Lord" probably means Jesus, just as 3:15 understands the Lord in Isa. 8:13 to be Jesus. The righteous are those who speak and do good rather than evil (vv. 10–11, 13–17). Although many commentators understand "those doing evil" to be those opposing the recipients, they are probably the recipients who have been the addressees throughout the household code. This explains the omission of the end of Ps. 33:17b LXX [34:16b] in this quotation ("to destroy the memory of them from the earth"), which applies to the truly evil but not to Christians, who may occasionally make the wrong choice to retaliate. The face of the Lord is an idiom for God's presence (cf. Gen. 3:8 MT), which is opposed to those doing evil, including Christians.

Theological Issues

The virtues of being agreeable, sympathetic, loving, compassionate, and humble are extolled for relationships within the family, within the Christian community, and between the Christian community and the world. These virtues are part of the blessing with which Christians should respond to insult and evil from others, especially non-Christians. Responding to evil with blessing is a call from God (3:9) and modeled on Jesus's example of blessing those who persecuted him. Blessing others is a form of the gospel and has power to transform the persecutor (2:12). Jesus's blessing of his persecutors led to the offer of salvation to the world, an offer we can extend by blessing our own persecutors.

We are called to bless our persecutors in part to maintain our blessing and inheritance, which might be jeopardized if we neglect to bless our persecutors. Evil and deceitful speech and wrongful acts jeopardize our inheritance, while seeking peace brings the presence of the Lord into our lives. Peace is the desired outcome in all relationships and certainly encompasses evangelism of persecutors, which would result in peace with them. Peace is a NT theme rooted in the teaching of Jesus (Matt. 5:9) and pursued by exercising virtues, several of which are listed in this section (Rom. 12:18; 14:19; 2 Tim. 2:22; Heb. 12:14; James 3:18).

1 Peter 3:13–22

Doing Good Rather than Evil amid Suffering, after Christ's Example

Introductory Matters

This section loosely follows the order of 2:18–25: a premise (2:18; 3:13), exhortation about Christian behavior in suffering (2:19; 3:14–16), an affirmation of doing good as the correct moral choice (2:20; 3:17), and the example of Christ, who suffered for doing good and was ultimately victorious (2:21–25; 3:18–22; Achtemeier 1996, 228–29). The previous quotation of Ps. 33:13–17a LXX (34:12–16a) in verses 10–12 and the following use of Isa. 8:12–13 LXX in verses 14b–16 provide authority for the exhortation in verses 13–17 for the recipients to do good rather than evil in the midst of suffering (Wagner 2008, 94–98).

> ### 1 Peter 3:13–22 in the Rhetorical Flow
>
> **God's provision for salvation, and Christians' status before God (1:1–2:10)**
>
> **Living honorably among the gentiles (2:11–4:11)**
>
> > Introduction to the main theme (2:11–12)
> >
> > The household code (2:13–3:7)
> >
> > Practicing mutual love and peace with all (3:8–12)
> >
> > ▶ Doing good rather than evil amid suffering, after Christ's example (3:13–22)
> >
> > > Doing good rather than evil amid suffering (3:13–17)
> > >
> > > Christ's suffering brings victory over the powers (3:18–22)

Tracing the Train of Thought

Doing Good Rather than Evil amid Suffering (3:13–17)

3:13. A rhetorical question shifts the focus from the recipients to their treatment by their neighbors: **Who then will harm you if you are an enthusiast for good?** What cannot be harmed is the grace, hope, glory, and inheritance that God promises and secures for Christians (1:3–9). The underlying premise is that God is on the side of those doing good and against those who do evil (Pss. 56:4; 91:7–10; 118:6–7; Matt. 10:28–31//Luke 12:4–7; Rom. 8:31). Even if those doing good suffer on earth, their eternal status with God is secure. The term "enthusiast" (*zēlōtēs*) is commonly used in Hellenism for the pursuit of moral ideals, such as honor, virtue, truth, piety, righteousness, and justice (Michaels 1988, 185), and in the NT of spiritual gifts (1 Cor. 14:12) and good works (Titus 2:14), the latter being the immediate reference here.

3:14a. The previous verse is now qualified with a probable adaptation of Jesus's beatitude on suffering and blessing (Matt. 5:10; cf. 5:11–12): **But even if you do suffer on account of righteousness, you are blessed.** Although the mood of the verb "suffer" (*paschō*) is optative, suggesting that suffering is a remote possibility, suffering for being righteous is a reality for the recipients (1:6–7; 2:12, 18–25; 4:12–19; 5:8–10). It is better to understand the verse as affirming that blessing can still occur even amid suffering. Blessed (*makarios*) is to receive divine favor, which includes an inherited blessing (1:4; 3:9; 4:14) and praise, glory, honor, and grace at the coming of Jesus Christ (1:7, 13).

3:14b–15a. A modified quotation of Isa. 8:12–13 LXX provides an added exhortation: **Do not fear them nor be intimidated, but in your hearts reverence Christ as Lord.** This verse is often translated "do not fear what they fear," but I read "fear" (*phobos*) as a cognate accusative with "them" (*autōn*) standing as a genitive of origin, indicating that "fear originates with the oppressors" (Achtemeier 1996, 232n45). Since Christians are blessed regardless of suffering, they need not fear their oppressors. Fearlessness is modeled by Christian wives exhibiting right conduct (3:6), and fear is reserved for God who judges all (1:17; 2:17). To reverence (*hagiazō*) Christ as Lord is to maintain one's perspective amid suffering by keeping in mind Christ's example of suffering and the ultimate blessing that will be shared with him (cf. Matt. 6:9; Luke 11:2).

3:15b–17. The recipients are now instructed on how to reverence Christ as Lord: **Always be prepared with a defense for everyone asking you for an account concerning the hope that is in you** (3:15b). A defense (*apologia*) is a formal response in court to specific charges (Acts 22:1; 25:16; 2 Tim. 4:16), as well as an argument made by someone when criticized or misunderstood (1 Cor. 9:3; 2 Cor. 7:11; Phil. 1:7, 16). Here the gospel is on trial by pagan neighbors, although official inquiries are not necessarily excluded (cf. Luke 12:1–12; 21:12–15; Knox 1953). Hope (*elpis*) is in God for resurrection through Christ's resurrection (1:3, 21) and in the grace to be revealed when Christ returns (1:13). The recipients are to be ready to defend their hope and the Lord they reverence to a world without hope (Eph. 2:12; 1 Thess. 4:13). The Greco-Roman world had lost hope in its own gods and was struggling to find meaning and purpose, and the Christian message is that Christ is hope (Col. 1:22, 27; 1 Tim. 1:1; Titus 2:13; 3:7).

The defense of Christian hope is to be done **yet with gentleness and reverence** (3:16a). Gentleness (*praytēs*), or humility, is an attitude that acknowledges human weakness and dependence on God's power. Reverence (*phobos*), or fear, is for God as well, not for those receiving a defense. Fear is reserved for God (1:17; 2:17): Christians are advised not to fear their opposition (3:6, 14), and Isa. 8:12–13 LXX (which has been in view since v. 14) concludes, "and he [the Lord] is your fear." While both gentleness and reverence are virtues rooted in an attitude toward God, they are expressed in relationships with people, including those asking for a defense. The exhortation is especially pertinent because in an honor-and-shame culture, the natural response of anyone offering a defense would be to do so at all costs, including slander. Christ has already been given as an example of not returning verbal abuse (2:23), with Ps. 34 further supporting this posture (3:10–12).

An accompanying characteristic of being gentle and reverent in giving a defense (and not a new imperative; Elliott 2000, 62) is **having a good conscience, so that when you are slandered, those mistreating you for your good behavior in Christ will be put to shame** (3:16b; cf. 2:12). Conscience (*syneidēsis*) is a spiritual awareness of our relationship with God (2:19; 3:21), and a clear conscience denotes our personal integrity in that relationship. Slander (*epēreazō*) is verbal abuse targeting one's good behavior (cf. 2:12; 3:9; 4:4, 14). Good behavior in Christ is living according to his teachings (2:15, 19–20; 3:11, 13, 17; 4:19), which creates and maintains a good conscience, puts the slanderers to shame (*kataischynthōsin*), and thus is a successful, gentle, and reverent defense against slander. This shame is both in this life—having their slander shown to be pointless (cf. 2:15)—as well as eschatological—shamed by God (cf. 2:6; see also 2:7–8; 4:5, 17–18). The OT promises that the faithful will not be put to shame, but their enemies will be shamed (Pss. 6:10; 22:5; 25:2–3; 31:1, 17; 35:4; 70:2; 127:5; Jer. 17:13, 18)—and now those trusting in Jesus will not be put to shame (2:6, quoting Isa. 28:16 LXX).

3:17. Now comes a reason for providing a defense for slander that is gentle and reverent, with a good conscience: **For it is better to suffer for doing good, if the will of God wants it, than for doing evil** (cf. 2:20). Suffering for doing good is a test from God (1:6–7; 4:12–16, 19). Christ exemplified this suffering (2:21–24; 3:18; 4:1), and God approves and rewards such a righteous sufferer, as he approved Christ (2:20; 3:18–22; 5:10).

Some have argued that this verse is a proverb, or *Tobspruch*, noticing the fate of Christians who now are doing good and suffering from neighbors and comparing that with the fate of neighbors who are doing evil and later will suffer God's judgment. They propose that the quotation of Ps. 34 in 3:10–12 divides humanity into those doing good and those doing evil, in the context of God's favor and disfavor (Michaels 1988, 191–92). Yet broadening the comparison from two sources of Christian suffering (doing good or doing evil) to a comparison of Christian and non-Christian behavior is unwarranted. In this letter, the contrast is between Christians' suffering for doing good or doing evil (2:20; 4:15–16), and the verb "suffer" (*paschein*) is never used in the NT of nonbelievers' suffering inflicted by God.

Christ's Suffering Brings Victory over the Powers (3:18–22)

The opening phrase, "For Christ also suffered," indicates that this section holds Christ up as an example (cf. 2:21–25). Christ's example of doing good amid suffering and his subsequent resurrection and exaltation is held up as a model and hope that Christian suffering is ultimately victorious through his victory. However, the specifics of the example are not so clear!

Interpretations of this section fall mainly into three differing trajectories: (1) This section is read in connection with 4:6, which is understood as proclaiming the gospel to the human dead. The dead here are then equated with the spirits of the evil generation that died in the flood of Gen. 6–8. (2) This section is related to Jesus's descent to the lower parts of the earth, understood as hell in Eph. 4:8–10. Jesus's proclamation here is then understood as his descent into hell during his three days in the tomb, either in order to assure the faithful under the old covenant that their salvation is now secure or to give the wicked a second opportunity for salvation. (3) During his time in the tomb or as he ascends to heaven, Christ announces his victory to the imprisoned evil angels of Noah's time (Gen. 6:1–4; *1 En.* 15.8–12). This last view, Christ's preaching to evil angels as he ascends, is the position of this commentator. (For further discussion, see Selwyn 1947, 314–62; Reicke 1946, 7–51; Perrot 1980; Dalton 1979; 1989; Westfall 1999; Klumbies 2001; D. Campbell and Van Rensburg 2008.)

3:18. Having discussed suffering for doing good in verses 13–17, Christ is now presented as an example of such suffering: **For Christ also suffered** (3:18a). Christ is the example not only for suffering unjustly (2:21–25) but also for suffering for doing good—both with redemptive power. Some scribes changed "suffered" to "died" because death is the reference at the end of this verse, and the death of Christ is central to the early confessions of faith (e.g., Rom. 4:25; 5:6–8; 1 Cor. 15:3; 2 Cor. 5:14–15; Gal. 2:21; 1 Thess. 5:9–10). However, "suffered" fits the immediate context (3:14, 17; 4:1) and the letter as a whole, in which Christ's suffering rather than his death provides an example for the recipients' lives (2:21–25; 4:13–16; 5:1, 9–10; Achtemeier 1996, 247).

Christ's suffering, which includes his death, is obviously more than an example of suffering for doing good because it was **for sins once for all** (3:18b; Rom. 6:9–10; Heb. 10:10–14). His was clearly a sacrificial death (1:19, 2:24) since the phrase "for sins" (*peri hamartiōn*) is used in the LXX (Lev. 5:6–7;

6:23; Ezek. 43:21) and the NT (Rom. 8:3; Heb. 5:3; 10:26; 1 John 2:2; 4:10) in connection with a sin offering. Unlike OT sacrifices, Christ's suffering for sin does not need to be repeated (Heb. 7:27; 9:12, 26, 28; 10:10–14). Christ's suffering frees humanity from sin to live for righteousness (2:24) and from the desires of the flesh to live by the will of God (4:1–2).

Christ's dying is a dying of **the righteous for the unrighteous** (3:18c). Christ's righteousness is the reason why he can be a unique, once-for-all sacrifice for sin (1:19; 2:22–23). The "unrighteous" is anyone before their conversion, before being made righteous through Christ (cf. 1:14, 18; 2:10, 25; 4:2–4, 18). Christ the righteous died *for* (*hyper*) the unrighteous, an expression used in early Christian proclamation for Christ's substitutionary atonement (John 11:50, 52; Rom. 5:6–8; 14:15; 1 Cor. 11:24; 15:3; 2 Cor. 5:15, 21; Gal. 2:20; 3:13; Eph. 5:25; 1 Thess. 5:10; Titus 2:14; *Diogn.* 9.2). This may be a reference to the Suffering Servant of Isa. 53:11: "The righteous one, my servant, shall make many righteous, and he shall bear their iniquities." This passage developed as part of the messianic tradition (Wis. 2:18; *1 En.* 38.2–3; 53.6) and was applied to Jesus by early proclamation (Acts 3:14; 7:52; 22:14; James 5:6; cf. 1 John 2:1, 29; 3:7; Ruppert 1972a; 1972b; 1973; Lohse 1963, 64–110).

The recipients are told that the reason Christ suffered for sins is **that he might bring you to God** (3:18d), that is, provide access to God (cf. Rom. 5:2; Eph. 2:18; 3:12). Christ can now provide this access because, as a consequence of being a righteous offering, he was resurrected by God and resides at God's right hand (3:18, 21–22). Some manuscripts read "bring *us* to God," but the context of verses 13–17 is in the second person.

Christ could effect this access to God **by being put to death in the flesh but made alive in the spirit** (3:18e). The formulaic contrasts of Christ's dying and living, or rising (Mark 8:31; 9:31; 10:33–34; Rom. 4:25; 6:10; 8:34; 14:9; 1 Cor. 15:3–4), and being in the flesh and the spirit (Rom. 1:3–4; 1 Tim. 3:16) are common in the NT. "Christ," the subject of the sentence, is modified by two passive participles: "put to death" (*thanatōtheis*), with the human authorities in Jerusalem as implied agents, and "made alive" (*zōopoiētheis*), with God understood as the agent (cf. 1 Pet. 1:3, 21), for the latter verb typically refers to the resurrection (John 5:21; Rom. 4:17; 8:11; 1 Cor. 15:22; Eph. 2:5; Col. 2:13; Achtemeier 1996, 249).

The two datives "in the flesh" and "in the spirit" are datives of respect (as in 4:6): put to death in respect to the flesh and made alive in respect to the spirit. Flesh (*sarx*) is human flesh as well as the physical dimension of life that is susceptible to evil and death (1:24; 2:11; 3:21; 4:1–2, 6). Spirit (*pneuma*) means "the intelligent and transcendent aspects of the human person that can be responsive to grace" (Senior 2003, 101), life "controlled and animated by God's life-giving Spirit" (Elliott 2000, 647). This understanding of these two datives conforms with two similar creeds pairing flesh and spirit in relation to Jesus (Rom. 1:3–4; 8:1–11; 1 Tim. 3:16 [although some understand the "spirit" here as "Spirit"]).

Some interpreters understand these two datives as instrumental: put to death by flesh (Jesus's accusers) and made alive by the Spirit, with a capital *S* (cf. John 6:63; Rom. 8:11; Achtemeier 1996, 250–51). However, as noted above, flesh in 1 Peter clearly refers to the mortal state, and in this tight contrast, spirit naturally refers to the spiritual state. Besides, this letter credits God rather than the Spirit for raising Jesus from the dead (1:3, 21).

Figure 7. Looking out of an ancient prison.

3:19. Here the letter speaks of Christ after the resurrection and in the spirit, **in which state he even went and made a proclamation to the spirits in prison.** The prepositional phrase with relative pronoun, "in which" (*en hō*) has been understood to refer to the preceding dative of respect, "in the spirit," but a dative of respect is never the antecedent of the relative pronoun in the NT (Selwyn 1947, 197). Rather, the relative pronoun refers to the *state* in which Jesus made the journey and his proclamation described in all of verse 18—after his death *and* resurrection. Christ went to the spirits in prison during his ascension to heaven (v. 22). *Thus the reference is not to Christ descending into hell in the spirit during his stay in the tomb.*

Christ went and preached "even" (*kai*) to the spirits in prison, that is, "to the most remote and unlikely audience imaginable" (Michaels 1988, 206). This description dramatizes that the victory of Christ is universal, as explicitly stated in verse 22 (Phil. 2:9–11; Eph. 1:20–22; cf. Col. 1:15–17). But who are the spirits in prison? They come from the days of Noah (v. 20) and have been variously identified as (1) humans who perished in Noah's flood, to whom Christ came in spirit during his three days in the tomb (cf. 4:6; Clement of Alexandria, *Strom.* 6.6); (2) the angels who fathered human children, whose wickedness precipitated the flood judgment (Gen. 6:1–4; *1 En.* 15.1–7; *2 En.* 18.1–5; Spitta 1890; Dalton 1989, 151); or (3) the souls of these children who perished in the flood and whose spirits became demons, according to some traditions (*1 En.* 15.8–12; see Reicke 1946, 7–51). The first identification of the spirits as human is ruled out because the word "spirit" (*pneuma*) is rarely used of a human, dead or alive, and if it is, it is qualified (cf. Heb. 12:23). Also, a prison (*phylakē*) is not used to describe the realm of the human dead

(Dalton 1989, 160), nor are the human dead confined anywhere in the flood tradition. The third identification seems viable at first, for "spirit" is frequently used of both good (Heb. 1:14; Rev. 1:4; 3:1; 4:5; 5:6) and evil supernatural forces, such as the demons that Jesus confronted in his ministry (Matt. 8:16; 12:45; Luke 10:20). However, these forces are free to roam the earth and are not imprisoned.

The second identification is most likely, for Jewish tradition describes the evil angels of Gen. 6:1–4 as bound in prison for their disobedience in fathering children with human women and creating evil offspring (*1 En.* 10.4–6, 12–14; 14.5; 18.14–16; 21.1–10; 54.1–6; *2 En.* 7.1–3; *Jub.* 5.6), a tradition that carries over into the NT (Jude 6; 2 Pet. 2:4). In this tradition, primarily found in *1 Enoch*, Enoch ascends to heaven, goes to these angels on his way, and announces their destruction (*1 En.* 12.4–6; 13.1–14.7; 15.1–16.3). This tradition is the closest parallel to the depiction of Christ here. Also pertinent is the tradition of Jesus's making a heavenly journey or ascent (Eph. 4:9–10; Heb. 4:14); ascent by others is also found in the literature of the period (Himmelfarb 1993).

Prison (*phylakē*) is a place of confinement, either for humans while living (not dead), as in a jail, or for evil spirits (BDAG 1067–68; *TDNT* 9:241–44). In Jewish and early Christian tradition, evil spirits are confined in a variety of locations, including in the earth (*1 En.* 10.4; 14.5; 15.8, 10; 67.7; *Jub.* 5.6; 2 Pet. 2:4; Jude 6; Rev. 20:3), in the heavens (*2 En.* 7.1–3; 18.3; Eph. 6:12), or at the end of both heaven and earth (*1 En.* 18.12–14; 21.1–10). The location meant here is uncertain, but according to tradition the angels are to remain in confinement until they are destroyed at the consummation (Jude 6; 2 Pet. 2:4).

The purpose of Christ's visit to the prison is to announce or proclaim (*kēryssō*) something. If referring to the gospel, this verb usually takes an object like "gospel" (Matt. 24:14; Col. 1:23; 1 Thess. 2:9). Since it does not here and the audience is unredeemable, the proclamation is probably not preaching forgiveness and redemption in an effort to convert those in prison. Rather,

First Enoch

First Enoch is one of three pseudepigraphical works attributed to the Enoch of Gen. 5:21–24. His mysterious translation into heaven and access to that domain led writers to attribute to him these books describing heavenly realities. *First Enoch* is a combination of five apocalypses spanning the mid-third century BCE to mid-first century CE. The first, based on Gen. 6:1–4, is the Book of the Watchers (chaps. 1–36), which describes how angels descend to earth, have sex with women, father an evil generation of giants, and corrupt humanity, which brings the judgment of the flood. It also tells how these evil angels are imprisoned until final judgment. This account lies in the background of 1 Pet. 3:18–21.

Christ came to proclaim to the evil spirits that since he has conquered sin and death, their final destruction is sure (3:22; cf. 4:5, 7, 17–18).

Christ's proclamation has been understood to occur in a descent to hell or the netherworld (Rom. 10:7; Eph. 4:8–10), but the verb here, "went" or "journeyed" (*poreuomai*), does not imply a downward motion. However, it can mean "ascend" and is used to describe Christ's ascent into heaven (John 14:2–3, 12, 28; 16:7, 28; Acts 1:10–11), as here in verse 22. Christ is proclaiming his victory to the imprisoned spirits as he ascends to heaven.

3:20. The spirits in prison are those **who formerly disobeyed when the patience of God was waiting eagerly in the days of Noah, during the building of the ark** (3:20a). In the Second Temple period, God's punishment of the evil angels and saving of Noah and his family were understood to be a prototype of God's judgment of evil and salvation of the righteous in general (Heb. 11:7; 2 Pet. 2:4–5, 10; 3:4–7; Unnik 1979; Elliott 2000, 655–56). The verb "disobey" (*apeitheō*) and similar terms are used to describe the behavior of the angels in taking human wives, thus violating their place in creation (*1 En.* 6.3; 9.7–9; *Jub.* 5.1–11; Jude 6; 2 Pet. 2:4). It is the verb used throughout 1 Peter to portray those who are persecuting the recipients (2:8; 3:1; 4:17), thus making this prototype pertinent to the destruction of the enemies of the recipients as well as the salvation of the recipients.

God's patience (*makrothymia*) refers to the period between the sin of the angels and the coming of the floodwaters, when the ark was being built, a period in tradition of 120 years, based on Gen. 6:3 and the human lifespan (*Tg. Onq.*, *Tg. Neof.*, and *Tg. Ps.-J.* on Gen. 6:3). Often lost in translation and recaptured here, God's patience is personified as "waiting eagerly" (*apekdechomai*), or "champing at the bit," to bring judgment but also as amazingly restrained in waiting 120 years for a payoff **in which a few, that is eight souls, were saved through water** (3:20b). "Souls" (*psychai*) here refers to the whole person rather than to the transcendent essence of a person (cf. 1:9, 22; 2:25; 4:19). The people saved include Noah and his wife and his three sons and their wives (Gen. 7:13; 2 Pet. 2:5).

If God was patient enough to save eight people, God will certainly act to save all the recipients, and in the same way—through water. The passive form of the verb "saved" (*diasōzō*) indicates that God is doing the saving, as in the accounts of the saving of Noah and his sons (*1 En.* 106.16; *Jub.* 7.34; 10.3). "Through water" can be an instrumental dative indicating that Noah was saved using water, but water in this tradition is a force of destruction, and the ark itself is what saved Noah and his family. "Through water" more likely is a locative dative indicating that Noah was saved by traveling through water (Wis. 14:1–7). In the next verse the water of baptism provides the perfect counterpart in saving people from death as they pass through water—Noah from his sinful generation and Christians from their own sin (Achtemeier 1996, 265–66).

3:21. Noah's and Christians' experiences are now compared: **Baptism, which corresponds to this, now saves you too** (3:21a). "Corresponding to" (*antitypon*) can also be translated "copy, antitype, or representation" (BDAG 90–91) and suggests that baptism is an inferior copy of the floodwaters. However, here the reference is to baptism as a counterpart to the floodwaters, emphasizing the unity within God's redemptive plan. Paul does the same thing by understanding the passing under the cloud and through the Red Sea as corresponding to baptism (1 Cor. 10:1–2; for full discussion, see Ostmeyer 2000).

Baptism corresponds to "this," that is, the water and Noah's entire salvation experience. As Noah passed through the water from evil and death to life, so converts pass through the water from evil and death to new life. This is the only reference in the NT to baptism as saving (*sōzō*). The wording implies that the water has some saving power, which sounds strange to anyone who has ever read Paul's Letters, in which "Jesus saves." But even Paul acknowledges that without baptism there is no share in the death, burial, and resurrection of Christ (Rom. 6:1–11; cf. Col. 2:12).

Fortunately, the remainder of the verse explains how baptism saves: **not as removing dirt from the body, but as a pledge to God out of a good conscience** (3:21b). Baptism is making a pledge (*eperōtēma*) to God out of a good conscience, given at the cleansing of conversion. At that time, obedience to Christ (1:2, 22; 2:1–3; Heb. 10:22) replaces obedience to the flesh, which controls the lives of unbelievers (1:14; 2:11; 4:2). This good conscience (*syneidēsis*) is not the absence of guilt, as we understand the term, but honesty and subordination before God, which issues in obedience to God's will (2:19; 3:16). Such a conscience motivates a pledge to continue living in obedience (4:2).

Some have translated the verse as "an *appeal or pledge* to God *for* a good conscience," a translation that the Greek will also support but which implies that conversion and a good conscience occur at baptism. However, baptism is a witness to conversion and a good conscience, not the moment thereof.

This pledge out of a good conscience and the salvation of which it is a part are made possible **through the resurrection of Jesus Christ** (3:21c). God saved Noah, and God gives life through the resurrection of Jesus (1:3). Baptism is a pledge that the salvation wrought by the cross has become effective in the lives of believers (1:3–5, 9–10, 21; 2:2, 5, 10, 24; 3:7; 4:6).

3:22. After digressing to describe the salvation of the obedient, the focus returns to Christ's journey: **who, having gone into heaven, is on the right hand of God, with angels, authorities, and powers subject to him.** Having ascended and announced his victory to the disobedient angels, Christ now resides at God's right hand. In the ancient world the right hand was a position of honor and power, second in command. Jesus is affirmed to possess the victorious position that he proclaimed (v. 19) and to have been glorified by God (1:21; cf. 1:11; 4:13; 5:1). Jesus at God's right hand is proclaimed throughout the NT (Mark 12:35–37//Matt. 22:41–46//Luke 20:41–44; Mark 14:62//Matt. 26:64;

Mark 14:62; 16:19; Luke 22:69; Acts 5:30–31; 7:55–56; Rom. 8:34; Col. 3:1; Heb. 1:13; 8:1; 10:12; 12:2), a position understood as the fulfillment of prophecy based on Ps. 110:1 (109:1 LXX; Acts 2:33–35; 1 Cor. 15:25; Eph. 1:20; Heb. 1:13). The idea of subjection of the powers to Christ comes in part from Ps. 8:6 (8:7 LXX; 1 Cor. 15:27 and Eph. 1:22, both after a quotation of Ps. 110:1 [109:1 LXX]; Heb. 2:5–9). While Pss. 8 and 110 anchor the ideas expressed here, the wording is the author's.

The authorities (*exousiai*) and powers (*dynameis*) are supernatural beings that influence humanity (Rom. 8:38; 1 Cor. 15:24; Eph. 1:21; 3:10; 6:12; Col. 1:16; 2:10, 15) and together with angels represent all power, whether good or evil, in the universe. This is the only place in the NT that includes angels with authorities and powers (cf. Rom. 8:38), and this mention of angels further supports the identification of the spirits in prison in verse 19 as angels (Elliott 2000, 688). These angels, powers, and authorities are now subjugated to Christ and no longer have ultimate power over the lives of the Christians, although they instigate others to persecute the Christians (cf. 5:8). While hidden now, Christ's rule over these powers will become apparent with the judgment by Christ (4:13; 5:10–11).

Theological Issues

Christians are to be "enthusiasts for the good," that is, actively seeking to be virtuous in our interactions with others and producing good works. Christianity is not an armchair religion but one of active involvement in the world, of building and expanding the kingdom of God. We are assured that if suffering results for doing good, we are still blessed. No person(s) or circumstances can take away our hope and inheritance. Our only fear is a reverent fear of Christ, which reminds us of our true allegiance and the source of our blessing and strength in times of suffering.

The advice to always be ready to make a defense for our hope with gentleness and reverence reminds us of two important practical points of evangelism: we need to (1) fully understand what our hope is and how to defend it and then (2) present the gospel in a nonoffensive way that acknowledges our own weakness. A gentle and reverent defense of the gospel, undergirded by honesty in relationship to God, exhibited in good conscience, puts slanderers to shame. This shame is not meant to embarrass them but is a tool of evangelism. Recognizing the truth of our hope and conduct may lead slanderers and detractors to conversion (2:12; cf. 3:1–2).

The thought that suffering for doing good is the will of God is unsettling, but as suffering was God's will for our Lord, so it is for his followers who model their lives after him (2:21–25). This passage reassures us that when we suffer for doing good, we are following the example of Christ, who ultimately was vindicated, as his followers will be. Jesus's experience of persecution to death by itself would not necessarily motivate us to follow his example! However, his suffering was unique in that he was righteous and died for the unrighteous, was resurrected, and can now bring his fellow sufferers to God. So now no matter what we endure in this life, we will see God, and that brings hope amid suffering.

We are also comforted by this passage to learn that God was willing to wait so long to rescue only eight people! Here we are reminded of God's patience, love, and concern for the redeemed and the lengths that God has taken to bring them safely home, including the ultimate sacrifice of the Son. This is a passage that gives us hope and assurance of God's love when we fail and think that God can no longer love us.

It is in conversion that we are cleansed, and we devote ourselves to obeying God's will. It is in baptism that we pledge to continue to be aware of God's will and the work of God through Christ's resurrection. Baptism is a pledge that the benefits of that resurrection have become efficacious in our lives.

Christ's proclamation to the fallen angels in prison and his ascension to the right hand of God are full assurance that his victory over evil is complete: these forces can no longer have the final say in the destiny of humans. We have no problem affirming that Christ rules from God's right hand, he is victor over evil, and victory will someday be revealed in full. However, we do have a problem believing that angels fathered children and God has them imprisoned somewhere awaiting judgment. (Do angels have DNA? Is it identical to our own so that propagation is possible? If so, would not angels be mortal?) So here we must look to what the text affirms—Christ's victory—and not to a literal understanding of the tradition in which it is encapsulated.

1 Peter 4:1–6

Living in the Spirit and Doing the Will of God

Introductory Matters

This section resumes the focus of the previous section on suffering for doing good, suffering at the hands of the unredeemed (3:13–17; 4:1–4), and the vindication of this suffering as exemplified by Christ (3:18–22; 4:5–6). The section compares the former sinful life of the recipients with the sinful life of their persecutors, a life that they left behind because Christ has finished with sin (3:18), and so they can and should as well (3:21; 4:1–3).

Tracing the Train of Thought

4:1. After the theologically packed verses of 3:18–22, describing Christ's redemptive work, the letter continues with the consequence of that work: **Since therefore Christ suffered in the flesh, you also should equip yourselves with the same insight** (4:1a). This verse picks up all of 3:18–22, especially verse 18, saying that Christ suffered for doing good, died for sins once for all, and can lead Christians to

> ### 1 Peter 4:1–6
> ### in the Rhetorical Flow
>
> **God's provision for salvation, and Christians' status before God (1:1–2:10)**
>
> **Living honorably among the gentiles (2:11–4:11)**
>
> Introduction to the main theme (2:11–12)
>
> The household code (2:13–3:7)
>
> Practicing mutual love and peace with all (3:8–12)
>
> Doing good rather than evil amid suffering, after Christ's example (3:13–22)
>
> ▶ Living in the Spirit and doing the will of God (4:1–6)

95

God. The recipients need to equip themselves with the same insight (*ennoia*) or disposition in moral action (BDAG 337; cf. Heb. 4:12).

An option for translation determines how to understand the insight mentioned. What follows may be the *reason* for equipping with the same insight, translating the next word *hoti* as "because": "because the one suffering in the flesh is through with sin." The insight is that suffering in the flesh like Christ (3:18) is discipline that helps a person stop sinning, a tradition found in the OT (Elliott 2000, 716–18). However, this translation is unworkable because the suffering in 1 Peter is a result of ceasing from sin, not a means to that end.

What follows may be the *content* of the insight, translating *hoti* as "that": **that the one suffering in the flesh is through with sin** (4:1b). The insight is that the willingness to stop satisfying sinful desires of the flesh and to suffer in the flesh for doing good like Christ is proof that one is done with sin (Achtemeier 1996, 278). The willingness to turn from sin and suffer at the hands of unrepentant neighbors is a sign that one has indeed conquered sin in Christ (2:20–24; 3:14–17; 4:15–16). This translation is more likely in light of the letter's themes.

This military metaphor of equip or arm (*hoplizō*) indicates that putting away sin requires hand-to-hand combat with it (cf. 2 Cor. 6:7; 10:3–5; Eph. 6:11–17; 1 Thess. 5:8). The weapon is the insight that the one who suffers has ceased from sin. In 1 Peter sin is the act of doing wrong, contrary to God's will (2:22, 24; 3:18; 4:8), not a condition or power that needs to be overcome, as in Paul (Rom. 5:12–13, 20–21; 6:1, 10, 12–23; 7:13; 13:14). With this weapon of insight, Christians in their behavior are in league with Christ and control the battle against evil.

The one suffering here can be Christ or the Christian. If a reference to *Christ*, it at first seems to imply that Christ was sinning and then turned from it. This is the only way he could be an example for sinful humanity in the complete sense. However, elsewhere we know that Christ did not sin (1:19; 2:22; 3:18), so it really means that Christ has dealt with the sin of humanity once and for all, and thus now he is through with it. If the one suffering is the *Christian*, it may be a reference to baptism, in which believers pledge themselves to be mindful of the will of God (3:21), to die to sin and live to righteousness (2:24), and to be willing to suffer at the hands of their neighbors (4:3–5). While Christians may be the primary referent, Christ is a secondary referent. It is only because Christ is through with sin, once and for all (3:18; Heb. 9:28), that Christians are enabled to do the same.

4:2. The reason for the previous exhortation to live by the insight that the one who suffers has ceased from sin is now provided: **So as not to live out the remaining time in the flesh according to human desires, but by the will of God** (cf. Gal. 2:19–20). The remaining time can be either the stretch before Christ's return (cf. 1:5–6; 4:7, 17; 5:10) or the rest of the recipients' lives. Since the context speaks of the return of Christ (4:7) and time in the flesh (*sarx*) in this letter is the human condition and not an eschatological reference (1:24; 3:18; 4:1, 6), the former interpretation is preferred (Achtemeier 1996, 281), but the latter interpretation is also in view. While the recipients await Christ's return, they are not to live according to the desires of the flesh, as they lived before conversion—desires guided by selfish needs and pleasures, without regard for God (1:14; 2:11), and pursuing the excesses of their culture as outlined in verses 3–4 (cf. 1 John 2:16). Rather, the remainder of the recipients' lives should be conducted by the will of God, that is, in doing good (2:15; 3:17; 4:19) and being disciplined, obedient children, holy, and conducting their lives in reverent fear of God, who judges (1:13–17).

Figure 8. An ancient mosaic of the god of wine, called Dionysus by the Greeks and Bacchus by the Romans. The worship of this god often included drunkenness and frenzied dancing.

4:3. Here is the reason why the recipient should now live by the will of God: **For the time that has passed was sufficient for you to do the will of the gentiles** (4:3a). The will (*boulēma*) of the gentiles is living by human desires rather than the will (*thelēma*) of God (v. 2), something the recipients have spent quite enough time doing in their pre-Christian lives. The adjective "sufficient" (*arketos*) is used ironically to imply that the time spent doing what the gentiles want is "more than enough." Since the letter appropriates the language of Israel for Christians, it assumes that the recipients, who are actually gentiles, are now God's people and refers to the unredeemed as gentiles (cf. 2:12).

The "gentiles," the unredeemed, want the recipients to be like them, **living in immorality, lusts, drunkenness, excessive partying, drinking parties, and detestable idolatry** (4:3b). "Living in" is literally "walking in" (perfect participle of *poreuomai*) and refers to a series of ethical decisions, either good or bad. Here a vice list, similar to those in Judaism and Christianity depicting the unredeemed and the unfaithful redeemed, describes a series of unethical decisions made by the unredeemed (*As. Mos.* 7.1–10; Wis. 14:22–31; Mark 7:22; Rom. 1:29–31; 13:13; 1 Cor. 5:10–11; 6:9–10; Gal. 5:19–21; Col. 3:5). Because of their excessive nature, such vices were impugned by Greek, Roman, and Jewish moralists as well (Diogenes Laertius, *Lives* 10.132; Plutarch, *Mor.* 12B; Philo, *Mos.* 2.185). In part these six vices describe the desires of former ignorance (1:14) and empty living inherited from the ancestors

(1:18). The first two are particularly sexual—immorality or self-abandonment (*aselgeia*) and lusts (*epithymiai*). The former is found in NT vice lists and refers to behavior at odds with accepted morality (Mark 7:22; Rom. 13:13; 2 Cor. 12:21; Gal. 5:19), and the latter describes the broad range of human desires that control a person before conversion (1:14; 2:11; 4:2). The next three vices are similar: drunkenness (*oinophlygia*), excessive feasting or partying (*kōmos*), and drinking parties (*potos*). Drunkenness is excessive drinking; excessive feasting (Rom. 13:13; Gal. 5:21) is associated with the worship of Dionysus, which involved drunken orgies; and drinking parties involve excessive drinking and carousing. The last vice, the most important in a list, is detestable idolatry (*athemitos eidōlolatria*) and indicates that all six vices are probably the excesses of pagan religion, rituals, sacred meals, and feasts. The Jewish and NT vice lists often contain warnings against idolatry, informed by the first commandment of the Decalogue (Gal. 5:20; Col. 3:5). Judaism and Paul considered idolatry the source of all other vices (Wis. 14:27; Rom. 1:18–32).

4:4. Now the letter describes the reaction of unrepentant neighbors to the Christians who now live by the will God: **In view of this, they are surprised that you are not running around with them in the same outpouring of reckless abandon, and they slander you.** The letter's recipients no longer participate in a flood of reckless abandon (*anachysis*), that is, a broad range of pleasure-seeking activities that include drunkenness and sexual acts, as outlined in the previous verse. Their neighbors are surprised (*xenizō*) by new and different behavior, and they slander the recipients for behavior at odds with their own (3:16), understanding that such change is an implicit condemnation of their own behavior. Also, nonparticipation in cultural activities was frowned upon at this time. Nonparticipation in the emperor cult could be considered treasonous, and forsaking observances to the gods was counted as exposing the population to divine wrath. The slander is probably directed both at the recipients, as has been the case in the letter so far (2:12, 15; 3:9, 16; 4:14), and at their God, as the reference to God's judgment in the next verse implies.

4:5. The fate of those slandering Christians and God is now described. They may seem to have the upper hand now, **but they will give an account to the one who is ready to judge the living and the dead.** This is subtle irony, for whereas these neighbors call the Christians to give an account of their hope (3:15–16), they will be called to give an account before God on the day of judgment. This is legal language for giving an account in court (*apodidōmi*). In the three other NT passages that speak of judging the living and the dead (Acts 10:42; Rom. 14:9; 2 Tim. 4:1) and in early Christian literature, Christ is the judge (2 *Clem.* 1.1; Pol. *Phil.* 2.1; *Barn.* 7.2). However, in this letter (1:17; 2:23; 4:17–19; 5:10) and in other early Christian tradition, God is the judge (Matt. 10:32–33; Rom. 2:5–11; 3:6; 14:10–12; 1 Cor. 5:13; Heb. 10:30–31; 13:4). A bridge between these two portrayals of judgment in early Christian tradition is the additional element that Christ is the agent of judgment for God (Rom. 2:16; 1 Cor. 4:5).

4:6. The seemingly obscure conclusion to this section has fueled centuries of discussion. It begins, **For this reason the gospel was preached even to the dead** (4:6a). This is one implication of the fact that God is to judge the living and the dead (v. 5): they need to hear the gospel (cf. Rom. 14:9). The impersonal passive verb "preached" (*euēngelisthē*) does not specify the preacher. It could be Christ who preached to the dead, but the active form of this verb in the NT outside the Gospels usually takes Jesus Christ as the object and not as the subject (Acts 5:42; 8:35; 11:20; 17:18; Gal. 1:16), and in this epistle the passive form takes the gospel about Christ as the object (1:12 [things preached]; 1:25 [word of God]. Evangelists preaching the gospel are the likely preachers here (Kelly 1969, 173–74; Achtemeier 1996, 287; Elliott 2000, 732). Christ did not preach the gospel to the dead; rather, evangelists preached the gospel about him to the dead.

But who are "the dead"? Here are four classic proposals: (1) "The dead" refers metaphorically to people dead in sin before conversion (Eph. 2:1; Col. 2:13; cf. Rev. 3:1). However, this position ignores the context here of final judgment, in which the dead are the physically dead (v. 5). (2) Link this verse with 3:19, and understand "the dead" as the generation that died in the flood or as the dead in general (as in v. 5) who heard the gospel from Christ either when he was in the tomb or on his way to heaven (depending on how 3:19 is interpreted; Horrell 2003). However, here Christ is not the one doing the preaching but is the subject of the preaching. Also, as the end of this verse indicates, these dead are judged by human standards, not by God's standards. The judgment of these dead is in the time of the letter, not in the final judgment. (3) The dead are the faithful or "Christians" before Christ, like the prophets (1:10–12) and the holy wives (3:5–6) of the old covenant. The gospel was preached to them as a promise of salvation when they were yet alive (1:12; Michaels 1988, 235–38). (4) Most likely the dead are a portion of all the dead mentioned in verse 5. They are the Christians who had the gospel preached to them (1:12, 25) but have since died. The unredeemed use human standards to judge these dead as having had a false hope, for the claim of the dead to live in the spirit is not tangible (Spitta 1890, 63–66; Senior 2003, 116; Elliott 2000, 732–34). Paul faced a similar problem among the Thessalonian churches (1 Thess. 4:13–18), but unlike at Thessalonica, there is no indication in the letter that the fate of the Christian dead is a major concern of these recipients.

The purpose of the gospel being preached to the recipients, including those now dead, is **that even though judged in the flesh by human standards, they might live in the spirit by God's standard** (4:6b). Although preaching of the gospel resulted in judgment in the flesh, the ultimate purpose of the preaching is to live in the spirit. This past judgment that the faithful received from others for responding to the gospel while in the flesh (2:12; 3:9, 16; 4:1–4,

14) stands in contrast to the faithful Christians living in the spirit by God's standard in resurrected life (1:3–5; cf. 1:9; 5:6, 10). Christ is the example of judgment in the flesh and then living by the spirit, and his example enables the same in the lives of his followers (2:21–25; 3:18). God's standard may be the mercy that gives new birth (1:3–5; 2:10), which more than compensates for temporary suffering or doubts about spiritual matters caused by death. Also in mind may be the classic examples of the faithful (Heb. 11; *1 Clem.* 9–12, 16–18) who also heard the gospel, were condemned by their neighbors, and now live in the spirit by God's mercy.

Theological Issues

Christ has finished with sin through his suffering in the flesh. Now Christians are no longer bound to sin and can be finished with sin as well. A consequence of Christ's dealing with sin and our living according to his example is living the remainder of life, from conversion and baptism onward, by the will of God rather than the desires of the flesh (v. 2). Being finished with sin like Christ, Christians are no longer bound by the desires of the flesh and can do God's will. Suffering at the hands of our neighbors will be one result verifying that we have ceased from sin (v. 1).

The early Christians were serious that postconversion sin is not acceptable, disrupts the walk of obedience with God, and needs immediate, prayerful repentance. Modern Christians often claim the salvation offered through Christ and the washing away of sins as if this decision were no more than taking medicine to cure a disease, without any further consequences for behavior—like undergoing open-heart surgery without any change of diet to preserve future health. But sin, like a bad diet, is to remain in the past (vv. 3–4).

Since God will be judging the living and the dead, the gospel needs to be preached. Those who hear it and respond are judged by their neighbors, but they will live in the spirit, prepared for God's judgment. The need and privilege of living in the spirit should be extended to neighbors regardless of consequences. God is a God of life and wants those who have received spiritual life to extend it to others.

1 Peter 4:7–11

The Need for Mutual Responsibility in Light of the End

Introductory Matters

This section concludes the body middle of the letter (2:11–4:11) with exhortations (vv. 7–10) and a doxology ending in "Amen" (v. 11), thus providing a transition to the body closing (4:12–5:11). It forms an *inclusio* with the opening of the body middle in 2:11–12, repeating the topics of the end or consummation (4:7; 2:12) and giving glory to God (4:11; 2:12). So far in the body middle, the focus has been on how Christians are to understand and relate to those outside their group (2:11–4:6), but now it turns briefly to how they are to relate to one another. The key topic of this section is mutual responsibility, which informs the commandments to love (v. 8), be hospitable (v. 9), and serve others (vv. 10–11)—all for the glory of God (v. 11; cf. Rom. 12:3–13). The exhortation is set in the context of the coming judgment, which should motivate appropriate behavior (v. 7). This topic of

> **1 Peter 4:7–11 in the Rhetorical Flow**
>
> God's provision for salvation, and Christians' status before God (1:1–2:10)
>
> Living honorably among the gentiles (2:11–4:11)
>
> > Introduction to the main theme (2:11–12)
> >
> > The household code (2:13–3:7)
> >
> > Practicing mutual love and peace with all (3:8–12)
> >
> > Doing good rather than evil amid suffering, after Christ's example (3:13–22)
> >
> > Living in the Spirit and doing the will of God (4:1–6)
> >
> > ▶ The need for mutual responsibility in light of the end (4:7–11)

101

the consummation not only concludes the body middle but also introduces the body closing (4:13), where it becomes a focus (4:17–18; 5:1, 4, 6, 10).

Tracing the Train of Thought

4:7. This section begins with an assessment of God's timetable: **The end of all things has drawn near** (4:7a). The end (*telos*) is the consummation of all things (cf. 1:9; 4:17). The perfect tense of the verb "draw near" (*engizō*) emphasizes that the end is not only present but also poised and ready to materialize. This is part of the eschatological perspective of the letter that Christ's return (1:7, 11–13, 20; 4:13; 5:1, 4), God's judgment (1:17; 2:23; 4:5–6, 17–19), and Christians' reward of salvation (1:3–5, 9–10; 2:2; 3:21) are imminent. This perspective brings a particular urgency to obeying the following exhortations. The announcement of the imminent end by using the verb "draw near" (*engizō*) and derivatives often forms the basis for exhortations, as it does here (Mark 1:15; Rom. 13:11–14; Phil. 4:4–6; Heb. 10:23–25; James 5:7–11).

In light of the imminent end and judgment, an appropriate exhortation is **therefore be serious and self-controlled** (4:7b; cf. Rom. 12:3; 1 Tim. 3:2, Titus 2:2). To be serious (*sōphroneō*) is to assess things accurately and respond with sound judgment (BDAG 986). To be self-controlled (*nēphō*) is to be alert, with nothing clouding the mind such as the drunkenness from which the recipients have retreated (4:3; BDAG 672). Self-control is necessitated by salvation and grace (1:13; cf. Rom. 13:11–13) and by the devil's desire to destroy faith (5:8–9).

Being serious and self-controlled is **for the sake of your prayers** (4:7c). This portion of the verse is obscure because the introductory preposition (*eis*) has many meanings. Translating it as "by" (rather than "for the sake of"), prayer assists a Christian in being serious and self-controlled; translating it as "for," being serious and self-controlled prepares a Christian for prayer (Senior 2003, 119, 123). However, in light of other references to prayer (3:7, 12), right conduct is needed for prayers to be effective, something quite necessary when the end and judgment are imminent (cf. Elliott 2000, 749).

4:8. Love is given a primary place in mutual relations: **Above all, have unwavering love for one another** (4:8a). There is wordplay with the preceding verse: since *all* things are ending, above *all*, love should be exercised. We expect love to be elevated as the primary virtue, as it is in early Christian tradition generally (John 15:12–17; 1 Cor. 13:1–13), but the focus here is on love for fellow Christians, with no reference to non-Christian neighbors (1:22; 2:17; 3:8; 5:14).

The reason for consistently loving other Christians is given: **for love covers a large number of sins** (4:8b). This reason is found in the OT and early Christian tradition, with the form here being closest to the Hebrew of Prov. 10:12, as adopted by early Christianity (James 5:20; 1 Clem. 49.5; 2 Clem. 16.4). "Conceals" or "hides" (*kalyptō*) is used synonymously in the LXX in the sense of "forgive" (Ps. 31:1 [32:1]), as is its compound form (*epikalyptō*; Ps. 84:3 [85:2]; Rom. 4:7). Love covering sins is not merely Christians turning from sin and loving one another so that sin disappears from the community (cf. 2:24; 4:1–4; contra Michaels 1988, 247), for here sin is covered rather than disappearing. Nor is the idea that those loving others overlook their sins (*1 Clem* 49.5; contra Achtemeier 1996, 295–96), for love is the agent here, not the person loving. Nor is the idea that Christians love and forgive each others' sins (contra Elliott 2000, 751), for in the context of Prov. 10:12, God is the one forgiving sins. Rather, Christ's sacrifice takes away sin (1:18–19; 2:24; 3:18), and that sacrifice becomes effective in covering sin when love is exercised. In *1 Clement* the exercise of love brings God's forgiveness and the covering (*epikalyptō*) of sins (50.5–6; cf. 49.5). Loving others brings God's love into play. Whether mutual love forgives the sins of the one loving and/or the sins of the one loved is unclear (cf. *1 Clem.* 50.5), but the emphasis on mutuality in community indicates that love covers the sins of both.

4:9. The exhortation continues by further developing the topic of love: **Be hospitable to one another.** The early church depended on hospitality in the use of private homes as house churches (Rom. 16:3–5, 23; 1 Cor. 16:19; Col. 4:15; Philem. 2) and welcoming itinerant prophets and teachers (Matt. 10:5–15; *Did.* 11–13; 3 John 5–8; cf. 2 John 10–11). Hospitality can be inconvenient and draw upon limited household resources, especially if hosting a house church on a regular basis. This might explain the added admonition to offer it **without complaining** (cf. Phil. 2:14).

4:10. To mutual love and hospitality is now added service: **Inasmuch as each has received a gift,** they are to use it to **serve one another** (4:10a). A gift (*charisma*) is a gift of grace that God gives each and every Christian, to be used to serve (*diakoneō*) the Christian community as a whole (Rom. 12:3–8; 1 Cor. 12–14; Eph. 4:7–16). This service includes love and hospitality on the part of all Christians, as well as preaching, teaching, and other manifestations of the gifts of grace (Rom. 12:6–8; 1 Cor. 12:7–11; Eph. 4:11).

As excellent stewards of God's diversified grace (4:10b), Christians are called to serve the community with the spiritual gifts from God. An excellent

---

Hospitality

With the lack of lodging, or at least safe and clean lodging, it was expected in the Greco-Roman world that travelers who came to your home late in the day would be fed, housed overnight, and given enough food to get to the next stop on their journey. With Christianity, hospitality is a virtue and expression of mutual love (Rom. 12:9–13; Heb. 13:1–2; Clement of Alexandria, *Strom.* 2.9) to be exercised by both leaders (1 Tim. 3:2; 5:10; Titus 1:8) and the entire community (Rom. 12:13; Heb. 13:2; *1 Clem.* 10–12).

The Steward

The steward (*oikonomos*) was a trusted and trained slave appointed by the head of the household to manage the affairs of an estate (Luke 12:41–48; cf. Gal. 4:1–2). These duties included oversight of other slaves, crops, and sales of produce. In the NT and early Christian tradition, it is used metaphorically to describe Christian leadership (Col. 1:25; Titus 1:5–10) and all Christians as trusted stewards of God's mysteries (1 Cor. 4:1–2) in God's household (Ign. *Pol.* 6.1).

---

steward (*oikonomos*) is a careful manager of a household and its resources—here the household of God (2:5; 4:17). These gifts are a manifestation of the diversified grace of God (Rom. 12:6; Heb. 2:4) through the Holy Spirit (1 Cor. 12:7); a grace coming in many forms, including being chosen by God (1:2) and receiving salvation (1:10, 13), eternal life (3:7), eternal glory (5:10), and more (5:5, 12).

4:11. The discussion now lists two broad categories of spiritual gifts and how they are to be exercised with God in mind (2:19; 3:21). The first category of spiritual gifts is that of speaking (*laleō*): **Whoever speaks, as one speaking the oracles of God** (4:11a). Speaking is a general term for all spiritual gifts involving speaking, including preaching, teaching, evangelism, prophecy, and tongues and their interpretation. When exercising these gifts, speakers must realize that they are giving the oracles of God (*logia theou*), which typically refers to prophetic utterance (Num. 24:4, 16 LXX) and God's revelation in general (Ps. 106:11 LXX [107:11]; Heb. 5:12), especially the law (Acts 7:38) and the OT (Rom. 3:2). Here the traditional understanding of law and prophecy as the oracles of God is expanded to include the exercise of the speaking gifts as God's oracles, emphasizing the sanctity of the exercise of vocal gifts in community (cf. 2 Cor. 2:17). As Paul J. Achtemeier (1996, 298–99) puts it so well, "The content of one's speech must bear the character of God's words and thus the divine intention, not the speaker's own."

The second broad category of spiritual gifts is that of serving (*diakoneō*): **If any serve, it is as by means of the strength that God provides** (4:11b). Unlike verse 10, where serving is understood broadly, here it more narrowly refers to a wide variety of gifts that serve the needs of others, including leading worship, administration, helping, hospitality, and healing. Again the focus is on God, who supplies the strength to exercise all gifts of service (cf. Phil. 2:13).

The reason spiritual gifts are exercised with God in mind is **so that God may be glorified in all things** (4:11c). God is the focus of the gifts, not only as supplier of the words and the strength for their execution, but also as their goal: God's glory in all things (2:12; 4:16; 5:10–11). "All things" includes not only the ministries mentioned in verses 7–11 but also all speaking and doing. Everything should bring God glory (cf. 1 Cor. 10:31; Col. 3:17). Christian conduct should motivate unbelievers to glorify God at the judgment (2:12). Glorifying God through all things is possible **through Jesus Christ** (4:11d) and his work of redemption.

The mention of God's strength and glorification leads to a further affirmation of these realities in a doxology: **His is the glory and the power forever and ever. Amen** (4:11e). It is unclear if the doxology is directed to Jesus Christ or to God. On the one hand, Jesus is the nearest antecedent and has been described previously as having been given glory (1:21; 3:21–22), a glory that will eventually be fully revealed (4:13). On the other hand, thematically and structurally God is the likely referent. God's power and glory are mentioned earlier in this very verse, doxologies praising God begin (1:3) and end the letter (5:11), and the hope that gentiles glorify God begins this section of the letter (2:12).

Theological Issues

First Peter has a vibrant eschatology: "The end is near" (v. 7). However, it is not interested in establishing the date of the end—only that the end has consequences for living now. It shares a common expectation in the NT that Christ's return is soon and Christians need to prepare for his return by living according to God's will (4:2). Today we may or may not share this imminent eschatology. Christ has not returned for two thousand years, but the arrival of the kingdom of God inaugurated the final period of human history. So Peter's call to a serious and self-controlled life before God is as pertinent now as it was then.

We are encouraged to have a constant love for fellow Christians (v. 7). This is not an easy task, for not all Christians are lovable, and none are lovable all the time! But that constancy of love reflects the quality of the love that Christ gives to us and is the glue that keeps the Christian community together. Love also makes the love of Christ and its forgiving power effective in the community. When we love one another, we forgive, and we can be forgiven as we forgive others (Matt. 6:12).

Hospitality is an expression of love that we can extend to family, friends, and fellow Christians that visit or stay with us (v. 9). However, it is not a virtue that we can exercise in quite the same way as in the first century. We cannot let travelers knock on the door and put them up for the night! Unlike in biblical times, there are now many safe and clean places to find food and lodging. But we can exercise this virtue in a variety of other ways, such as making sure that visitors find Christ in our home, being foster parents, or making sure that the homeless in our community can find food and shelter. Our society may have changed, but the basic needs of love and hospitality remain.

Expressions of love and hospitality are to be accompanied by the exercise of spiritual gifts (vv. 10–11). We are now members of the household of God, and as such we need to be good stewards of the grace that God has given us in managing that household as we fulfill our role within it. The gifts of speaking need to be exercised in the character and purpose of God's word for the community. This is a call for careful sermon, teaching, and presentation preparation, as well as for watching everything we say. All gifts of service are to be done in God's strength, fully aware that God is supplying the energy and power in their exercise. We need to be mindful that God is present and working through us; it is not just we ourselves doing things. In other words, by exercising our spiritual gifts, we are the voice and hands of God to others, and in that exercise God will be glorified.

PART 3

1 Peter 4:12–5:14

*Exhortations on Faithful Suffering
among the Gentiles, and Conclusion*

This section is the body closing of the letter, which functions to reiterate topics previously mentioned, as well as to expand them in new ways, often by interweaving them. A shift to the body closing is indicated by the vocative "beloved" (*agapētoi*), which also began the body middle in 2:11, and by a command, which begins both the body opening (1:13) and middle (2:11). Unlike the opening of the body middle (2:11), the anticipated appeal does not immediately follow but rather comes in 5:1, where it is directed to the elders.

---

1 Peter 4:12–5:14 in Context

**God's provision for salvation,
and Christians' status before
God (1:1–2:10)**

**Living honorably among the
gentiles (2:11–4:11)**

▶ **Exhortations on faithful suffering among the gentiles,
and conclusion (4:12–5:14)**

**Suffering faithfully among the
gentiles (4:12–19)**

**Concluding exhortations
(5:1–11)**

Epistolary postscript (5:12–14)

1 Peter 4:12–19

Suffering Faithfully among the Gentiles

Introductory Matters

The major topic of suffering is central to this section, reiterating and extending aspects of the topic as previously discussed (1:6–7; 2:18–25; 3:9–18; 4:1–4) and as found in Christian tradition (Matt. 5:11–12//Luke 6:23). Suffering is explored as an expected part of the Christian life (vv. 12–13), as a test (v. 12), a reason for rejoicing (v. 13; 1:6–7), sharing Christ's suffering (v. 13), meaningless as a consequence of wrongdoing (v. 15), a means for glorifying God (v. 16), and indicative that final judgment is near (vv. 17–18). What is new so far in the letter is that suffering is intrinsic to being a Christian and indicates that the end is near.

**1 Peter 4:12–19
in the Rhetorical Flow**

God's provision for salvation, and Christians' status before God (1:1–2:10)

Living honorably among the gentiles (2:11–4:11)

Exhortations on faithful suffering among the gentiles, and conclusion (4:12–5:14)

▶ Suffering faithfully among the gentiles (4:12–19)

Tracing the Train of Thought

4:12. The vocative **Beloved** (*agapētoi*) not only begins the body closing of the letter but also reaffirms the familial love binding the community together (1:8, 22; 2:17; 3:8; 4:8; 5:14). An exhortation follows: **do not be surprised by the fiery ordeal happening to you as a test for you, as though something strange were happening**

to you (cf. 1 John 3:13). Unbelieving neighbors were surprised when the recipients changed their behavior after their conversion (4:4), and their hostile response should come as no surprise to the recipients. As indicated by the following reference to "Christ's sufferings" (v. 13) and the allusion to Jesus's beatitude that those who follow him will be persecuted (v. 14), suffering is an expected part of the Christian life (Matt. 10:24–25; John 15:18–21; 1 Thess. 3:3; 2 Tim. 3:12). Persecution is especially expected during the ordeal of the righteous before the judgment (vv. 17–18; Rev. 11:1–13; 12:1–18). The "fiery ordeal" (*pyrōsis*) is a word used in the LXX to describe removing the dross from metals melted in a crucible and God's refining or testing God's people (Zech. 13:9; Ps. 65:10–12 [66:10–12]; Prov. 27:21). The fiery ordeal is a God-given test (*peirasmos*) of faith commitment, as it is in 1:6–7.

4:13. Having taught how not to respond to trials (v. 12), the letter proceeds to teach how to do so: **But rejoice insofar as you share Christ's sufferings** (4:13a). Christ has been held up as an example of endurance in suffering (2:19–23; 3:17–18; 4:1), but now the topic intensifies to include Christians' sharing his suffering (2 Cor. 1:5–7; Phil. 3:10). Rejoicing in shared suffering is not a masochistic approach to the Christian life. It is not suffering itself that is the cause of rejoicing but suffering unjustly for doing right as Christ did (2:19–20; 3:14, 17) and for the name of Christ and being a Christian (4:14, 16).

Rejoicing in this suffering is **so that when his glory is revealed, you may rejoice exceedingly** (4:13b). This is not *causative*, for the recipients do not need to suffer in order to participate in future joy (contra Achtemeier 1996, 306). Rather, it is *consequential*, for Christ's glory was a consequence of his sufferings, as testified in the prophecies concerning him (1:11). While the recipients are sharing Christ's suffering, they can rejoice, because when he returns and God reveals Christ's glory (1:21; 3:22), that glory belongs to them as well (1:5–9, 13; 5:1, 4, 10). This future glory provides the motivation to rejoice while suffering now. Jewish and Christian tradition teaches that the righteous suffer (2 *Bar.* 25; Matt. 10:24–25; Mark 8:34; 13:9–13; John 15:20; 2 Thess. 2:3–10), and it is proper to rejoice in suffering for God (2 Macc. 6:26–31; Jdt. 8:25–27; James 1:2–4) with the motivation of reward (Wis. 3:1–9; Matt. 5:11–12//Luke 6:22–23), which in the NT is sharing Christ's glory (Phil. 3:10–11; 2 Tim. 2:10–13).

4:14. It is further explained how sharing Christ's suffering leads to joy: **If you are mocked for the name of Christ, you are blessed** (4:14a). "Mock" or "heap insults upon" (*oneidizō*) describes mocking God, Christ, and the people of God (Ps. 118:42 LXX [119:42]; Isa. 37:17 LXX; Matt. 27:44; Rom. 15:3). Unbelieving neighbors were mocking the recipients because of the "name of Christ," a probable reference to allegiance to Christ and identification as a Christian (4:16; Elliott 2000, 779–81). It is already established that suffering for righteousness leads to God's blessing (3:14), and here is added early Jesus tradition that those suffering for Christ's sake will be blessed (Matt. 5:11–12//Luke 6:22–23).

The mocked are blessed **because the spirit of glory, which is the Spirit of God, rests upon you** (4:14b). This is an allusion to Isa. 11:2 LXX, which refers to the messianic shoot from the root of Jesse, upon which the spirit of the Lord rests; this text was used to identify Jesus as the Messiah when the Holy Spirit descended on him at his baptism (Matt. 3:16). The blessing of the recipients is from the same Spirit of God resting on them and provides a reason why they can rejoice in suffering: it gives them a foretaste of glory to be fully experienced when Christ returns (1:7; 4:13; 5:1, 4, 10). This role of the Spirit is another aspect of being alive and living in the Spirit (3:18; 4:6). Elsewhere in the NT the Spirit is mentioned as residing with the Christians in time of suffering (Matt. 10:19–20; Luke 12:11–12; John 14:26) and transforming them into the image of Christ's glory (2 Cor. 3:8; 4:17; Col. 3:4).

4:15. Contrast now amplifies the exhortation: **But let none of you suffer as a murderer, thief, wrongdoer, or as a busybody.** This vice list helps define suffering for the name of Christ in the previous verse by giving its opposite. While this list is used for clarification, we cannot rule out the possibility that the recipients are in danger of committing these vices, especially in light of previous exhortation to suffer for doing right rather than wrong (2:20; 3:17; cf. 2:12, 14). Prohibitions against murder and thievery are found in the NT, several explicitly based on the Ten Commandments (Exod. 20:13, 15; Mark 10:19 par.; Rom. 2:21; 13:9; cf. 1 Cor. 6:10). Wrongdoing is a strong topic in this letter (2:12, 14, 20; 3:17). The last vice, busybody (*allotriepiskopos*), is set off for emphasis and reflects the Roman hatred of people who meddled in the affairs of others (Plutarch, *De curiositate*, in *Mor.* 515B–523B). Paul too speaks against busybodies (2 Thess. 3:11; 1 Tim. 5:13). Possibly the Christians understood themselves as the guardians of public morality in the fashion of the Cynics, who thought they should oversee others (Balch 1981, 93–94). "Busybody" may also indicate embezzlement of the goods of others that one oversees (Achtemeier 1996, 310–13) and movement beyond prescribed social boundaries, which would further cast suspicion on Christianity (J. Brown 2006).

4:16. The previous statement is now qualified: **Yet if you suffer as a Christian, do not be ashamed, but rather glorify God because of this name.** Suffering for wrongdoing is dishonorable, but suffering for being a Christian is not. Instead of being ashamed for preaching and living the gospel, Christians should glorify God for the privilege of bearing the name Christian—even when suffering (cf. Rom. 1:16; 2 Tim. 1:8–14). Neighbors may shame Christians for testifying to their faith (3:15–16), but ultimately they will never be put to shame because God is the final arbiter of honor and shame (2:6; 5:10; Phil. 1:20). Being called a Christian reflected the convention of the time, designating followers by their leader's name, and here the name has a derogatory connotation (Acts 11:26; 26:28; Elliott 2000, 789–90).

4:17. The letter now provides a motivation for suffering for Christ's name and not for wrongdoing (vv. 14–16): **For it is time for judgment to begin** (4:17a).

The Name "Christian"

The name "Christian" was first used by the detractors and accusers of Christians as a derogatory title, impugning their honor (Acts 11:26). It was in part to slander those "foolish" enough to follow a Galilean prophet crucified for rebellion against Rome. Rather than recoiling from this name, Christians adopted it as their main designation and used it to define themselves against the world (Horrell 2007).

Final judgment has come (4:7, 12), and suffering is its precedent (Mark 13:19// Matt. 24:21; Rom. 8:18; 2 Thess. 1:4–12) and tests whether the faith of Christians is genuine (1:6–7; 2 Thess. 1:4–5). The focus is not that Christian suffering is part of the judgment of the end (cf. Achtemeier 1996, 315), but as the context indicates, the judgment of the end determines what kind of suffering is appropriate: suffering for the name of Christ and not for wrongdoing (cf. 4:7–11).

God is the Judge (1:17; 2:23; 4:5), and that judgment begins **with the house of God** (4:17b), an expression not found elsewhere in the NT. It is found in the OT and subsequent literature that God's judgment begins with God's people (*2 Bar.* 13.8–10; *T. Benj.* 10.7–11) and at the temple, God's house (Isa. 10:11–12; Jer. 25:28–31; Ezek. 9:5–6; Mal. 3:1–6). God's own house is a mixed metaphor for the church as the spiritual house of God (2:5; cf. 2:9) as well as the church as a household of God (1:14, 17; Achtemeier 1996, 315–16).

This motivation is further amplified with a lesser-to-greater contrast between the believer and the unbeliever, implying greater judgment for the latter: **if it is for us first, what is the end for those disobeying the gospel of God?** (4:17c). To disobey (*apeitheō*) is to refuse to believe the gospel and trust in God's work in Jesus Christ (2:7–8; 3:1; cf. 2 Thess. 1:8). It is implied that the end (*telos*) of those who reject the gospel will be the lack of salvation (cf. 1:9).

4:18. To amplify the point that the recipients need to suffer for doing right rather than for doing wrong, because judgment begins with God's people, the writer quotes Prov. 11:31 LXX to present another lesser-to-greater contrast: **and if the righteous person is saved with difficulty, what will become of the ungodly person and sinner?** The righteous person, the Christian, is saved (1:3–10; 2:2; 3:21), but salvation is difficult and includes suffering (cf. Mark 8:35; 10:26–27; 13:13, 19–20). If the righteous person is barely saved, it is implied that the ungodly person will not be saved. However, the nature of their fate is not stated, as is typical elsewhere in the letter (2:8; 3:12b, 16b–17).

4:19. This section concludes: **Therefore let those suffering according to God's will entrust their souls to a faithful Creator, while continuing to do good.** Suffering is not God's will, although God uses it as a test of faith (4:12; cf.

1:6–7), and it naturally results from following God's will and imitating Christ (2:21–25; 3:13–18; 4:1, 13). If the recipients suffer for doing God's will, for doing good (2:15; 3:17; 4:2), then they should continue to do good (2:14–15, 20; 3:6, 11, 13, 16–17) and trust that God will bring this test of faith to a triumphant end—their salvation (1:6–9; 4:13–14; 5:10). All Christians need to trust in God (1:21), especially during suffering (2:23), because God protects the faithful until God reveals the honor and salvation awaiting them (1:3–9; cf. 3:13). Their model, Christ, entrusted himself to God, and so should they (2:23; Luke 23:46). The reference to God as faithful Creator emphasizes that God is all-powerful and can and will bring the divine will and purposes for the world to completion.

Theological Issues

Suffering for doing good is a test used by God to refine faith and prove whether or not it is genuine (v. 12). Conversion entails a turn from attitudes, values, behaviors, and practices that the secular world embraces. Our turning away is an implicit critique of others still living without Christ, and their reaction is often to lash out at us. Such persecution and suffering tests whether we are true to our new commitment to Christ or simply mouthing the words as we return to our old ways in order to appease our critics.

Suffering unjustly like Christ results from trying to live the Christian life faithfully in a hostile world. Rejoicing in this suffering is grounded in the events of Christ's suffering, death, and glorification and the promise that we too will follow his path to glory (v. 13). Rejoicing in suffering is possible because it leads to the blessing of God and an experience of the Holy Spirit that gives us a foretaste of the glory we will one day share fully with Christ (v. 14).

Christians are prohibited from doing wrong and thereby bringing suffering upon themselves (v. 15). While most of us are not worried about being murderers and thieves, we do need to be on the alert to avoid the other vices in the list: wrongdoing and being busybodies. Wrongdoing is broad and includes any behavior that does not further the kingdom of God in the world. It is anything from foul language and unsavory hand gestures, to arrogance and seeking revenge. Being a busybody is as hated today as it was when this letter was written, but it still provides the petty side of us a way to feel superior to others. Here we are urged to give the secular world no basis in our behavior for criticism or persecution.

Though we may be distressed and shamed by persecution for doing good now, we will ultimately be honored by the God who is the final arbiter of honor and shame (v. 16). The judgment of God provides a strong motivation for doing good rather than evil, especially when it is emphasized that judgment begins with God's own people (vv. 17–18). Judgment both encourages ethical conduct and discourages unethical behavior. Fully acknowledging judgment is also a potent motivator for evangelism. Everyone we meet will face God's judgment, and that should motivate us to present the gospel to those who have yet to accept it and nurture those already in the faith, especially if they are wavering.

No matter what suffering we may endure for our faith, we continue to do good because God is the Creator (v. 19). As Creator, God's purposes and will define what is appropriate behavior in the world. If we live accordingly and yet thereby suffer, God as Creator is able to bring God's purposes and promises to completion—providing us further motivation to obey in spite of any hardship. Christ himself provides the model of such trust amid great suffering. It is not that God wills our suffering, but when it occurs, God requires us to remain faithful. God will restore our honor and will honor our faithfulness at judgment with our salvation, just as God honored Christ's faithfulness before us.

1 Peter 5:1–11

Concluding Exhortations

The NT Letters typically conclude with exhortation. Once the theological foundation for the Christian life has been laid, exhortation on how to live that life faithfully is built upon it. Here the exhortation is divided into two sections (vv. 1–5; vv. 6–11) by a transitional particle (*oun*).

Introductory Matters

These exhortations further define the roles and responsibilities among the recipients as first outlined in 4:7–11. In light of suffering and impending judgment outlined in 4:12–19, strong leadership, faithful followers, and humility are needed to keep the community strong. In a time of crisis, those in authority are urged to lead effectively, and those they lead are to respect them.

The exhortation is traditional, being given to bishops (*episkopos*, 1 Tim. 3:1–7; Titus 1:7–9), deacons (*diakonos*, 1 Tim. 3:8–13), and elders (*presbyteros*, 1 Tim. 5:17–19; Titus 1:5–6). It is particularly akin to Paul's address to the Ephesian elders (Acts 20:18–35; Senior 2003, 137–38). The exclusive use of elders here indicates that the more developed hierarchy of bishop, elder, deacon manifested in the Pastorals (1 Tim. 3:1, 8; 5:17; Titus 1:7–9) and letters of Ignatius (*Magn.* 6.1–2; 13.1–2; *Trall.* 2.1–3; *Phld.* 10.2) has not yet developed in these churches.

Tracing the Train of Thought

Appeal to Elders and the Young (5:1–5)

5:1. This section begins with an appeal, a common element in letter closings in the NT, typically revealing a reason why the author writes (Rom. 15:30; 1 Cor. 16:15; Heb. 13:22): **I appeal to the elders among you** (5:1a). While elder (*presbyteros*) may refer simply to age in contrast to youth (v. 5), the context indicates a leadership role. However, it is uncertain how carefully defined or formal this role may have been. Elder is an early form of Christian leadership (Acts 14:23; 20:17; 1 Tim. 5:1, 17–19; Titus 1:5–6; James 5:14; 2 John 1; 3 John 1), often understood to be modeled on the leadership in Jewish communities and synagogues based on seniority, life experience, and wisdom (1 Macc. 11:23; 12:35; Mark 7:3; 8:31; 11:27; 14:53; 15:1). However, a more immediate model was the elder within the household where churches met (1 Tim. 5:1; Titus 1:5–6; 2 John 1; see Elliott 2008).

The author next builds collegiality by citing three characteristics he shares with the elders addressed. First he appeals **as a fellow elder** (5:1b), even though as an apostle he has more authority than any elder. Second, he is a **witness to the sufferings of Christ** (5:1c). "Witness" can refer to eyewitness *of* or bearing witness *to* something. If eyewitness *of* is the reference, the focus is on Peter's witness of Christ's sufferings. However, while Peter saw the daily suffering of Jesus, he was not an eyewitness to the interrogation or crucifixion of Jesus, having deserted Jesus with the other apostles (Mark 14:27, 50). If eyewitness *to* is the reference, the focus is on the author and the elders as joint witnesses to the suffering of Christ by preaching the gospel. Suffering is the central topic of this letter's witness (1:11; 2:21, 23–24; 3:18; 4:1, 13), and the portrayal of Peter in the NT is one of witness *to* the gospel, especially in the speeches and responses attributed to him in Acts (2:14–36 [v. 32]; 3:12–26 [v. 15]; 4:8–12; 5:30–32; 10:34–43 [vv. 39–41]. Third, the author is **one who shares in the glory to be revealed** (5:1d), a common hope of the entire Christian community (1:7, 13; 4:13; 5:10; cf. 4:14; Rom. 8:18), symbolized by the crown of glory to be given the elders (5:4) and the triumphant coming of Christ to reward the faithful (1:3–5, 9, 13, 21).

5:2. Having worked to establish collegiality with the elders, the author exhorts them to **shepherd the sheep of God among you** (5:2a).

1 Peter 5:1–11 in the Rhetorical Flow

God's provision for salvation, and Christians' status before God (1:1–2:10)

Living honorably among the gentiles (2:11–4:11)

Exhortations on faithful suffering among the gentiles, and conclusion (4:12–5:14)

Suffering faithfully among the gentiles (4:12–19)

▶ Concluding exhortations (5:1–11)

Appeal to elders and the young (5:1–5)

Summarizing exhortations (5:6–11)

The metaphor of shepherd derives from OT images of God as shepherd of God's sheep, the Israelites (Ps. 23:1–4; Jer. 13:17; 23:1–3), and leaders as shepherds (Isa. 63:11; Jer. 23:4; Ezek. 34:23–24). This leader-as-shepherd metaphor underlies Gospel tradition of Jesus's role in gathering God's people (Mark 14:27//Matt. 15:24; 26:31; John 10:1–18; cf. Mark 6:34), his portrayal of leadership in the church (Matt. 18:12–14), and his command to Peter to "Shepherd my sheep" (John 21:15–17 AT; R. Brown, Donfried, and Reumann 1973, 139–47, 163–64). It continues in the NT (Acts 20:28; Eph. 4:11) and early Christian tradition (*1 Clem.* 16.1; 44.3; 54.2; 57.2; Ign. *Phld.* 2.1; *Rom.* 9.1; *Herm. Sim.* 9.31.5–6). The elders are to care for the portion of the larger flock of God in their care. While Jesus is the "Chief Shepherd" (5:4) who shepherds the recipients (2:25), the flock belongs ultimately to God.

What is meant by shepherding is now described, using a general verb and three antitheses that unfold its meaning. The general verb and first antithesis are **overseeing, not by compulsion, but willingly, in accord with God** (5:2b). "Overseeing" (*episkopountes*) is an adverbial participle introducing the three antitheses explaining *how* to shepherd. Elders are not to serve out of compulsion (*anankastōs*) simply because their age and experience qualifies them to be leaders, but lead willingly (*hekousiōs*) in accord with God, meaning God's will (cf. 2:15; 3:17; 4:2, 19).

The second antithesis is overseeing **not for dishonest gain, but eagerly**. The elders are also not to serve for dishonest gain (*aischrokerdōs*), for greed satiated by fraud (cf. 1 Tim. 3:3; *Did.* 15.1; Pol. *Phil.* 5.2), something that disqualifies deacons (1 Tim. 3:8) and bishops as well (1 Tim. 3:8; Titus 1:7). This antithesis indicates that the recipients supported the elders. Such support would include food, shelter, clothing, and wages (Matt. 10:10; Luke 10:7–8; 1 Cor. 9:6–14; 2 Cor. 11:9; Gal. 6:6; 1 Tim. 5:17–18; *Did.* 11.4–6; 12.2–3; 13.1–7). The antithesis may also indicate that elders are in charge of the recipients' shared funds (cf. Acts 5:1–5; 2 Cor. 8:20; Pol. *Phil.* 11.1–4). In either case, greed might influence the decision to lead. Rather, overseeing is to be done "eagerly" (*prothymōs*), that is, "ready and willingly," and not for dishonest gain.

5:3. The third antithesis is overseeing **not as domineering those that are your portions, but by being a model to the flock**. "Domineering" (*katakyrieuō*) is subduing an enemy or an unwilling populace (BDAG 519). "Portions" (*klēros*) has rich meaning, but here are the portions of the flock of God under the care of the elders (v. 2). "Model" (*typos*) is usually a moral example and here probably refers specifically to being a model of humility (v. 5). Paul is a model for his churches (1 Cor. 4:16; Gal. 4:12; Phil. 3:17; 1 Thess. 1:6; 2:14; 2 Thess. 3:7, 9), as are Timothy and Titus for their churches (1 Tim. 4:12; Titus 2:7). A strong parallel passage is Jesus's exhortation that while secular leaders dominate (same verb), Christian leaders should humbly serve, using himself as an example (Mark 10:42–45//Matt. 20:25–28//Luke 22:25–27 [different verb]).

In this letter, Christ is the model for all Christians (2:21–23), the shepherd and guardian of their souls (2:25), and Chief Shepherd (5:4)—thus worthy of imitation by other shepherds.

5:4. Having been instructed on how to lead their flocks, the elders are provided with a motivation for faithful leadership: **And when the Chief Shepherd is revealed, you will receive the unfading crown of glory**. Christ was called a shepherd (2:25) but is now called the Chief Shepherd (*archipoimēn*) to distinguish him from elders who are also shepherds and to provide a model for their leadership (cf. Heb. 13:20). The revelation of Christ to the world occurred at his incarnation (1:20) and will occur again at his second coming (1:7, 13; 4:13). The passive voice of the participle translated "reveal" (*phaneroō*) here and in 1:20 indicates that God is the one revealing Christ according to God's plan. Christ's revelation manifests his glory (4:13; 5:1); brings glory, grace, and salvation to the faithful (1:5, 7, 13; 5:1); and will bring an unfading crown of glory to the elders who faithfully shepherd their flocks.

Typically crowns of honor were given to statesmen, benefactors, and victors in military and athletic contests (Danker 1982, 468–71). Crowns given to these latter two groups were made of olive leaves, pine boughs, ivy, parsley, or celery—which all quickly fade (1 Cor. 9:25; 2 Tim. 2:5)—but Christian honor is forever. The adjective "unfading" (*amarantinos*) is derived from the amaranth, a dark-red flower that was known not to fade like most vegetation (Elliott 2000, 835). The crown of glory is part of the imperishable, undefiled, and unfading inheritance that God is keeping for the faithful (1:4–5), a glory in which all share (5:1). The crown is singular, symbolizing the glory shared by all the faithful (1:7, 13; 5:1, 10; cf. 4:14). In the NT, the crown is a symbol of God's future reward of the faithful (1 Thess. 2:19; 2 Tim. 4:8; James 1:12; Rev. 2:10; 3:11).

5:5. The exhortation turns from the elders to the youth: **In turn, younger people, be subject to the elders** (5:5a). The identity of the younger people (lit., "younger men") is debated, with suggestions such as those younger in the faith (Elliott 1970, 379–86; Elliott 2000, 838–40; 1 Cor. 16:15–16; 1 Tim. 3:6); a younger official group in the church (Spicq 1969, 516–27; cf. Acts 5:6, 10; Titus 2:6–8); and, most likely, the remainder of the recipients from whom the elders were chosen (*1 Clem.* 3.2–4; Achtemeier 1996, 331–32). These younger people are to be subject to the elders, who ideally are providing eager and model leadership. The same verb for "be subject" (*hypotassō*) was used previously to describe the Christian attitude to human institutions, slaves to masters, and wives to husbands (2:13, 18; 3:1, 5); it denotes proper respect for authority and experience. This is traditional exhortation to respect leaders (1 Thess. 5:12–13; 1 Cor. 16:15–16; Heb. 13:17; *1 Clem.* 13.1–4; 57.1–2; 61.1; Pol. *Phil.* 5.3), not evidence that the younger people are challenging the leadership of the elders.

The exhortation continues, **All of you put on humble-mindedness with respect to one another** (5:5b). Since the letter addresses two groups separately and then both together, followed by an OT quotation (e.g., 3:8, where "all" includes all those addressed by the household code of 2:13–3:7, followed by an OT quotation in 3:10–12), and since the next verse includes all the recipients as needing to be humble, the "all" here probably includes both the elders and the younger. Everyone is to be humble with others. This reflects previous commandments to show love, hospitality, and service to one another (4:8–10), and to be humble (3:8). The metaphor is of putting on clothing (*enkomboomai*) and may refer to slaves putting on the apron over other clothing for more menial work (Pollux, *Onom.* 4.119; Achtemeier 1996, 332–33; Elliott 2000, 846–47). The metaphor recalls Jesus's putting on a towel to wash the disciples' feet (John 13:4) and the humility that such an action entailed—another example of Jesus's serving as a model for the recipients (2:21–23; 4:1).

While such exhortation to humility is common to the Jewish and Christian tradition (Eph. 4:2; Phil. 2:3; Col. 3:12; cf. Rom. 12:10; Eph. 5:21), it would be unusual in the Greco-Roman world, which generally regarded humility as more appropriate for servants than for free people or people with high social status. A quotation of Prov. 3:34 LXX provides theological grounding for the exhortation: because **"God opposes the arrogant, but gives grace to the humble"** (5:5c). This verse was part of early Christian instruction (James 4:6) and stresses both the present and future reality of God's grace and judgment.

Summarizing Exhortations (5:6–11)

This section is a loose commentary on Prov. 3:34 LXX, quoted in verse 5 (cf. James 4:6–10), developing its topics of God, arrogance (the devil), and humility. It also further develops the topic of suffering common in the letter, especially that God cares for the Christian who suffers (1:5, 21; 2:9–10; 3:12; 4:14, 19; 5:7) and that current suffering leads to future glory (1:6–7; 4:13; 5:10). In addition, this section places Christian suffering within the context of the cosmological battle between good and evil, a battle whose resolution comes with the return of Christ.

5:6. Summarizing exhortations begin with a commandment: **Therefore humble yourselves under the sovereign hand of God** (5:6a). This commandment is a logical corollary of the previous quotation of Prov. 3:34 LXX. If God opposes the arrogant and gives grace to the humble, then the faithful should be humble! "The sovereign hand of God" is a phrase especially used in connection with God's deliverance of Israel from slavery in Egypt (Exod. 3:19; 6:1; 13:3, 9, 14, 16). That God is sovereign (*kratos*) is reiterated in the doxologies of this letter (4:11; 5:11); in light of this sovereignty, humility is the proper human response.

Besides the wisdom of being humble before a sovereign God, the recipients receive a motive as well: **so that in time he may exalt you** (5:6b). On the eschatological day (4:7), the day of salvation (1:5) and judgment (4:17) when Jesus is revealed (1:7, 13; 4:13; 5:4), God will exalt those who humble

Figure 9. An ancient lion statue at the entrance to Ferrara Cathedral in northern Italy. Peter describes the devil as a roaring lion.

ermess/Photos.com

themselves. This topic of humility and exaltation is common in the OT (1 Sam. 2:7–8; Isa. 2:11; Job 5:11; Sir. 7:11) and the NT (Matt. 18:4; Matt. 23:12//Luke 14:11; 18:14; Phil. 2:8–9; James 1:9–11; 4:10). In this epistle, the humble-exalted reality is modeled on Christ's suffering according to God's will and his ultimate exaltation (2:21–25; 3:18–22), a model providing the recipients hope for their own exaltation (4:13; 5:10) as they suffer for doing God's will (2:20; 3:17).

5:7. Exhortations continue: **Cast all your worries on him, because he cares about you.** The aorist participle "casting" can have the force of an imperative and be another exhortation or can be explaining how to be humble before God as just commanded in verse 6 (RSV, NRSV, NEB, NIV). In support of the latter, casting one's worries on God is a humble act in which trust is put in God rather than oneself. However, the imperative force is best understood here in light of similar commandments on which this verse depends and to which it points (BDF 468; Elliott 2000, 851). This exhortation is reminiscent of a previous exhortation to "entrust yourself to a faithful Creator" (4:19). Here Ps. 54:23a LXX (55:22a) is used: "Cast your worries on the Lord." Also in mind may be the commandments of Jesus not to worry or be anxious (Matt. 6:25–34// Luke 12:22–31), commandments that filtered into early Christian tradition (Phil. 4:6–7; *Herm. Vis.* 3.11.3; 4.2.4–5). The authority of the OT and the Jesus tradition affirms that God cares for recipients who are suffering for their faith (1:5, 21; 2:9–10; 3:12; 4:14, 19).

5:8. Verses 8–10 place suffering in the context of the struggle between good and evil, with the promise of God's ultimate blessing on the good. This section reiterates and rewords 1:6–7 and 1:13, functioning like a rhetorical peroration, beginning with two strong commandments and an accompanying reason for them. The commandments are brief: **Be self-controlled, be on the alert** (5:8a). These two commandments (*nēphō*; *grēgoreō*) are used in the NT in eschatological contexts like this one, in which Christ's return is viewed as imminent and there is a need to be ready (v. 6; Matt. 24:42; 25:13; Mark 13:35, 37; Luke 12:37; 1 Thess. 5:6, 8). Being self-controlled harks back to 4:7, where being serious and self-controlled (*nēphō*) in prayers is necessary since the end is near.

The reason for these commandments is stark: **Your enemy the devil walks about like a roaring lion, seeking someone to devour** (5:8b). Up to this point the recipients have been suffering at the hands of humans, but now this suffering has a single, supernatural source: the devil, the enemy. "Enemy" (*antidikos*) can also mean accuser or plaintiff in a lawsuit, a meaning that fits early conceptions of the devil as an accuser of human virtue in God's court (Job 1:6–12; 2:1–6; Zech. 3:1–2; cf. Rev. 12:9–10; BDAG 88). However, in this context where the metaphor of a hungry lion and the destruction of Christians is in the forefront, the broader meaning of "enemy" is more appropriate. The author is convinced that the last days are upon the world (4:7, 12, 17), days in which evil is expected to increase.

The lion was a metaphor for the opponents of Israel (Ps. 51:34–38 [21:14, 22 LXX]; Jer. 50:17 [27:17 LXX]; 51:34–38 [28:34–38 LXX]; Ezek. 22:25; 1QH 5.5–7, 9, 13–14, 18–19; 4QpNah 1.5–6; Achtemeier 1996, 341), and the early Christian use of Ps. 22 indicates that Ps. 22:13 (21:14 LXX), referring to David's enemies as being like a "roaring lion," may have provided the metaphor here. Being devoured by the devil is to renounce Christ and return to pagan ways and gods in order to stop the suffering inflicted by neighbors. When sheep are attacked by lions, some separate from the flock, and such are attacked and eaten (Schwank 1962, 19; Golebiewski 1965). The recipients are urged to remain faithful to Christ, the Chief Shepherd of God's flock, and not become separate and vulnerable (5:1–4). For interesting parallels to this verse, see *Jos. Asen.* 12.9 and Eusebius, *Hist. eccl.* 5.1.25–26.

5:9. In light of the threat that the devil poses, the recipients are instructed: **Oppose him, steadfast in the faith** (5:9a). The devil's volley of slander and persecution can lead the recipients to deny Jesus Christ and revert to pagan ways. Remaining steadfast in the faith is the way to oppose the devil. It is to trust in God, who guards Christians through faith (1:5, 21) and protects the praise, glory, honor, salvation, and hope that is the outcome of their faith (1:7, 9, 21). Resisting the devil is a familiar exhortation in the NT and addresses the temptation to deny Christ, which all Christians experience, even if persecution is not in view (Eph. 6:12–13; James 4:7).

An added motivation for opposing the devil and remaining steadfast is **knowing that the same kinds of suffering are being fulfilled by your fellowship throughout the world** (5:9b); thus the recipients suffer with others (cf. 4:13). The changes that faith makes in peoples' lives, often in opposition to the mainstream, provoked a negative reaction throughout the Greco-Roman world. The suffering of Christians is also experienced as part of the eschatological battle between good and evil (4:7, 12, 17), and as the passive verb "fulfilled" (*epiteleō*) indicates, this suffering is part of the fulfillment of God's plan (3:17; 4:17–19; cf. Col. 1:24; Rev. 6:11) and something to be faithfully endured.

5:10. A further incentive to remain steadfast in the faith is now provided: **The God of all grace, who has called you to his eternal glory in Christ, after you have suffered a short time, will himself restore, support, strengthen, and establish [you].** God gives many gifts of grace (1:2, 10, 13; 4:10; 5:5, 12) and has called the recipients to share God's eternal glory in Christ (1:7; 4:13; 5:1, 4, 10; Rom. 8:30; 1 Thess. 2:12; 2 Thess. 2:13–14), who himself also suffered and now shares God's glory (1:11, 21; 4:13). The suffering is short-lived, but the resulting glory is eternal and is described as restoration, support, strengthening, and establishing. This is a description of the grace and exaltation promised at the end of time in 5:5–6, and as there, is given by God when Christ returns, although not excluded in this life as well. This verse reiterates promises opening the letter: suffering that tests faith will be short and result in exaltation (1:6–7, 13).

The pronoun "you" expected at the end of the verse is missing because the emphasis is on God's power and promises and/or the grace that God gives all Christians in the world undergoing suffering (v. 9).

5:11. A doxology concludes this section: **To him is the sovereignty forever and ever. Amen.** This is a shortened form of the doxology of 4:11, although this time directed to God rather than Jesus Christ. God has many characteristics, but sovereignty (*kratos*) is the focus here, to emphasize that the promises of God, especially to bring grace to those suffering, are reliable (cf. 5:6).

Theological Issues

Leadership today is not granted solely or even primarily on the basis of age, as it was in the time of this letter. However, the point still remains that God calls leaders according to God's will, and those called to be leaders should accept that call willingly, even if there is a little self-doubt about accepting that call (vv. 1–2). Answering the call to lead can be motivated by greed—not just greed for money, as here in 1 Peter (v. 2), but also greed for power, prestige, and fame. Leaders are urged to be examples of humility to those they lead (v. 3), an example that Jesus provided. A motivation to lead willingly, without greed, and humbly is eternal reward, secure in heaven (v. 4). It is not that reward is the sole motivation for ministry, but in times of struggle and suffering, which a good ministry will ultimately entail, reward provides an eternal perspective that helps the persecuted see beyond current limitations and disappointments and stay energized for ministry.

The exhortation to the young to subject themselves to the elders is that long-standing principle that those with more experience in the art of living have wisdom by which those that are younger can benefit (v. 5). But as we know, the younger do not always appreciate that fact and, in that transition to adulthood, assume that their newfound independence is also newfound wisdom! Generally, those who have faithfully walked in the faith are better guides than those newer in the faith. This section of the letter demonstrates that strong leadership, faithful followers, and humility are needed to keep the Christian community strong and healthy.

God is sovereign in the world as Creator and the one who both exalts and judges. Our wise response is to recognize this sovereignty by humbling ourselves before God (v. 6). Humility may mean that we suffer unjustly without retaliating, knowing full well that God can and will exalt us eventually. God's sovereignty also means that our worries and anxieties are not something we should bear but something we should cast on God, who has all things in divine control (v. 7). When we dwell on our problems, we are not being humble but arrogant and trusting in our own strength, as if we were sovereign. Although we will naturally have some concern about issues we face and make plans to avoid or solve problems, we should be humble enough to seek God's will amid these problems and remember that God cares and is working with our faithful plans to help resolve our anxieties.

The suffering that we encounter in the Christian life is part of the cosmic battle between good and evil (vv. 8–9). Although Christ has conquered evil, we await the consummation of all things to see all evil finally expunged from the universe. The letter is not working with the modern idea that evil is simply the result of selfish choices, prejudicial traditions, or exclusive and aggressive power structures. These are certainly sources of evil, for even within the letter the slanderers are supported by social norms. However, in addition the letter assumes that forces of evil, including the devil himself, are real powers that influence our lives through others, like the slanderers. They are not just real forces but also aggressive forces, seeking to bring Christians back to their old ways and to abandon future glory.

In this battle with an aggressive enemy, we are to remain steadfast in our faith (v. 9). That can be difficult when suffering is severe, but we are not alone in our suffering, and all who suffer are suffering according to the plan of God. "Misery loves company" is true, and it is easier to suffer when we know that God is using that suffering as part of a mysterious divine plan in which others are involved. If that is not enough, we are assured that the ultimate end of suffering is that God will restore, support, strengthen, and establish the faithful at the return of Christ (v. 10), and undoubtedly in this life as well. These last promises to the sufferer may seem a bit unrealistic. The author assumes that Christ's return is imminent (5:6, 10) and suffering will be short-term. However, the suffering we endure may be long-term, and it is harder to look to the future final glory for comfort. The call to be steadfast in the faith has new urgency when the time of suffering is elongated.

1 Peter 5:12–14

Epistolary Postscript

Introductory Matters

This section is the epistolary postscript or conclusion of the letter. It is divided into five parts common to epistolary postscripts in the NT: the commendation of the messenger and the message (v. 12a), the purpose of the letter (v. 12b), an official and personal greeting from the writer to the recipients (vv. 13–14a), a reference to a kiss (v. 14a), and a wish for peace (v. 14b). There is a great effort to form an *inclusio* with the beginning of the letter, including repetition of the following topics: Christ (1:1; 5:14), chosen / chosen together (1:1–2; 5:13), resident foreigners and Diaspora (1:1) or Babylon (5:13), grace (1:2; 5:12), and peace (1:2; 5:14).

> **1 Peter 5:12–14 in the Rhetorical Flow**
>
> God's provision for salvation, and Christians' status before God (1:1–2:10)
>
> Living honorably among the gentiles (2:11–4:11)
>
> Exhortations on faithful suffering among the gentiles, and conclusion (4:12–5:14)
>
>   Suffering faithfully among the gentiles (4:12–19)
>
>   Concluding exhortations (5:1–11)
>
> ▶ Epistolary postscript (5:12–14)

Tracing the Train of Thought

5:12. The author commends the letter, beginning with the phrase **by Silvanus** (5:12a). Silvanus may be unknown to us outside this reference, but he is usually identified as a companion of Paul and Timothy (2 Cor. 1:19; 1 Thess. 1:1; 2 Thess. 1:1), perhaps to be equated with the Silas (the Aramaic version of "Silvanus") mentioned first in Acts as a leader at the Council of Jerusalem (15:22, 27, 32, 40) and then as a companion of Paul on his mission to the Greek cities of Philippi (16:19, 25, 29), Thessalonica (17:4), Berea (17:10, 14–15), and Corinth (18:5).

This phrase "by Silvanus" means not that Silvanus was Peter's secretary in writing the letter but that he carried the letter to the churches (Achtemeier 1996, 349–50; Richards 2000; contra Kelly 1969, 214–16). The vast majority of commendations using "by" (*dia*) in papyrus letters and early Christian letters refer to the carrier of the letter (Acts 15:23; Ign. *Phld.* 11.2; *Smyrn.* 12.1; *Rom.* 10.1; *Pol.* 8.1; Pol. *Phil.* 14.1). Also, if Silvanus had a large role in the writing of the letter, it is likely that his name would appear alongside Peter's in the letter opening, as it is alongside Paul's in 1 Thess. 1:1 and 2 Thess. 1:1, and he would probably not commend himself here at the end (Michaels 1988, 306–7; Achtemeier 1996, 349–51). If Silvanus is Silas in Acts, he has a similar role as carrier of the letter from the Jerusalem church (15:22–23, 27).

The author then commends Silvanus, referring to him as **a faithful brother as I regard him** (5:12b). Paul has similar commendations for his letter carriers (Rom. 16:1–2; 1 Cor. 16:17–18; 2 Cor. 8:16–19; Eph. 6:21–22; Phil. 2:25–30; Col. 4:7–9; Philem. 10–12; cf. Titus 3:13) as did other early Christian leaders (Ign. *Phld.* 11.2; *Symrn.* 12.1; *Rom.* 10.1; Pol. *Phil.* 14.1). A commendation may be needed because Silvanus is unknown to the recipients, for there is no record of Silvanus ministering in the areas addressed by this letter. Acts even records the Spirit's directing Paul and Silas away from ministry in Asia and Bithynia (16:6–8). The commendation helps ensure that Silvanus will find needed hospitality when he arrives (cf. 4:9) by assuring the recipients that he is trustworthy. This is important since the letter carrier would often explain and supplement the letter's contents. If Silvanus is Silas, he filled a similar role in expounding the contents of the letter from the Jerusalem Council that he delivered to the churches (Acts 15:27, 32).

Having commended the letter carrier, the author commends the purpose and content of the letter: **I have written a few lines to you, exhorting and bearing witness that this is the true grace of God; stand firm in it** (5:12c). The reference to writing a "few lines" (*di' oligōn*) is customary in ancient letters, for long letters were considered to try the recipients' patience (cf. Eph. 3:3; Heb. 13:22; Demetrius, *Eloc.* 228; Isocrates, *Ep.* 2.13; 8.10; Pliny, *Ep.* 3.9.27; Ign. *Rom.* 8.2; Pol. 7.3; *Barn.* 1.5). The purpose of the letter is to give ethical exhortation (*parakaleō*, as in 2:11; 5:1) and witness (*epimartyreō*; cf. *martys* in 5:1); the latter is used in contexts where the benefactions of a patron are extolled (Danker 1982, 442–78; Elliott 2000, 877). This witnessing is fitting because the benefactions of God are central to the letter. It is emphasized that the contents of the letter, the "this," are a gift of God's grace (cf. 5:10; not suffering, as suggested by Brox 1986, 244–45). As such, the recipients are to stand firm (*histēmi*), not in the epistle itself, but in the grace of God to which it bears witness (cf. 2 Cor. 1:24; Eph. 6:14). This final command to stand firm (*histēmi*) in God's grace contrasts with the command to oppose or stand against (*anthistēmi*) the devil (5:9).

5.13. The letter turns to personal greetings: **She who is chosen together with you and residing in Babylon greets you, as does Mark, my son.** The feminine referent is not specified and is sometimes understood to be Peter's wife (Bigg 1901, 197). This identification corresponds nicely with the fact that Peter was married (Mark 1:30//Matt. 8:14//Luke 4:38) and traveled with his wife (1 Cor. 9:5), but this is a very obscure way to refer to one's wife! The feminine referent has also been identified as a woman leader well known to the recipients and needing no further introduction (Applegate 1992), but why not name her as Silvanus and Mark are named? Most commentators understand the referent to be the feminine word "church" (*ekklēsia*; cf. 2 John 1, 13), as was the assumption of ancient scribes who added this word to the text (Codex Sinaiticus, Vulgate), but the word "church" is not found anywhere in the letter. The referent could also be to the fellowship, or brotherhood, of Christians (*adelphotēs*) in 5:9 (also 2:17), which is feminine and nicely complements the family metaphors in this closing section (Senior 2003, 154; Elliot 2000, 882).

"Babylon" cannot be the actual Mesopotamian city, which at that time was in ruins, or the military outpost in the Nile Delta by that name, for tradition does not associate Peter with these regions. Rather, it is a reference to Rome. This association was particularly pertinent because Rome shared Babylon's idolatry and immorality. If this epistle is pseudonymous, Rome's destruction of the temple in Jerusalem in 70 CE makes the connection with Babylon even more natural (*2 Bar.* 11.1–2; 67.6–7; 2 Esd. [*4 Ezra*] 3:1–2, 28; *Sib. Or.* 5.143, 159–60; Rev. 14:8; 16:19; 17:5, 18; 18:2, 10, 21). "Babylon" complements the metaphor of exile and Diaspora that begins the letter (1:1; 2:11), forming an *inclusio* and indicating that the author shares with the recipients the exile from their heavenly home (1:4–5; Hunzinger 1965; Thiede 1986). Also, Christian tradition places Peter and Mark together at Rome, as is the case here (Eusebius, *Hist. eccl.* 2.15.1–2; 3.39.15).

Mark is probably not a literal son of Peter (contra Haselhurst 1926) but one who had come to faith through the ministry of Peter. The designation "son" picks up the family metaphor used throughout the letter to designate relationships among Christians. On analogy, Paul liked to describe his close converts as children—Timothy (1 Cor. 4:17; 1 Tim. 1:2, 18; 2 Tim. 1:2; 2:1; cf. Phil. 2:22), Titus (Titus 1:4), Onesimus (Philem. 10)—and his churches as his children (1 Cor. 4:14–15; Gal. 4:19; 1 Thess. 2:11). Mark is likely John Mark of Acts, who was a traveling companion of Barnabas and Paul (12:25; 13:5, 13; 15:37–39) and may have met Peter when Peter visited Mark's mother's home (12:12); the Mark of Paul's Letters (Col. 4:10; 2 Tim. 4:11; Philem. 24); and the Mark of tradition, who used what he learned from Peter to write his Gospel in Rome (Eusebius, *Hist. eccl.* 2.15.1–2; 3.39.14–15; 6.25.5; Black 1994, 60–67).

5:14. The letter continues with a greeting: **Greet one another with a kiss of love** (5:14a). The kiss was practiced within the family and as a greeting among friends (Luke 7:45; Acts 20:37; Adinolfi 1988, 183–86). This commandment emphasizes mutual love once more (1:22; 2:11, 17; 3:8; 4:8, 12); continues the familial tone of the conclusion, where Silvanus is a brother and Mark a son of Peter; and reminds the recipients that they are part of the larger Christian family.

The letter concludes with a peace wish: **Peace to all of you who are in Christ** (5:14b). The wish reiterates the earlier commandment to seek peace and pursue it (3:11) and, unlike the holy kiss that is given between Christians, is extended to everyone, including persecuting neighbors. The peace is "in Christ," that is, peace for those who rely on Christ for their redemption and sure inheritance, a peace that transcends temporary suffering.

Theological Issues

Using family language, the epistolary conclusion emphasizes the close ties that Christians share with one another in Christ. Silvanus is a brother and Mark is a son. Greetings with a kiss, typically reserved for family and close friends, urges the recipients to express mutual love. It is within this close, shared relationship made possible by being in Christ that we find peace amid suffering. This peace is not the absence of conflict but the eternal view, which recognizes that everything here is fleeting, including suffering, and that an eternal and imperishable inheritance is awaiting us in heaven. In the interim, this knowledge of God's grace provides strength and endurance when suffering comes and threatens to pull us away from our faith.

Second Peter

Terrance Callan

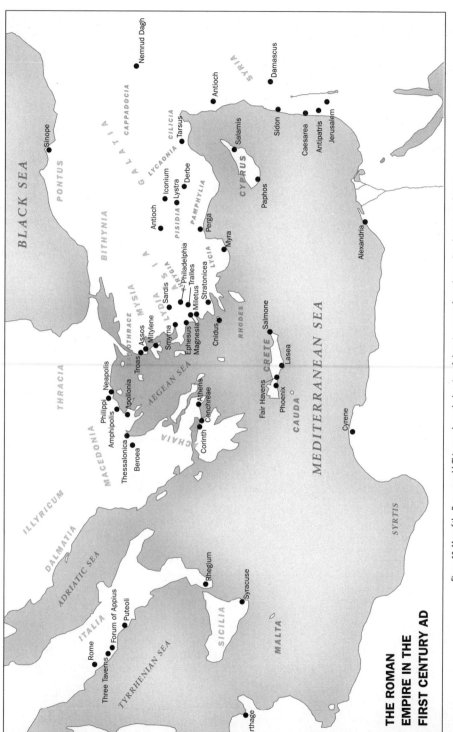

Figure 10. Map of the Roman world. This map shows the location of places important for understanding the context of 2 Peter.

Introduction to Second Peter

The Form of 2 Peter

In form 2 Peter is a letter. It has a letter salutation in 1:1–2 that greatly resembles the salutations of other NT Letters (see commentary). The author of 2 Peter also identifies his composition as a letter in 3:1. However, the addressees of 2 Peter are indicated very generally in 1:1 as those who have received faith equal in honor to ours (i.e., the author of the letter and others). This is a more general specification of addressees than that found in any other NT letter except Jude 1. This might mean that the letter is addressed to Christians generally, not to a specific group of Christians. For this reason Jude and 2 Peter are often called Catholic, or General, Letters. However, both Jude and 2 Peter might have been intended for specific groups even though these groups are not identified in the salutation. This would be especially true for 2 Peter if 3:1 implies that it has the same addressees as 1 Peter.

Second Peter also has the form of a testament. This is a Jewish literary form in which someone bids farewell to his associates, offering them ethical advice and/or revelations about the future to guide them after his death. Since Hans Windisch (1951, 87–88), commentators have generally agreed that 2 Peter should be seen as an example of a testament.[1] Richard J. Bauckham (1983, 131–35; 1988, 3734–35) discusses this at greatest length. The testamentary character of 2 Peter is especially clear in 1:12–15, where Peter refers to his coming death and says that his purpose in writing is to continue reminding the addressees about his teaching after his death. It is also clear in 2:1–3 and 3:1–4, where Peter predicts the rise of false teachers (Bauckham 1983, 132).

---

1. See Schelkle 1961, 181; Reicke 1964, 146; Spicq 1966, 193–94; Grundmann 1974, 55–58; Knoch 1990, 200–202; Paulsen 1992, 89–90; Vögtle 1994, 122; Harrington 2003, 229. Unconvinced are M. Green 1987, 36–38; Davids 2006, 148–49; G. Green 2008, 164–67; and Harvey and Towner 2009, 10–11.

Examples of Testaments

The *Testaments of the Twelve Patriarchs*, a document of uncertain date, is either a Jewish composition with Christian additions or a Christian composition that incorporates Jewish sources and traditions. It is divided into twelve parts. In each part, one of the twelve sons of Jacob reviews his own life, offers ethical instructions based on the events of his life, and makes predictions about the future. Unlike the *Testaments of the Twelve Patriarchs*, the Jewish apocalypse *2 Baruch* (a pseudonymous work attributed to Baruch, secretary of the prophet Jeremiah; cf. Jer. 36:4) is not, as a whole, a testament. It was written in about 100 CE and survives principally in a Syriac translation. In it, Baruch foresees God's salvation of Israel and tries to explain the presence of evil in the world. At the end of this apocalypse, Baruch writes a testamentary letter to the captives in Babylon, by means of which he assures them of God's salvation before he dies.

The best-known example of the testament is the *Testaments of the Twelve Patriarchs*. The clearest example of a testament in letter form is *2 Bar.* 78–86 (Bauckham 1983, 133); another possible example is 2 Timothy. Luke T. Johnson (2001, 320–24) argues that 2 Timothy is not a testament, but perhaps mainly to evade the implications of this for the authenticity of 2 Timothy. A regular feature of testaments is that they are pseudonymous (Bauckham 1983, 134). The *Testaments of the Twelve Patriarchs* were not actually written by the twelve sons of Jacob, nor was the testamentary letter of Baruch written by Jeremiah's secretary. The testamentary character of 2 Peter makes it likely that 2 Peter was not actually written by Peter.

Invention, Arrangement, and Style

By the first century the Greco-Roman world had a long tradition of extensive reflection on the effective composition of speeches and, indirectly, of other forms of verbal expression. Various features of 2 Peter make it likely that such reflection was operative in the mind of its author; unless he misjudged his audience, it must also have been operative in at least some of their minds. As it applies to prose composition, this reflection is organized into three general categories: invention, arrangement, and style. *Invention* refers to creating the content of the composition; *arrangement* concerns the order in which the contents are presented; and *style* concerns the manner in which the contents are presented. Duane F. Watson (1988) has discussed all three of these in 2 Peter; Joseph B. Mayor (1907, xxvi–lxvii), Joseph Chaine (1939, 14–18), Thomas J. Kraus (2001), and Terrance Callan (2003) have discussed the style of 2 Peter. Watson also summarizes what is generally involved in invention, arrangement, and style.

The content of a composition consists mainly of arguments that support its contentions. The arguments pertinent to a composition like 2 Peter fall into three categories: ethos, pathos, and logos. Argument from ethos is based on the writer's personal moral uprightness. Argument from pathos appeals to the emotions of the addressees. Argument from logos uses reasoning, which may be either induction from examples or deduction from premises. The form of deduction most important for a composition like 2 Peter is the enthymeme, usually a proposition with a reason given for it. Arguments are formulated by using topics, or conventional relationships among ideas.

The arrangement of a composition like 2 Peter has at least three parts. The first is the opening of the letter, intended to make the addressees attentive, well disposed, and receptive to the message that follows. The last is the close of the letter, which recapitulates its arguments and makes an emotional appeal. In between lies the body of the letter, which presents its main arguments.

The style of a composition can be considered under two headings: vocabulary and syntax. Vocabulary can be ornamented using rare words, new coinages, metaphors, and other tropes. Syntax can be ornamented by avoiding the hiatus of vowels[2] and the harsh clash of consonants and by the use of rhythm and figures of speech and thought. It can also be ornamented by use of the period, suspending the completion of a sentence's sense until the end. Depending mainly on the quantity and quality of ornament used, compositions are said to exhibit grand, middle, or plain style. Second Peter is written in grand style—specifically, an Asian version of the grand style.

The Style of 2 Peter

The style of 2 Peter is striking (on this, see Callan 2003). One of its notable features is the frequent repetition of words. Another is that 2 Peter contains a large number of words not found elsewhere in the NT. According to Richard J. Bauckham, 2 Peter contains fifty-seven such words. Of these words, twenty-five are found in the Greek translation of the OT, seventeen are found in other contemporary Jewish literature, and one is found in the Apostolic Fathers. Most of the remaining fourteen words are very rare; two of them are not found elsewhere in extant Greek literature: *paraphronia* (madness) in 2:16 and *empaigmonē* (scoffing) in 3:3 (Bauckham 1983, 135–36).

According to Bauckham (1983, 137), "The incidence of rare words is part of a general impression 2 Peter gives of aiming at ambitious literary effect." Bauckham also mentions the author's characteristic use of pairs of synonyms and the already-noted repetition of words in support of this. Other indications of 2 Peter's literary ambition are the complex sentences found in 1:3–7

2. Hiatus is the break in pronunciation caused when successive words end and begin with vowels.

and 2:4–10a; the many figures of speech used in 2 Peter, especially the chain of virtues in 1:5–7 and the image in 1:19; and the poetic rhythm found in parts of 2 Peter.

The poetic rhythm of 2 Peter (and some of the other features mentioned above) probably results from the author's attempt to write in the style known as Asianism (Reicke 1964, 146–47; Kelly 1969, 228; Bauckham 1983, 137; Watson 1988, 145–46; Callan 2003). This was one of two principal tendencies in Greek prose style that flourished in the rhetorical schools during the Hellenistic and Roman periods; the other was Atticism. Unfortunately, few examples of Asianism survive, and we derive our understanding of it largely from hostile criticism of it.

Just as Asianism was criticized in its own time, many today find the style of 2 Peter unappealing. However, if 2 Peter is written in this style, its author's literary aspirations are clear. Bo Reicke (1964, 146–47) compares it to European art and literature of the Baroque period, a parallel that may allow us to be more appreciative of the style of 2 Peter.

Following Cicero, Eduard Norden (1898, 134–47) describes two kinds of Asianism: the delicate and the bombastic. The former was characterized by (1) replacement of the period with short, choppy sentences, (2) each of which had a marked rhythm, and (3) unusual usage, such as nonsensical metaphors and absurd paraphrases. The bombastic style shared the second and third characteristics with the delicate style but used long instead of short sentences.

Reicke (1964, 147) describes the second kind of Asianism as "characterized by a loaded, verbose, high-sounding manner of expression leaning toward the

The Nemrud Dagh Decree

The Nemrud Dagh decree was inscribed on the mausoleum of Antiochus I (86–38 BCE), king of Commagene, in the middle of the first century BCE. The mausoleum was built on a mountain, known today as Nemrud Dagh, in present-day Turkey. The inscription describes some of Antiochus's accomplishments and lists regulations for the rites to be held forever at the site of his tomb. Some idea of its ornate style can be gained from the following excerpt:

> "I considered piety not only the most secure possession but also the most pleasurable enjoyment for human beings, and the same judgment I held to be the cause of my prosperous power and of its most blessed use; and for my entire life I appeared to all as one who considered reverence the most faithful guardian of my reign and an inimitable source of delight; in consequence of which I was able to survive hazards and achieved remarkable mastery of hopeless situations and in the fullness of my many years found blessedness." (Danker 1982, 238)

Figure 11. The east terrace of Nemrud Dagh, in Turkey. One copy of the Nemrud Dagh inscription was carved on the backs of the monumental statues of seated figures, whose lower sections can be seen in this photograph.

novel and bizarre, and careless about violating classic ideals of simplicity." This is the kind of Asianism that 2 Peter represents. The attempt to write in this style accounts for all the features of 2 Peter mentioned above: unusual vocabulary; figures of speech, including use of synonyms and repetition of words; complex sentences; and rhythm. Stylistically 2 Peter resembles the Nemrud Dagh decree (Callan 2003).

Date of Composition

The most important basis on which to assign a date to 2 Peter is the reference to Paul in 3:15–16 (see commentary on this passage). In 3:15 the author of 2 Peter first refers to what Paul wrote to the recipients of 2 Peter, then says that Paul says the same thing in all his Letters. This implies the existence of a collection of Letters of Paul.

Exactly when such a collection was made is unknown. Some argue that Paul himself began such a collection (Trobisch 1994; Murphy-O'Connor 1995, 114–30). Most see the collection as likely to have been made around 100 (e.g., Kümmel 1973, 480–81). The earliest explicit reference to more than one letter of Paul is probably found in the letters of Ignatius of Antioch, written about 108. In his letter *To the Ephesians* (12.2), Ignatius says that Paul makes mention of the Ephesians in every letter. In his letter *To the Romans* (4.3), Ignatius

Ignatius of Antioch

Ignatius of Antioch (ca. 35–108 CE) was bishop of Antioch in Syria. As he was being taken to Rome to be executed, he wrote seven letters that are now included in the collection known as the Apostolic Fathers. From Smyrna, Ignatius wrote letters to three churches (in Ephesus, Magnesia, and Tralles) whose delegates had met him in Smyrna. He also wrote a letter to the church in Rome, preparing for his arrival. When Ignatius had proceeded to Troas, he wrote letters to two churches he had just visited (in Philadelphia and Smyrna) and one to Polycarp, the bishop of Smyrna. In all of these letters except the one to Rome, Ignatius argues against false teachers within the church and emphasizes the bishop's importance in preserving the unity of the church. Ignatius's letter to the church in Rome urges the Roman Christians not to try to prevent his martyrdom.

says that he does not command the Romans as Peter and Paul did; this could be a reference to Paul's Letter to the Romans. Thus Ignatius probably knows of at least Paul's Letters to the Ephesians and Romans. He probably knows them by way of a collection of Paul's Letters that includes them.

In 3:16 the author of 2 Peter says that the ignorant and unstable twist difficult elements of Paul's Letters, as they do the other Scriptures. This implies that the author of 2 Peter puts the Letters of Paul into the same category as the Jewish scriptures, which were also accepted as authoritative by Christians. This presumably happened some time after the collection of Paul's Letters. By about 140 Marcion used a collection of ten Letters of Paul that he regarded as authoritative.

It seems likely that 2 Peter was written sometime between 100 and 140, perhaps about 125 (so also Mayor 1907, cxxvii; Senior 1980, 99). Other commentators assign different dates. Richard J. Bauckham (1988, 3740–42) gives the most comprehensive survey. Dates proposed by the commentaries I have consulted include the following:

ca. 60 (Bigg 1901, 242–47)
63 (Wohlenberg 1915, xxxvii)
mid-60s (Mounce 1982, 99)
64–110 (Davids 2006, 130–31)
ca. 65 (Moo 1996, 24–25)
65–68 (Harvey and Towner 2009, 15)
ca. 70 or 80 (Chaine 1939, 34)
80–90 (Bauckham 1983, 157–58)
ca. 90 (Reicke 1964, 144–45; Spicq 1966, 195)
late first or early second century (Perkins 1995, 160; Harrington 2003, 237)

Marcion

Marcion (ca. 110–160 CE), the son of the bishop of Sinope in Pontus, was excommunicated by the church of Rome in 144 CE. Thereafter he established his own schismatic church, which continued to exist for several centuries. The views of Marcion are known from the arguments of church fathers against him. He apparently considered salvation by grace alone the essence of the Christian faith and found this understanding expressed in the Letters of Paul and the Gospel of Luke, both edited to remove Judaizing corruptions. Marcion thought this perception of Christianity implied rejection of the OT.

---

ca. 100 (Schelkle 1961, 178–79)
100–110 (Kelly 1969, 237; Knoch 1990, 213)
100–125 (James 1912, xxx; Paulsen 1992, 94; Vögtle 1994, 128–29)
110–50 (Grundmann 1974, 65)
130 (Sidebottom 1967, 99)

The dates suggested by Bigg, Wohlenberg, Mounce, Moo, and Harvey and Towner are based on the view that Peter is the actual author of 2 Peter; I and most others argue that he is not (see below). Chaine's date is based on the time when the views rejected by 2 Peter first appeared. Reicke's date is based partly on the idea that 2 Pet. 2:10 is a positive reference to magistrates and society; I interpret the passage differently (see my remarks on 2:10 in the commentary proper). The dates offered by Bauckham, Spicq, Kelly, and Knoch are based on parallels between the thought of 2 Peter and that of other early Christian writings. The dates of Bauckham and Harrington are based on the view that 2 Pet. 3:4 means that the generation of the apostles has died; I interpret this passage differently (see my comments on 3:4). Perkins, Schelkle, and Bauckham mention 2 Pet. 3:15–16; Perkins and Schelkle interpret its implications for the date of 2 Peter in somewhat the same way I do, although they arrive at a somewhat earlier date than I have suggested. Chaine denies these implications (1939, 28–29).

The Author of 2 Peter

The author identifies himself as "Simeon Peter, slave and apostle of Jesus Christ" (1:1). This unambiguously claims that the author is Peter, chief of the twelve apostles of Jesus. Many other details of the letter are consistent with this. According to 1:14, Jesus has revealed that the author will soon die; in John 21:18–19, Jesus predicts the death of Peter. According to 1:16–18, the author has witnessed the transfiguration of Jesus; Mark 9:2–8 and parallels

The *Acts of Peter*

The *Acts of Peter* was written in Greek in the latter part of the second century CE and survives mainly in a Latin translation. The document narrates a contest between Peter and Simon Magus in Rome and ends with the martyrdom of Peter, who was crucified upside down. This occurred in the reign of Nero, who ruled the Roman Empire from 54 to 68 CE. Although the *Acts of Peter* does not mention this, a great fire burned Rome in 64 CE. Nero blamed Christians for the fire and executed many of the Christians then living in Rome, perhaps including Peter.

say that Peter witnessed Jesus's transfiguration. In 3:1 the author says that he is writing a second letter, which suggests that 1 Peter is the previous letter.

Nevertheless, most commentators do not think Peter was the actual author of the letter (Bauckham 1988, 3719–24). Of the twentieth- and twenty-first-century commentaries I have consulted, only seven[3] argue that Peter was the author of 2 Peter. Briefly, the reasons most do not regard Peter as the author of 2 Peter are the following, in order of importance:

- The letter was probably written too late to have been composed by Peter. *Acts of Peter* 36–41 (ca. 200) says that Peter was crucified in Rome during the reign of Nero, during the mid-60s. Thus Peter died too early to have written the letter.
- As we have seen, the letter is also a testament, and testaments are regularly pseudonymous.
- The language and style of the letter seem unlikely to have been used by Peter; the literary skill and ambition that are manifested in the Asian style of 2 Peter seem unlikely to derive from Peter. In addition, the language and style of 2 Peter differ from the language and style of 1 Peter.[4]
- It seems unlikely that Peter would have made use of Jude in the way 2 Peter does (see the discussion of this below).

Compare the somewhat different list given by Bauckham (1988, 3722–24).

Bauckham (1988, 3736–40) surveys various explanations that have been offered for the composition of 2 Peter in the name of Peter. He suggests that

3. That is, Bigg 1901, 242; Wohlenberg 1915, xxvii; Mounce 1982, 99; M. Green 1987, 13–39; Moo 1996, 23–24; G. Green 2008, 150; and Harvey and Towner 2009, 9–16.

4. Over time, as testamentary literature became less common, fewer readers perceived the testamentary form of 2 Peter and so sought ways to explain why it differed from the language and style of 1 Peter. One of the earliest explanations was to say that its language and style derived from Peter's secretary.

it is one means by which the church of Rome, whose representative was Peter, exercised pastoral responsibility for other churches.

The Recipients of 2 Peter

In 3:1 the author of 2 Peter says that he is now writing a second letter to the addressees. If he means that his first letter was 1 Peter, this might imply that the recipients of 2 Peter are the same as the recipients of 1 Peter: residents of Pontus, Galatia, Cappadocia, Asia, and Bithynia (1 Pet. 1:1; Chaine 1939, 32–33; Grundmann 1974, 58; Knoch 1990, 199; Mayor [1907, cxxxv] rejects this idea).

In 3:15 the author of 2 Peter says that Paul also wrote to the recipients of 2 Peter. We have no knowledge of any letter of Paul directed to Pontus, Cappadocia, or Bithynia. Paul did write to the Galatians, however, and he wrote letters to the Ephesians, Colossians, and Laodiceans (see Col. 4:16), all living within the Roman province of Asia.

If 2 Pet. 3:14–15a is intended as a summary of what Paul wrote to the recipients of 2 Peter, verse 14 ("Be eager to be discovered by him spotless and unblemished in peace") might be seen as referring to Eph. 4:3 ("being eager to keep the unity of the Spirit in the bond of peace"). A reference to Eph. 4:3 would be consistent with understanding 2 Pet. 3:1 as implying that 2 Peter is written to the addressees of 1 Peter.

Location of 2 Peter in the History of the Christian Movement

Second Peter is especially rich in relationships to other texts, what Vernon K. Robbins (1996, 40–58) calls oral-scribal intertexture. Several times 2 Peter quotes from another text, either reproducing its exact words, or reproducing its exact words with one or more differences. Instances of this kind of recitation follow in order of their appearance in 2 Peter:

1:2a = 1 Pet. 1:2a
1:17b = Matt. 17:5 with differences
2:17b = Jude 13b with one difference
2:20b = Matt. 12:45//Luke 11:26 with one difference
3:2 = Jude 17 with several changes
3:8b = Ps. 90:4 (89:4 LXX) with several changes
3:10a = 1 Thess. 5:2
3:13a = Isa. 65:17; 66:22 with several changes

The Story of Ahiqar

The Story of Ahiqar, a document dating from the fifth century BCE that survives in Syriac and Arabic versions, is a wisdom writing. It includes many proverbs with which Ahiqar teaches his adopted son wisdom and ends with a number of comparisons with which Ahiqar criticizes him. The comparison that seems to be the source of 2 Pet. 2:22b is 8.15 in the Arabic version: "O my son! thou hast been to me like the pig who went into the hot bath with people of quality, and when it came out of the hot bath, it saw a filthy hole and it went down and wallowed in it" (*APOT* 2:772). *Ahiqar* 8.18 in the Syriac version parallels this but is not as close to the text of 2 Peter.

An instance of reciting a saying by using words different from the authoritative source is found in 2:22. The verse cites a double proverb. The first part derives from Prov. 26:11; the second part seems to come from *The Story of Ahiqar* 8.15 Arabic (cf. 8.18 Syriac). Bauckham (1983, 273) thinks the two may have been joined by Hellenistic Jews before being incorporated into 2 Peter.

Second Peter includes several examples of reciting a text substantially in one's own words:

1:14 may be such a recitation of John 21:18–19.

1:16–18 may be such a recitation of Matt. 17:1–8; as noted above, 1:17b reproduces the exact words of Matt. 17:5 with some differences.

2:15–16 is a recitation of Num. 22, perhaps as interpreted in targums (Aramaic translations of the OT).

3:1–2 is probably such a recitation of 1 Peter.

3:15–16 is a recitation of the Letters of Paul.

Second Peter also includes examples of recitation that summarize a span of text including various episodes:

2:4–8 summarizes Gen. 6:1–19:29

3:5–6 summarizes Gen. 1–7

In all but the first two instances (1:2a, 17b), 2 Peter's recitation of the exact words of a source also recontextualizes them. In 2:1–3:3, in addition, 2 Peter thoroughly recontextualizes Jude 4–18 (on this, see Callan 2004).[5] This is the most significant literary relationship between 2 Peter and another text.

---

5. See also Mayor 1907, xxi–xxv; Chaine 1939, 18–24; Windisch 1951, 91–92; Schelkle 1961, 138–39; Sidebottom 1967, 68–69; Kelly 1969, 226–27; Grundmann 1974, 102–7; Knoch 1990, 205–6; Senior 1980,

Figure 12. Parallels between Jude and 2 Peter

(underlined words are identical; italicized words are different forms of the same root)

Jude 4–18 (NRSV, adapted)	2 Peter 2:1–3:3
	[2:1] But there were also false prophets among the *people*, as among you there will also be false teachers, who
[4] For certain intruders have stolen in among you, people who *long ago* were designated for this <u>judgment</u> as ungodly, who pervert the grace of our God into *licentiousness*	will secretly introduce heresies of *destruction*,
<u>even denying</u> our only <u>master</u> and Lord, Jesus Christ.	<u>even denying</u> the <u>master</u> who purchased them, bringing on themselves imminent *destruction*.
	[2:2] And many will follow their *licentiousnesses*, because of whom the way of truth will be slandered.
	[2:3] And in their greed they will buy you with counterfeit words, whose <u>judgment</u> *long ago* is not idle and their *destruction* does not sleep.
[5] Now I desire to remind you, though you are fully informed, that the Lord, who once for all saved a *people* out of the land of Egypt, afterward *destroyed* those who did not believe.	
[6] And *the angels* who did not keep their own position, but left their proper dwelling, *he has kept* in eternal chains in *gloom* <u>for the judgment</u> of the great Day.	[2:4] For if God did not spare *the angels* who sinned but, having cast them into Tartarus, delivered them to chains *of gloom, kept* <u>for judgment</u>; . . .
[7] Likewise, *Sodom and Gomorrah* and the surrounding <u>cities</u>, which, in the same manner as they, indulged in sexual immorality and went <u>after</u> other <u>flesh</u>,	[2:6] and if he condemned the <u>cities</u> of *Sodom and Gomorrah*, having reduced them to ashes in a catastrophe,
serve as *an example* by undergoing a punishment of eternal fire.	having made them *an example* of the things about to happen to the impious, . . .
	[2:9] then the Lord knows how to rescue the pious from trial and how to keep the unjust confined for the day of judgment,
[8] Yet in the same way these dreamers also *defile the flesh*, reject *dominion*,	[2:10] and especially those who go <u>after the flesh</u> in desire for *defilement* and despise *dominion*.

102; Bauckham 1983, 142–43; 1988, 3714–16; Watson 1988, 160–87; Paulsen 1992, 97–100; Neyrey 1993, 122; Vögtle 1994, 122–23; Perkins 1995, 178; Gilmour 2002, 90–91, 120; Harrington 2003, 232–33; Davids 2006, 136–43; G. Green 2008, 159–62. Bigg (1901, 216–24) argues that Jude depends on 2 Peter; so also Wohlenberg (1915, xli–xliii) and Moo (1996, 16–18). Lapham (2003, 152–54, 157) argues that in the process of transmission, both 2 Peter and Jude have undergone redactive cross-interpolation.

Jude 4–18 (NRSV, adapted)	2 Peter 2:1–3:3
and *slander* <u>the glories</u>.	Stubborn bold ones, they do not tremble, *slandering* <u>the glories</u>,
[9]But when the *archangel* Michael contended with the devil and disputed about the body of Moses, he *did not dare to bring* a <u>judgment</u> *of slander* against him, but said, "The *Lord* rebuke you!"	[2:11]where *angels*, being greater in strength and power, *do not bear* against them a *slanderous* <u>judgment</u> from (the side of) the *Lord*.
[10]<u>But these people</u> *slander* whatever they do not understand, and *they are corrupted* by those things that, <u>like irrational animals</u>, they know *naturally*.	[2:12]<u>But these, like irrational animals</u> begotten *naturally* for capture and corruption, slandering things of which they are ignorant, *will* also *be corrupted* in their corruption, . . .
[11]Woe to them! For they go the *way* of Cain, and abandon themselves to <u>Balaam's</u> *error* for the sake of *reward*, and perish in Korah's rebellion.	[2:15]Abandoning the straight *way*, they *have gone astray*, having followed in the *way* <u>of Balaam</u>, son of Bosor, who loved the *reward* of wrongdoing. . . .
[12]<u>These are</u> blemishes on your love-feasts, while they feast with you without fear, feeding themselves.	[2:17]<u>These are</u>
They are <u>waterless</u> clouds carried along <u>by</u> the winds; autumn trees without fruit, twice dead, uprooted;	<u>waterless</u> springs and mists driven <u>by</u> a storm;
[13]wild waves of the sea, casting up the foam of their own shame; wandering stars,	
<u>for whom the gloom of darkness has been kept</u> forever. . . .	<u>for whom the gloom of darkness has been kept</u>.
[16]These are grumblers and malcontents; they indulge their own *desires*; their mouth speaks <u>boastful words</u>, flattering people to their own advantage.	[2:18]For speaking <u>boastful words</u> of futility, they entice with the *desires* of the flesh, with licentiousnesses, those who are just escaping from the people who live in error, . . .
	[3:1]<u>Beloved</u>, I now write this second letter to you, in which I arouse in your remembrance the pure understanding
[17]But you, <u>beloved</u>, must *remember* <u>the words spoken beforehand by the apostles</u> of our <u>Lord</u> Jesus Christ;	[3:2]to *remember* <u>the words spoken beforehand by</u> the holy prophets and the commandment of your <u>apostles</u> of our <u>Lord</u> and savior,
[18]for they said to you, "<u>In the</u> *last* time there will be <u>scoffers, going according to</u> their own ungodly *desires*."	[3:3]first knowing this, that <u>in the</u> *last* days <u>scoffers</u> will come with scoffing, <u>going according to</u> their own *desires*. . . .

It seems that 2 Peter's use of Jude can best be described as a rather free paraphrase (Sidebottom 1967, 95, 112). Working from the written text of Jude, the author of 2 Peter rewrote Jude, avoiding direct quotation but using much of Jude's language. The procedure was similar to that used by the author of a work like the one you are now reading who paraphrases the work of others in developing his own presentation. Bauckham (1983, 236, 260) says, "This

1 Enoch and the *Assumption of Moses*

First Enoch is a Jewish apocalypse written in about 160 BCE that survives principally in an Ethiopic translation. Enoch, the alleged author of this pseudonymous work, is one of the patriarchs who lived before the flood. He is shown the secrets of the universe, including God's salvation of Israel at the end of time. Jude 14–15 quotes *1 En.* 1.9. The *Assumption of Moses*, also known as the *Testament of Moses*, is a Jewish apocalypse perhaps dating from the first century CE. Before his ascension to heaven, Moses outlines the course of history from his own time until God's final salvation of Israel. Jude 9 refers to a dispute between Michael the archangel and the devil over the body of Moses. The extant text of the *Assumption of Moses* does not describe such a dispute, but many argue that it was described in the lost ending of the text (Bauckham 1983, 65–76).

dependence is never slavish. The author takes what he wants from Jude, whether ideas or words, and uses it in a composition that is very much his own. . . . It is characteristic of our author's use of Jude that he gets an idea from Jude and then gives it a fresh twist or development of his own." G. Green (2008, 161–62) characterizes 2 Peter's use of Jude as *imitatio*.

To summarize, 2 Peter is related to the following writings of the OT: Genesis, Numbers, Isaiah, Proverbs, and Psalms. And it is related to the following writings of the NT: Matthew, possibly John, 1 Thessalonians and the Letters of Paul in general, 1 Peter, and Jude. At the appropriate points, the commentary discusses these relationships in more detail. The author knows and uses much of what is now the Christian Bible. He does not take over from Jude the quotation of *1 Enoch* in Jude 14–15 or Jude's possible allusion to the *Assumption of Moses* in Jude 9. Perhaps he purposely avoids referring to these texts that are not now authoritative for Christians.

Attestation

Origen (ca. 185–254) is the earliest extant writer to mention the Second Letter of Peter by name. He does so in his *Commentarii in evangelium Joannis* on John 5:3, quoted in Eusebius, *Hist. eccl.* 6.25.8 (Bigg 1901, 201; Spicq 1966, 190; Bauckham 1983, 163).

> And Peter, on whom the Church of Christ is built, against which "the gates of Hades will not prevail," has left one acknowledged epistle, and let it be granted that there is also a second, for it is doubtful.

Origen also cites or alludes to 2 Peter a number of other times (Bigg 1901, 201; Spicq 1966, 190). As can be seen in the quotation above, Origen refers to the

Origen and Eusebius

Origen (ca. 185–254 CE), one of the first great theologians of the Christian church, was head of the catechetical school of Alexandria early in his life and spent his last years in Caesarea Maritima, in Palestine. He wrote interpretation of the Bible, as well as dogmatic, practical, and apologetic works. Eusebius (ca. 275–339 CE) was bishop of Caesarea Maritima. In addition to writing his *Ecclesiastical History*, he produced many other works, especially dogmatic and apologetic writings.

existence of doubts that Peter wrote 2 Peter. Eusebius, writing around 324, mentions the consequent uncertainty about the canonical status of 2 Peter in *Hist. eccl.* 3.3.1; 3.25.3. However, 2 Peter was included in the NT by Athanasius in 367.

The earliest probable allusions to 2 Peter are found in the *Apocalypse of Peter* (Bigg 1901, 207; Spicq 1966, 189; Bauckham 1983, 162). For example, sections 22 and 28 of the Greek fragment of the *Apocalypse of Peter* refer to blaspheming "the way of righteousness." This phrase may have been taken from 2 Pet. 2:21. Second Peter also frequently refers to blaspheming or slandering (2:2, 10, 11, 12); 2 Pet. 2:2 speaks of "slandering the way of truth." An even more probable allusion is found in *Barn.* 15.4. This passage quotes an unidentified "he" as saying, "Behold, the day of the Lord shall be as a thousand years." This is almost certainly a reference to 2 Pet. 3:8, because this is 2 Peter's own expansion of the quotation from Ps. 90:4, which says only that in God's eyes a thousand years are as one day. Such allusions are compatible with a date of around 125 for 2 Peter. Bigg (1901, 202–10) discusses many other possible allusions, both earlier and later (see also Bauckham 1983, 162–63).

The earliest extant copy of 2 Peter is found in a papyrus manuscript known as 𝔓[72], dating from about 300. It contains Jude and 1 Peter along with 2 Peter. These documents were part of a codex that included eight other writings, both

The *Apocalypse of Peter*

The *Apocalypse of Peter* is a Christian apocalypse written about 120–140, a fragment of which survives in Greek, as does a more extensive Ethiopic translation of the text. When Jesus is seated on the Mount of Olives, his own disciples ask him to reveal to them the signs of his parousia and the end of the world. After Jesus's initial answer, Peter questions him further, and Jesus describes at length the punishment of sinners and reward of the righteous. The document ends with an account of Jesus's transfiguration.

The *Epistle of Barnabas*

The *Epistle of Barnabas*, a writing of uncertain date, thought by most to have been written between 70 and 140, is included among the Apostolic Fathers. Its author argues against the validity of the Jewish law in its literal sense, though in his view it remains valid when interpreted figuratively, either as a prediction of the future or as allegorical statements of ethical norms. The document ends with a description of the two ways—the way of light and the way of darkness.

---

biblical (i.e., Pss. 33–34) and nonbiblical Christian writings (e.g., the *Homily on Passover* by Melito, bishop of Sardis, who died ca. 180).

Overview of 2 Peter

The opening section of 2 Peter begins with the salutation of the letter. This is followed by a statement of the letter's general theme. Since Jesus Christ has given his followers benefits, including the promise of sharing in divine nature, they need to show their gratitude for these benefits by living virtuously, and

---

An Outline of 2 Peter

The letter opening (1:1–15)

  Salutation of the letter (1:1–2)

  Theme of the letter (1:3–11)

    Preamble (1:3–4)

    Resolution (1:5–11)

  Occasion of the letter (1:12–15)

The letter body (1:16–3:13)

  Two arguments against opponents (1:16–2:10a)

    First reply: Argument from the transfiguration (1:16–18)

    Second reply: Argument from prophecy (1:19–2:10a)

      Appeal: Attend to prophecy (1:19–21)

      The coming of false teachers predicted (2:1–3)

      Destruction of false teachers and salvation of the righteous predicted (2:4–10a)

  Critique of opponents (2:10b–22)

    Moral failings of opponents and their punishment (2:10b–17)

    Negative effects of the opponents' teaching (2:18–22)

  Occasion of the letter restated, and argument against opponents resumed (3:1–13)

    Restatement of the letter's occasion and purpose (3:1–4)

    Resumption of argument against opponents (3:5–13)

The letter closing (3:14–18)

  Concluding exhortation (3:14–18a)

  Final doxology (3:18b)

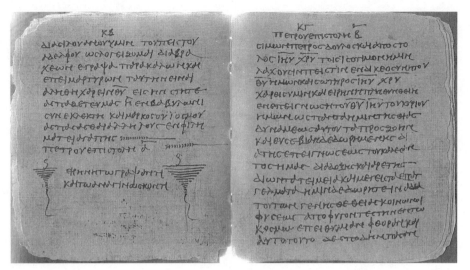

Figure 13. Facsimile of 𝔓⁷². This facsimile was published in *Beati Petri Apostoli Epistulae: Ex Papyro Bodmeriana VIII transcriptae*, ed. Carlo M. Martini (Milan: Pizzi, 1968). The page on the left contains the end of 1 Peter; the page on the right contains 2 Peter 1:1–5a.

this in turn will enable them to receive the fulfillment of the promise. The occasion of the letter is that Peter's death is near. He writes so the addressees can remember his teaching after his death.

The body of 2 Peter makes it clear that the author expounds his teaching because some people do not await the future fulfillment of Christ's promises and so do not emphasize the need for virtuous living. The author begins by offering two arguments against the claim that expectation of Christ's return in glory is a cleverly devised myth. The first argument is that Christ's transfiguration shows he will come in glory; the second is that the prophetic word predicts both the rise of false teachers who will deny the second coming of Christ and the second coming itself. The author digresses from his argument to criticize the immorality of those false teachers and any who follow them. After this digression, the author says again that he writes to remind the addressees about the words of the prophets. In the last days, scoffers will deny the second coming of Christ. The author appeals to various arguments from Scripture to refute their denial.

In the closing section of the letter, the author again exhorts the addressees to reject the false teachers and contends that the Letters of Paul say the same thing, although they can be difficult to understand.

2 Peter 1:1–15

The Letter Opening

Introductory Matters

The opening section of 2 Peter consists of three parts. The first is the salutation of the letter; the second introduces the theme of the letter; and the third states the occasion of the letter. A generally similar letter opening can be seen in many NT Letters, as in Rom. 1:1–15; 2 Cor. 1:1–11; Gal. 1:1–9; 1 Pet. 1:1–9.

Commentators disagree about the syntax of 2 Pet. 1:1–7. Some understand verses 3–4 as a continuation of the letter salutation (vv. 1–2); others understand verses 3–4 as the beginning of a sentence that continues in verses 5–7; still others interpret verses 3–4 as an independent sentence. For a thorough exploration of this disagreement and an argument that verses 3–4 are the beginning of a sentence that continues in verses 5–7, see Terrance Callan 2005. I regard verses 1–2 as the salutation of the letter, verses 3–11 as stating the theme of the letter, and verses 12–15 as presenting the occasion of the letter.

The Letter Salutation

Second Peter 1:1–2 makes use of the formula "Sender to Recipient, Greeting," by far the most common way to begin a Greek letter in the Roman period (Exler 1923). This formula was also used to begin Aramaic letters at this time (Fitzmyer 1979). Use of this formula informs readers and hearers that what follows is a letter. This formula is used in the NT letter openings listed above and is found in all other NT Letters; it is a defining feature of a first-century letter.

In Greek letters a noun in apposition or an adjective is often added to the name of the addressee; likewise the greeting is often expanded slightly (Exler 1923). This tendency is taken much further in 2 Peter, as it is in most NT Letters. Two nouns in apposition are added to the name of the sender, with another noun in the genitive case dependent on them. The addressees are not named but instead are described in a complex participial phrase. The greeting is a complex wish for the addressees.

The sender of the letter is Simeon Peter, the leader of Jesus's followers, to whom Jesus gave the name Peter (i.e., Rock; see Matt. 16:18). Apart from this passage, Peter's name is given as Simeon only in Acts 15:14; elsewhere he is called Simon, an alternative form of the same name. Simeon was the name of one of Jacob's twelve sons and thus one of the twelve tribes of Israel. Three other men with this name are mentioned in the NT (Luke 2:25, 34; 3:30; Acts 13:1).

The greeting in 1:2 "may favor and peace be multiplied for you" (*charis hymin kai eirēnē plēthyntheiē*) has probably been adapted from other NT Letters. "Favor and peace to you" (*charis hymin kai eirēnē*) is part of the greeting in every letter of Paul except 1 and 2 Timothy and Titus. "May favor and peace be multiplied for you" (*charis hymin kai eirēnē plēthyntheiē*) is also found in 1 Pet. 1:2. Since 2 Pet. 3:1 seems to indicate that the author knows 1 Peter, it is likely that 2 Peter's greeting is a recitation of the greeting from 1 Peter (Gilmour 2002, 92).

Second Peter 1:1–2 mentions a number of social and cultural topics. Peter in 1:1 refers to himself as the slave of Jesus Christ. In this way he metaphorically places himself in a familiar social position, that of a slave. Most slaves had very low status in society, but some had very high status. As an example of the latter, some slaves of the Roman emperor were entrusted with significant responsibilities. Paul calls himself a slave of Christ in the salutations of Romans and Philippians, as does Jude in the salutation of that letter. Paul calls himself a slave of God in the salutation of Titus; James calls himself slave of God and Christ in the salutation of that letter.

In 1:1 Peter also refers to himself as an apostle of Jesus Christ. This is another familiar social role, that of the envoy or messenger. In other Christian texts, "apostle" particularly designates a special envoy of Christ. Paul calls himself an apostle in the salutations of Romans, 1 and 2 Corinthians, Galatians, Ephesians, Colossians, 1 and 2 Timothy, and Titus, as does Peter in the salutation of 1 Peter.

In referring to Jesus as Christ, this passage identifies Jesus as the Messiah expected by Jews (see Cullmann 1959, 113–17; Hahn 1969, 136–48; Fuller 1965, 23–31; Callan 1994, 7–14). This same identification is common to all early Christian literature. In referring to Jesus as Savior, the passage describes him with a term often used for gods and notable men in both Jewish and Greco-Roman culture, and especially for rulers in the latter. Jesus is also described as Savior in other early Christian literature, especially the Pastoral Epistles (see Cullmann 1959, 238–45). Second Peter uses the title "Savior" for Jesus five times, more frequently than any other NT writing.

The passage also refers to the social and cultural value of honor versus shame when it speaks of the addressees' having received faith equal in honor to that of Peter and others (1:1). The topic of the patron-client relationship between God/Jesus and the addressees appears in the reference to the benefaction of God/Jesus in verse 1 and in the call for recognition of their patronage in verse 2. These and other social and cultural dimensions of 2 Peter have been discussed most fully by Jerome H. Neyrey in his commentary on 2 Peter and Jude (1993).

Decrees Honoring Benefactors

Frederick W. Danker (1978) argued convincingly that 1:3–11 follows the form of a decree honoring a benefactor, with verses 3–4 forming the preamble and verses 5–11 the resolution of the "decree." Thus the letter begins with the statement that Christ has bestowed some gifts and promised others (the preamble) and the exhortation to show one's gratitude for them (the resolution). This effectively introduces the twofold theme of the letter: Christ's gifts will be completed at his second coming; one shows gratitude for them by a life of virtue, which is also necessary for one to receive their completion.

Danker gives the following example of a decree honoring a benefactor, saying that it is typical of hundreds of others:

> In the month of Aphrodision, during the magistracy of Apollophanes, son of Apollo, on the sixth. Xenon, son of Aphthonetos was chairman, and Pantaleon, son of Kleandres, proposed the following:
>
> Whereas [*epeidē*] Theocles, son of Thersites, of Meliboea has proved himself a perfect gentleman [*kalos kai agathos*] in his relations with Iasos and has rendered exceptional service to our citizens who visit Meliboea, be it resolved [*dedochthai*] that Theocles, son of Thersites, be declared our public friend and representative [*proxenos*]; that he be granted exemption from whatever imposts our city has authority to exact and be free to come and go both in war and in peace, without formality of treaty; that he enjoy the privilege of a front seat at the games; and that he be officially recognized with the rest of our city's representatives. (Danker 1978, 65)

The following decree of the inhabitants of Stratonicea honoring Zeus Panhemerios and Hekate is much closer to 2 Pet. 1:3–11 in its content:[1]

---

1. This is my translation of the text given in *CIG* 2.2715 a, b. Deissmann (1901, 360–68) and Charles (1997, 146–48) have discussed the similarity of this inscription to 2 Peter. In three cases, Deissmann restores lacunae in the inscription differently from the editor of *Corpus inscriptionum graecarum*.

During the magistracy of Ptolemy the clever, when Sosandros son of Diomedes, secretary of the council, said: "The city has been saved [*sesōsthai*] again from many great and pressing dangers by the providence of the very great [*megistōn*] gods who protected it, namely, Zeus Panhemerios and Hekate, whose inviolate temples and suppliants and holy assembly were made clearly conspicuous by a decree of Augustus Caesar and the eternal [*aiōniou*] empire of the Roman lords [*kyriōn*]; and it is good to bring all eagerness into [*pasan spoudēn ispheresthai*] piety [*eusebeian*] toward them and to neglect no opportunity to show piety [*eusebein*] and to supplicate them; and statues of the aforementioned gods are set up in the august council chamber, representing the most illustrious virtues of divine power [*tēs theias dynameōs aretas*], on account of which the whole people together also sacrifices and offers incense and prays and gives thanks always to the so very illustrious gods and is accustomed to show piety [*eusebein*] toward them by means of procession with hymn-singing and worship"; it seemed good to the council now to choose thirty children of the wellborn, whom the superintendent will lead each day into the council chamber, with the public guardians of the children, clad in white and crowned with olive branch, and having olive branches likewise in their hand, who will together with harper and herald sing a hymn which Sosandros son of Diomedes, the secretary, would arrange; . . . [the resolution of the decree continues by addressing various contingencies related to this arrangement].

Like 2 Pet. 1:3–11, this decree honors divine benefactors. However, the preamble of the decree is much longer than the corresponding part of 2 Pet. 1:3–11, which is verses 3–4. And in content the preamble of the decree resembles not only 2 Pet. 1:3–4 but also the remainder of 1:1–11. This is mainly because the preamble of this decree not only describes the benefits conferred by the gods but also describes past responses to this benefaction.

Points of similarity include the following:

1. The decree states that Zeus and Hekate have saved Stratonicea; 2 Pet. 1:1 and 11 describe Jesus as Savior, and this is explicated in verses 3–4.
2. The decree describes Zeus and Hekate as very great; in 2 Pet. 1:4 the promises given by Jesus are said to be very great.
3. The inscription speaks of the eternal domain of the Roman lords; 2 Pet. 1:11 speaks of the eternal kingdom of our Lord and Savior Jesus Christ.
4. The inscription says that the people of Stratonicea should respond to the benefaction of Zeus and Hekate by bringing all eagerness into piety toward them; 2 Pet. 1:5–7 says that the addressees should respond to the benefaction of Jesus by bringing all eagerness into supplying abundantly a number of virtues, including piety.
5. Piety is mentioned additional times by both.

In two of those cases, I have followed Deissmann. Neither of these enters into the similarities with 2 Peter discussed below.

6. The inscription speaks of the statues of Zeus and Hekate as displaying the virtues of divine power; 2 Pet. 1:3 speaks of Jesus's divine power and his having called the addressees by means of his glory and virtue.

Neither of these decrees is identical in form to 2 Pet. 1:3–11. In the first decree the preamble is a clause introduced by *epeidē*, and the resolution is introduced by an infinitive dependent on the introduction to the decree. In the second decree, the preamble is an accusative-infinitive construction dependent on the introduction to the decree, and the resolution is introduced by the clause "It seemed good to the council." Closer parallels to 2 Pet. 1:3–4 are found in a decree in which the preamble is introduced by *epeidē* but what follows is a genitive absolute, and a decree in which the preamble simply consists of a genitive absolute (Danker 1978, 66). The closest parallel is provided by decrees included in a letter in which the preamble consists of a genitive absolute (Danker 1978, 79–80). The closest formal parallel to 2 Pet. 1:5–11 is provided by decrees in which the resolution is introduced by an expression meaning "therefore" (Danker 1978, 71). Danker argues not only that 2 Pet. 1:3–11 follows the form of a decree honoring a benefactor but also that its vocabulary derives from such decrees.

Such decrees are available to us because they were inscribed on stone in public places. This made it possible for the decrees to have a wide influence on those who used these public places and enabled the decrees to survive over time. Many of these inscriptions (including those mentioned above) have been transcribed and published. Of course, 2 Pet. 1:3–11 is not the record of an actual decree. No individual or group ever enacted it. Rather, the author uses the form of a decree to argue that in view of the benefits conferred on them by Christ, the addressees ought to respond with a life of virtue.

The reference in 2 Pet. 1:4 to the possibility that the addressees can become sharers of divine nature uses language familiar from Greek philosophical and religious thought, which had been picked up by Hellenistic Jews (Bauckham 1983, 179–81; Paulsen 1992, 108–10; Starr 2000).

Second Peter 1:3–11 refers to a number of social and cultural values. The value of honor versus shame appears in the references to the divine power, glory, and virtue of Jesus (v. 3). The topic of the patron-client relationship between God/Jesus and the addressees appears in references to the benefactions of God/Jesus in verses 3–4, and 9, in the call for recognition of their patronage in verses 5 and 8, and in the warning against forgetting it in verse 9. Finally, the topic of purity appears in references to piety (vv. 3, 6, 7), escaping corruption (v. 4), desire (v. 4), self-control (v. 6), and cleansing from sin (v. 9).

The Testament

Bauckham (1983, 194–203) argues that 1:12–15 displays features of the testament, a literary form known from Jewish literature. Bauckham thinks

2 Bar. 78–86, Baruch's epistolary testament, and Josephus, *Ant.* 4.309–19, Moses's last words, are particularly close parallels. Bauckham identifies five conventions of the testament form:

1. The hero knows his death is approaching.
2. He wishes his teaching to be remembered after his death (Bauckham 1983, 194).
3. An apocalyptic revelation is sometimes given the hero, forming the basis for predictions made in the testament (Bauckham 1983, 205).
4. A testament could include predictions of the last times and of false teachers to appear then (Bauckham 1983, 237–38, 282).
5. Many testaments include ethical exhortations with eschatological sanctions (Bauckham 1983, 323).

The first two of these appear in 2 Pet. 1:12–15 as part of the author's presentation of the letter as the testament of Peter, a statement of Peter's teaching that makes it available after Peter's death. The remaining conventions appear elsewhere in 2 Peter. All of these conventions also appear in *2 Bar.* 78–86 and Josephus, *Ant.* 4.309–19 but with a less apocalyptic character in the latter.

In 1:14 Peter says that Jesus Christ revealed the time of his death to him. Bauckham (1983, 200–201) discusses five possible predictions of Peter's death by Jesus and concludes that the only one likely to be referred to here is John 21:18. This is also the view of most other commentators (see Gilmour 2002, 95n30). Thus 1:14 is probably a recitation of John 21:18 in the author's own words.

This passage continues to develop the values of honor versus shame and the patron-client

**2 Peter 1:1–15
in the Rhetorical Flow**

▶ The letter opening (1:1–15)

Salutation of the letter (1:1–2)

Theme of the letter (1:3–11)

Preamble (1:3–4)

Resolution (1:5–11)

Occasion of the letter (1:12–15)

relationship. Authoring a testament honors Peter as chief apostle and patriarch (Neyrey 1993, 164). In his testament Peter functions as mediator of the patron-client relationship between God and the addressees (Neyrey 1993, 164–65). He solicits recognition of himself as mediator of the patron.

Tracing the Train of Thought

The letter opens with a salutation (1:1–2) followed by a decree-like statement of the letter's theme (1:3–11), which can be divided into two parts: a preamble recognizing the benefits conferred by Jesus Christ (1:3–4) and a resolution to show one's gratitude for those benefits (1:5–11). Closing this section is a statement of the testamentary occasion of the letter (1:12–15).

Salutation of the Letter (1:1–2)

1:1. The first part of the letter opening is the letter salutation. The sender of the letter is **Simeon Peter, slave and apostle of Jesus Christ.** In the first century, only one known follower of Jesus had the name Peter; the identity of the sender is completely unambiguous. Here and elsewhere identification of the letter as deriving from Peter is an appeal to the ethos of Peter as a reason for the addressees to accept the contents of the letter. The addressees of the letter are indicated less definitely—**to those who have received faith equal in honor to ours by the justice of our God and Savior Jesus Christ.** This could refer to all Christians everywhere. However, the remainder of the letter makes it clear that the author is writing to Christians who face a definite set of problems. Perhaps the testamentary character of 2 Peter explains why the situation of the addressees is not indicated more explicitly; 2 Peter is a record of Peter's teaching for all who come after him even though written with a specific situation in view.

The word translated **received** has the connotation of receiving by lot or divine will, implying that the addressees' faith is a gift from God. The author mentions **faith** only here and in 1:5 below, making it difficult to know exactly what "faith" means in 2 Peter. It is likely to be related to the knowledge of God and Jesus our Lord first mentioned in the following verse and a prominent theme of the letter thereafter. If so, faith has a more exclusively cognitive connotation for the author of 2 Peter than it does for Paul (contrast Rom. 1:5). Second Peter's understanding of faith might be similar to that of the Letter of James (cf. James 2:19). The statement that the addressees' faith is **equal in honor** to that of Peter and others can be seen as an attempt to make the addressees well disposed to the following message, as is appropriate for the opening of the letter. Their "faith equal in honor to ours" derives from **the justice of our God and Savior Jesus Christ.** This suggests that "justice" means equal treatment; God gives faith equally to all. However, elsewhere in

2 Peter "justice" refers to moral uprightness in general, and that is probably what it means here too; God gives faith to all because of God's own inherent rectitude. (On Jesus's being called God and Savior, see "Christology" in the Theological Issues section at the end of this chapter.)

1:2. The sender greets the addressees by saying, **May favor and peace be multiplied for you by full knowledge of God and Jesus our Lord.** Since the author has just said in 1:1 that the addressees have faith, it seems clear that they already possess knowledge of God and Jesus to some degree. The wish that grace and peace be multiplied by it presumes that at least its effects can be extended and leaves open the possibility that the knowledge itself can be increased. From what follows, it seems likely that the author intends the latter.

This first reference to **full knowledge** (*epignōsis*) introduces a topic that is prominent both in the remainder of the letter opening and in the rest of the letter. The reference to "full knowledge" in 1:3 presumes that at least the author already possesses full knowledge and explains why it is the source of grace and peace: it is the source of everything needed for life and piety. The reference to "full knowledge" in verse 8 indicates that full knowledge is something the addressees need to increase or at least preserve. They do so by growing in virtue. Thus the theme of the letter is that one who has received full knowledge makes a proper return for it and, even more important, continues in it until its completion, by a life of virtue.

The topic of knowledge also appears in the letter opening in references to the virtue of knowledge in 1:5–6, to the danger of forgetting in verse 9, and to the letter's purpose as reminding the addressees in verses 12, 13, 15. The author says that he will remind them of what he has just said although they already know it and are established in the truth (v. 12) because he considers it right to do so (v. 13) and knows that his death will come soon (v. 14). The addressees already possess knowledge, but they need to maintain and increase it. The author presents himself as acting properly on the basis of his knowledge. Exactly how the author understands knowledge as salvific is made more explicit later in the letter (i.e., in 2:10b–22).

Theme of the Letter (1:3–11)

The argumentative character of 1:3–11 is very marked; it consists of a series of interlocking enthymemes (see Watson 1988, 96–97). The first in this series is found in verses 3–7, which constitute an elaborate and ornate conditional sentence. Verses 5–7 draw a conclusion from the existence of the circumstances stated in verses 3–4.

1:3–4. *Preamble.* **Since his divine power has given us all things for life and piety through full knowledge of the one who has called us by his glory and virtue, through which [glory and virtue] he has given us the precious and very great promises in order that through these you might become sharers of divine nature, having escaped the corruption in the world by desire.** The antecedent of **his** is probably "Jesus our Lord" in verse 2 since it is the nearest substantive (Fornberg 1977, 144; Bauckham 1983, 177; contra Kelly 1969, 300). The antecedent of **us** is not completely clear. The contrast between it and **you** in verse 4 might indicate that "us" refers to the author and others as distinct from the addressees, like "ours" in verse 1 (Bigg 1901, 255; Grundmann 1974, 69). If so, verses 3–4 strongly emphasize that salvation is mediated by Peter and others. Understood this way, verses 3–4 say that Jesus's divine power has given Peter and others all things for life and piety (etc.) so that the addressees might become sharers of divine nature through (it would be implied) Peter's and others' transmission of what they have received to the addressees. The passage can bear this meaning, but nothing in 2 Peter explicitly suggests that it does.

Alternatively, the antecedent of "us" in 1:3–4 may be the author and addressees of 2 Peter, or Christians in general (Kelly 1969, 299–300; Bauckham 1983, 176–77), as in the immediately preceding "our" in verse 2. The author of 2 Peter uses the first-person plural in both of these ways, though its inclusive use is the more common. The only clear instances where the first-person plural refers to Peter and others as distinct from the addressees are in 1:1a, 16–18 (possibly also in 3:15b). Instances where the first-person plural refers to the author and addressees can probably be seen in 1:1b, 2, 8, 11, 14, 16; 2:20; 3:15a, 18. Since this is the more common usage, it is probably the meaning of "us" in 1:3–4. Understood this way, verses 3–4 say that Jesus's divine power has given both author and addressees all things for life and piety and so on.

Life and piety (1:3b) may be a hendiadys equivalent to pious life (Reicke 1964, 184; Bauckham 1983, 178; Watson 1988, 97–98), or it may mean life and the piety that leads to it. Especially if the latter is correct, this is an instance of mentioning two items in reverse of temporal and logical order; such reversals are somewhat characteristic of 2 Peter. In this case "life" refers to the fullness of life, the ultimate goal of humans (Paulsen 1992, 107). Piety is a central concern of 2 Peter. **The one who has called us** is probably Jesus; the author speaks of "full knowledge" of Jesus in 1:8; 2:20; and 3:18, suggesting that **full knowledge** of the one who has called us (1:3c) is "full knowledge" of Jesus (Bigg 1901, 253–54; Kelly 1969, 300–301; Bauckham 1983, 178). This is the call that the addressees are urged to make secure in 1:10. Jesus has called the author and addressees **by his glory** (1:3d). Jesus received glory from God the Father, who is also characterized by glory (1:17); therefore a doxology can be addressed to Jesus (3:18).

Through **his glory and virtue** (1:3d; possibly another hendiadys = glorious virtue), Jesus has also given the author and addressees **promises** for the future, in addition to already having given them everything pertaining to life and piety. Since the purpose of the promises (the antecedent of **these**) is that the addressees may become **sharers of divine nature** (1:4c), this is the ultimate content of the promises. In light of the remainder of the letter, we may suppose that these promises will be kept when Jesus returns (3:4, 9) and the new heavens and earth appear (3:13). The most salient characteristic of divine nature is incorruptibility; the immediately following reference to **having escaped the corruption in the world** (1:4d) makes it very likely that the author equates sharing divine nature with becoming incorruptible (Fornberg 1977, 86–88; Bauckham 1983, 180–81; Neyrey 1993, 157–58). If so, the hope of sharing divine nature is equivalent to the hope of putting on incorruptibility and immortality (cf. 1 Cor. 15:50–55). This will occur when they enter the eternal kingdom of Jesus (2 Pet. 1:11).

The addressees will become sharers of divine nature by having escaped the corruption in the world **by desire** (1:4d). Since according to 1:3 "full knowledge" of Jesus is the means by which his divine power has given us everything pertaining to life and piety, we may suppose that escaping the corruption of the world is equivalent to receiving everything pertaining to life and piety. Corruption means both physical (2:12) and moral (2:19) decay. Presenting the result of following Jesus as escape from the corrupt world and sharing divine nature makes use of terms taken from dualistic Greek philosophical and religious thought. In such thought, these terms have an ontological meaning. For 2 Peter, however, corruption is not intrinsic to the world but a result of desire; the negative effects of desire are also mentioned in 2:10, 18; 3:3. Similarly, people become sharers of divine nature; they do not share it by virtue of their essential character.

1:5–7. *Resolution.* These verses state the conclusion the author draws from this set of circumstances: **therefore, having brought in all eagerness beside,**

> **by your faith supply virtue,**
> **and by virtue, knowledge,**
> **and by knowledge, self-control,**
> **and by self-control, endurance,**
> **and by endurance, piety,**
> **and by piety, brotherly love,**
> **and by brotherly love, love.**

The addressees are to bring in **all eagerness**; the word translated **having brought in beside** is rare (1:5a). In 1:10 the author again urges them to be eager and in 1:15 says that he will be eager. The addressees are to **supply** various qualities. In return, according to 1:11, entrance into the eternal kingdom of Jesus Christ will be richly supplied to them.

By means of one quality, the addressees are urged to supply another quality, then by the second quality to supply a third, by the third a fourth, and so forth—until they have supplied seven qualities, eight if we include the faith with which they began. Each quality except the first and last is mentioned twice; each quality except the last is seen as a step on the way to the next quality. This is an example of the figure of speech called *gradatio*, or climax. Another example can be seen in Rom. 5:3–5. The seven phrases that comprise 1:5b–7 closely parallel one another and so display several other figures of speech: isocolon (having approximately the same number of syllables), polysyndeton (repeated use of conjunctions), and homoeoptoton (repetition of case endings; Watson 1988, 98).

Faith (1:5b), the first quality mentioned, is something the addressees are said to have received in 1:1. The second, **virtue** (1:5c), is said in verse 3 to have been the means by which Jesus called the author and addressees. This makes it seem likely that the addressees are being urged to imitate this characteristic of Jesus (M. Green 1987, 76–77). "Virtue" is probably a general term that includes the qualities that follow (Bauckham 1983, 185–86; Neyrey 1993, 156). In that case this is another statement of the letter's theme that **faith** (1:5b), meaning full knowledge, must lead to a moral life (Fornberg 1977, 97–98).

The third item listed, **knowledge** (*gnōsis*; 1:5d–6a), is cognate with "full knowledge" (*epignōsis*), which is fundamental for the author of 2 Peter, as we have seen. Use of different words might mean that the two are to be distinguished. However, the parallel formulations in 1:8; 2:20; and 3:18 (esp. the latter two) suggest that there is little difference in meaning between the two words. The presence of "knowledge" in this list may mean that Christians need to preserve and increase their full knowledge of Christ by means of a moral life.

The fourth item listed is **self-control** (1:6b), the opposite of desire. Earlier, 1:4 speaks of having escaped the corruption in the world by desire. Inclusion of "self-control" in the list of virtues indicates that freedom from corruption results from ongoing control of desire.

The fifth item listed is **endurance** (1:6c). This may specifically mean continuing to wait for fulfillment of the promises mentioned in 1:4.

The sixth item listed is **piety** (1:6d–7a). This is mentioned in 1:3 as something for which Christ has given Christians everything needed. Inclusion of "piety" in this list shows that they have not yet attained the fullness of piety. As is the case with "knowledge," addressees are being urged to grow in a quality they already possess to some degree.

The seventh item listed is **brotherly love** (1:7b). The penultimate result of all the other qualities is love of Christians for one another. The last item is **love** (1:7c). The ultimate result is simply "love," love for everyone and everything.

Second Peter 1:3–7 forms an enthymeme in which the gifts of Jesus listed in verses 3–4 are the basis on which progress in virtue is urged in verses 5–7. The argument can be restated:

One who receives everything needed for life and piety should live virtuously.
Jesus's divine power has given the addressees everything needed for life and piety.
Therefore, the addressees should live virtuously.

1:8. Verses 3–8 form yet another enthymeme, which reformulates the enthymeme in verses 3–7 and indicates why one who receives everything needed for life and piety should live virtuously. **For possessing and exceeding in these things renders you neither idle nor fruitless for full knowledge of our Lord Jesus Christ. Fruitless** is a metaphor for failing to be productive. Verse 3 has said that the addressees have received everything needed for life and piety through full knowledge of the one who called them, namely Jesus. The reformulation argues that this full knowledge must issue in a virtuous life in order to be sustained and developed. A virtuous life is needed to grow in full knowledge of Jesus, which in turn is the source of everything needed for life and piety. The argument runs thus:

> One should not be idle or fruitless for full knowledge of Jesus.
>
> Progress in virtue makes one neither idle nor fruitless for full knowledge of Jesus.
>
> Therefore, one should make progress in virtue.

1:9. Taken together, 1:3–7 and verse 9 form a parallel enthymeme, a negative reformulation of the enthymeme in verses 3–8. **For the one in whom these things are not present is blind, nearsighted, having experienced forgetfulness of the cleansing of his past sins.** Verse 9 presumes that having received everything needed for life and piety is a matter of cleansing from one's past sins and argues that failing to progress in virtue is to have forgotten that. The argument declares:

> One should not be blind or forget cleansing of one's past sins.
>
> Lack of virtue is blindness and forgetfulness of the cleansing of one's past sins.
>
> Therefore, one should not lack virtue.

Blind, nearsighted (1:9b) is another instance of mentioning things in reverse of the expected order (like life and piety in 1:3); the lesser condition, nearsightedness, should precede blindness, the more severe state. "Blind" and "nearsighted" are metaphors for failing to understand; the word translated "nearsighted" seems to have been coined by the author of 2 Peter. The one who lacks the qualities listed in verses 5–7 is blind with respect to everything pertaining to life and piety that Christ's divine power has provided through recognition of him (vv. 3–4). Such a person has forgotten **the cleansing of his past sins** (1:9c). **Cleansing** is a metaphor for remission of sins. This cleansing must be equivalent to having received everything pertaining to life and piety through full knowledge of Christ. The language of cleansing probably implies a reference to baptism (Bigg 1901, 260; Kelly 1969, 308; Bauckham 1983,

189–90). **Forgetfulness** (1:9c) is important to the author as a way to describe the problem against which he warns the addressees. It is the opposite of full knowledge. The author uses a verb cognate with "forgetfulness" in 3:5 to say that his opponents have forgotten the flood and in 3:8 to warn the addressees against forgetting that time is different for God. The author describes his purpose as reminding the addressees in 1:12, 13, 15; 3:1.

1:10. Second Peter 1:3–10a is yet another enthymeme, drawing the conclusion from verses 3–9 that the addressees should be eager to make secure their call and election. **Therefore, brothers, be more eager to make secure your call and election.** It is another indication why one who receives everything needed for life and piety should live virtuously. Verse 3 has said that the addressees received everything needed for life and piety through full knowledge of the one who called them, Jesus. Verse 10a argues that this call of Jesus must be made secure through a virtuous life. In verse 5 the addressees are urged to be eager to progress in virtue; here they are urged to be eager to make their call secure. The argument runs thus:

> It is good to have been called and elected.
> This call and election can be lost by failing to live a virtuous life (because such failure is blindness and forgetfulness of the cleansing of one's past sins).
> Therefore, the addressees should make their call and election secure by living virtuously.

The admonition to make their call and election **secure** (1:10a) echoes the reference to endurance in 1:6. The reference to **call and election** (1:10a) may be another instance of mentioning things in reverse of logical order (cf. 1:3, 9), since choice can be understood as logically preceding call. Note, however, that we find this same order in Matt. 22:14 and Rev. 17:14.

Then 1:10a forms two more enthymemes with verses 10b and 11. First, those who make secure their call and election will never stumble: **for doing these things you will never stumble** (1:10b). "Stumble" is a metaphor for failing to attain salvation. The argument states:

> One should avoid stumbling.
> Making one's call and election secure is a way to avoid stumbling.
> Therefore, one should make one's call and election secure.

1:11. Second, entry into the kingdom of the Lord and Savior Jesus Christ will be supplied abundantly to those who make secure their call and election. **For in this way entrance into the eternal kingdom of our Lord and Savior Jesus Christ will be richly supplied to you.** In verse 5 the addressees were urged to

159

be eager to supply progress in virtue. Verse 11 says that if they make their call and election secure, entry into the kingdom of the Lord and Savior Jesus Christ will be richly supplied to them. The virtue they are urged to supply will be matched, and even exceeded, by the entrance into the kingdom they will receive. The argument declares:

> One should enter the kingdom of Jesus Christ.
> Entry into the kingdom of Jesus Christ will be supplied to those who make secure their call and election.
> Therefore, one should make one's call and election secure.

Occasion of the Letter (1:12–15)

1:12. Second Peter 1:12–15 begins with an enthymeme formed by verses 3–12; verse 12 draws the conclusion from verses 3–11, and especially verses 10–11, that the author will always remind the addressees of what he has just said because of its benefit to them. **Therefore, I will always remind you about these things, although you know them and are established in the present truth.** **Established** is used as a metaphor for unwavering affirmation. This reminder is the antidote to forgetfulness, identified as a danger in verse 9. Verse 8 has said that progress in virtue makes one neither idle nor fruitless for full knowledge of Jesus; verse 10 has urged the addressees to make their call and election secure by living virtuously. The reminder of verse 12 is issued even though the addressees know what the author is telling them and are established in the truth. This is yet another expression of the letter's theme that the addressees must maintain the status they already have. It is also an attempt to make the addressees receptive to the reminder by saying that they do not really need it. The argument can be restated in this way:

> Knowing that one's call and election must be made secure by a virtuous life enables one to make them secure.
> Being reminded helps one to retain this knowledge.
> Therefore, the author will always remind the addressees.

1:13–15. This passage is less argumentative. Peter explains why and how he will remind the addressees and thus clarifies the occasion and purpose of the letter he is writing. **But I consider it just, while I am in this tent, to arouse you by remembrance, knowing that putting off my tent is imminent, as also our Lord Jesus Christ revealed to me, and I will be eager for you also to be able always to make remembrance of these things after my departure.** In the first place he reminds them because he considers it **just**. In 1:1 he has said that the addressees' faith is derived from God's justice; now he reminds them in order to manifest that same quality of justice in himself. Moreover, he reminds them because he knows that **putting off my tent is imminent** (1:14a), and he wants the addressees **to be able always to make remembrance of these things after my departure** (1:15b) by reading the letter he is now writing. In this way the letter serves as his testament. He is **eager** (1:15a) to make this possible, manifesting the eagerness to which he has exhorted the addressees in verses 5 and 10.

"Tent" is a metaphor for the body (Bigg 1901, 263; Kelly 1969, 313; Bauckham 1983, 198) or for ordinary life (cf. 2 Cor. 5:1, 4). Some commentators see "putting off" as implying that the tent is taken off like a garment, thus creating a mixed metaphor (Bigg 1901, 264; Kelly 1969, 313; Bauckham 1983, 199). However, this expression might simply refer to laying aside the tent. The mixed metaphor is explicit in 2 Cor. 5:2–4. "Putting off my tent" and "departure" are metaphors for death. Peter knows that he will soon put off his tent and depart because **our Lord Jesus Christ revealed** [it] **to me** (1:14b). The author probably thinks this revelation occurred when Jesus said to Peter, "But when you grow old, you will stretch out your hands, and someone else will fasten a belt around you and take you where you do not wish to go" (John 21:18).

Theological Issues

Christology

Second Peter 1:1 probably designates Jesus as God and Savior (Bigg 1901, 250–52; Reicke 1964, 150; Kelly 1969, 297–98; Bauckham 1983, 168–69; Callan 2001a). Grammatically parallel phrases (i.e., in Greek: article + noun + possessive pronoun + *kai* + noun + noun + noun) are found elsewhere in 2 Peter in 1:11 and 3:18, and probably in 2:20; in all of these cases, they designate Jesus as Lord and Savior. (The only other occurrence of a parallel phrase in the NT is in 2 Thess. 1:12, and it can be argued that there it refers to God and the Lord Jesus Christ as distinct from each other [R. Brown 1968, 15–16; 1994, 180; Harris 1992, 265–66].)

The next verse, 1:2, clearly distinguishes God and Jesus. The author of 2 Peter can refer to Jesus as God in one breath and distinguish God from Jesus in the next. This may be a calculated effort to maintain both ideas, though without explaining how both can be true (cf. John 1:1–2). Only in this verse does the author speak of full knowledge (*epignōsis*) of both God and Jesus; in verses 3 and 8 he speaks of full knowledge of only Jesus (cf. also 2:20–21; 3:18). Though distinct from God, Jesus is so completely identified with God that he alone can be mentioned instead of God and Jesus.

In line with this, the author speaks of Jesus's divine power in 1:3. He has divine power because he is God (Bigg 1901, 253). Also consonant with this is the description of the kingdom of Jesus as eternal in verse 11. Elsewhere in the NT only Luke 1:33 says that the kingdom of Christ will have no end; in 1 Cor.

Pliny

Pliny (ca. 63–113 CE), also known as Pliny the Younger to distinguish him from an uncle with the same name, served as Roman governor of the province of Bithynia and Pontus around 110. Ten books of his letters survive. The tenth book consists of letters he wrote to the emperor Trajan while he was governor and the emperor's replies. In the ninety-sixth letter of this book, Pliny tells the emperor how he has been dealing with the cases of people denounced to him as Christians and asks the emperor's opinion of his procedures. In the ninety-seventh letter the emperor approves them.

15:24 Paul says that it will not last forever. Likewise the author of 2 Peter says that the destiny of the addressees is to become sharers of divine nature (1:4).

Calling Jesus by the title "God" would most naturally mean either that he is identical with the one God or that there are two Gods. Because early Christians did not wish to assert either of these things, use of the title "God" for Jesus is rare in the NT, though more common in post-NT Christian literature. Early examples can be found in Ignatius of Antioch, *Smyrn.* 1.1; *Eph.* 1.1; 7.2; 15.3; 19.3; compare also Pliny's statement that early Christians chant in honor of Christ as if to God (*Ep.* 10.96.7). In the NT, Jesus is clearly called God only in John 1:1; 20:28; and Heb. 1:8, though there are several other passages (in addition to 2 Pet. 1:1) that are probably to be interpreted this way (Cullmann 1959, 306–14; R. Brown 1968, 1–38; 1994, 171–95; Harris 1992). Raymond E. Brown considers this interpretation probable in the case of the following passages: John 1:18; Titus 2:13; Rom. 9:5; 1 John 5:20. The adjective "divine" is used elsewhere in the NT only in Acts 17:29, where it refers to God.

Thus by calling Jesus by the title "God," the author of 2 Peter presents one of the most exalted evaluations of Jesus to be found in the NT, though it is not as fully developed as in John and Hebrews. Using the title "God" for Jesus takes advantage of a theological development among Greek-speaking Jews, influenced by contact with Hellenistic polytheism, that allowed for an extension of the sphere of divinity beyond God to encompass others (Callan 2001a). This theological development also underlies the idea that Christians are destined to become sharers of divine nature.

In subsequent centuries, speaking about Jesus as God would become a fundamental expression of faith in Jesus. This development was affirmed definitively at the Council of Nicaea in 325, which declared Jesus to be of the same substance as God. It is taken for granted by most Christians today, who might readily summarize their faith by saying that Jesus is God.

The author of 2 Peter gives further information about his understanding of the relationship between Jesus and God in 1:16–18, which will be discussed below.

Soteriology

This passage makes several references to the ultimate state of those who have been saved by Christ. In 1:3 the author says that Jesus has given his followers everything needed for life, probably meaning the fullness of life, or as we might say, eternal life. In verse 11 he says that the followers of Jesus will enter his eternal kingdom. And most striking of all, in verse 4 he says that they will share the divine nature.

The author of 2 Peter probably understands this to mean that they will be incorruptible. Understood in this way, becoming sharers of divine nature is very similar to the expectation found in Paul's Letters that the followers of Jesus will put on incorruptibility and immortality. However, in itself becoming sharers of divine nature could mean much more and has been taken to mean much more in the history of Christianity. It has been understood to mean becoming divine in a more comprehensive sense. For example, in his *Mystagogical Lectures* 4.3, Cyril of Jerusalem says, "For in the form of bread the body is given to you, and in the form of wine the blood is given to you, in order that you, having partaken of the body and blood of Christ, may be united in one body and blood with Christ. For thus we become Christ-bearers, since his body and blood are distributed into our members. Thus according to the blessed Peter we become 'sharers of divine nature.'" Cyril understands sharing the divine nature as the result of participating in the Eucharist, which unites the participant with Christ, who is understood to be divine.

This is surely not the literal sense of the phrase in 2 Peter. However, it may be entirely proper as one of its spiritual senses. The literal sense of Scripture is the meaning conveyed by its words, which is discovered by exegesis; the spiritual sense is based on the literal sense but goes beyond it by taking the realities about which it speaks as signs of further realities in light of Christian faith.

"Early Catholicism"

Many interpreters see the later writings of the NT as expressions of a theological outlook they call "early Catholicism." For Protestants, this is a

Cyril of Jerusalem

Cyril of Jerusalem (ca. 315–386) was bishop of Jerusalem and has been declared a doctor of the church. He was banished from Jerusalem three times while he was its bishop as a result of conflict between Arian and orthodox Christians. His principal surviving writing is a series of lectures. In nineteen of them he instructed those preparing to become Christians (the *Catechetical Lectures*); in the remaining five he continued their instruction after baptism (the *Mystagogical Lectures*).

Figure 14. Icon of Cyril of Jerusalem, from the Pillars of Orthodoxy Baptistry, Carlisle, PA.

pejorative term referring to the theological position(s) rejected by the Protestant Reformation. Ernst Käsemann (1964, 169) is the most important Protestant interpreter who has criticized 2 Peter as expressing an early Catholic viewpoint, and many others have followed him in this. Catholics evaluate the same thing differently, understanding it as a legitimate development in Christian theology (see Schelkle 1961, 241–45; Knoch 1990, 226–27). Because the meaning of "early Catholicism" is determined by one's confessional stance, it is probably not a helpful exegetical category.

"Early Catholicism" is also an unsatisfactory category because its meaning is rather vague. According to Bauckham (1983, 8), early Catholicism is characterized most of all by three things: (1) fading of hope for Jesus's parousia, (2) increasing institutionalization, and (3) crystallization of the faith into set forms. Bauckham (1983, 151–54; 1988, 3728–34) argues, correctly in my opinion, that 2 Peter does not manifest these three things. More specifically, Bauckham argues that 2 Peter expresses hope for the imminent arrival of the parousia and does not insist on formal creedal orthodoxy. The only way in which institutionalization appears in 2 Peter is in its emphasis on the role of the apostle and particularly the role of Peter. This is rather slight evidence of institutionalization. Walter Grundmann sees the understanding of baptism in 1:9 as another instance of "early Catholicism." Here baptism is seen only as cleansing from past sins, not as a new foundation for human life (Grundmann 1974, 74–75; cf. Paulsen 1992, 112). It is true that the verse mentions only cleansing from past sins, but it seems unreasonable to suppose that the author's full understanding of baptism is expressed in a single reference to it, which does not even mention baptism explicitly.

Thus even if "early Catholicism" were a more satisfactory characterization of a type of Christian theology, it would not be accurate to describe the theology of 2 Peter as early Catholic.

The Place of Ethics in Christian Life

As one part of his critique of 2 Peter as an expression of "early Catholicism," Ernst Käsemann (1964, 184) criticizes its ethical teaching, saying that it is not linked with justification. However, as we have seen above, 2 Peter presents Jesus as having given his followers all things for life and piety through full knowledge of him, and it argues that the addressees must continue in this full knowledge by living virtuously. As Bauckham (1990, 53–60) says, for 2 Peter the saving action of God in the past is the basis for ethical life in the present (cf. Paulsen 1992, 110). Jesus's followers accept salvation from him by faith (1:1), which is equivalent to full knowledge of God and/or Jesus (1:3); this full knowledge is the source of peace (1:2) and must continue and develop through a life of virtue (1:8). Likewise, faith must lead to virtue (1:5–7).

Second Peter 1:11 indicates that entry into the eternal kingdom of Jesus Christ will be richly supplied to those who have themselves supplied virtuous living (1:5). However, the latter is a response to the gift of everything for life and piety (1:3) and leads to entry into the kingdom of Jesus only because it is a way to continue acceptance of the gift and grow in it.

As is also true for the Letters of Paul, the incompleteness of salvation makes ethics necessary. It is possible to act in such a way as to negate one's salvation. Therefore, one must act so as to maintain the status of one who has been saved (Callan 2006b, 149–51). It is when salvation is complete that it is clear who has maintained that status and who has not.

Pseudonymity

Although 2 Peter presents itself as having been written by Peter, I have argued above that it was not. This is a point on which there is near unanimity among NT scholars. A document presenting itself in a way that is not factually accurate is problematic for those who believe that it is part of the inspired Word of God. Every pseudonymous NT document presents this problem. However, it is particularly acute in a case like that of 2 Peter, where the author not only uses a name other than his own but also makes use of biographical details from the named author's life. The Pastoral Epistles are similar in this respect, especially 2 Timothy.

In 2 Pet. 1:14 "Peter" says Jesus has revealed to him that he will soon die, apparently referring to what Jesus says to Peter in John 21:18. Even more striking, in 2 Pet. 1:16–18 "Peter" says that he has witnessed Jesus's transfiguration, narrated in Mark 9:2–8 and parallels.

If 2 Peter is pseudonymous, the identity of the author of 2 Peter is clearly not part of God's revelation through this document. However, it may be part of God's revelation that Jesus revealed to Peter the imminence of his death and that Peter witnessed Jesus's transfiguration. Both of these references confirm information found in other NT texts. It may also be part of God's revelation that Peter would have addressed the circumstances to which 2 Peter is directed as 2 Peter does. But whether or not that is the case, God's revelation through 2 Peter is the way it analyzes the situation of the addressees and exhorts them. The significance of the document's content for those who believe that it is God's Word need not be diminished at all by recognition that its apparent author is not its actual author.

Recognizing that 2 Peter is partly in the form of a testament also provides a context for its pseudonymity. Since pseudonymity was a convention of the testament form, the original addressees of 2 Peter may well have understood it as making use of this convention. Just as recognizing parables as fictions keeps us from thinking that there was a historical Good Samaritan (cf. Luke 10:29–37), so recognizing 2 Peter as a testament may originally have kept people from thinking that it derived from the historical Peter.

2 Peter 1:16–3:13

The Letter Body

The body of 2 Peter communicates the principal message of the letter. This message has been announced in the letter opening and will be summarized briefly in the letter closing but is presented most extensively in the letter body.

The body of 2 Peter is divided into three main sections. In the first section (1:16–2:10a), the author formulates two arguments against those who deny that Jesus will come again. In the second section (2:10b–22), the author criticizes the immorality of his opponents and their followers. In the third section (3:1–13), the author refers again to the occasion of the letter (mentioned earlier in 1:12–15) and makes additional arguments against those who deny Jesus's second coming.

2 Peter 1:16–2:10a

Two Arguments against Opponents

Introductory Matters

Second Peter 1:16–2:10a is the first of three divisions in the body of 2 Peter (i.e., 1:16–3:13). It consists of two arguments against the author's opponents: 1:16–18 contains the first argument, and 1:19–2:10a the second.

Argument from the Transfiguration (1:16–18)

This argument continues 2 Peter's use of the testament form. The testament often includes a revelation given to the testator that forms the basis for the testator's teaching (Bauckham 1983, 205; Watson 1988, 102; 2002, 199; Vögtle 1994, 164).

Following Richard J. Bauckham (1983, 205–10), Duane F. Watson argues that 2 Pet. 1:16–18 is not dependent on the accounts of the transfiguration found in the Synoptic Gospels (i.e., Mark 9:2–8 par.). However, he sees the words of the voice in verse 17b as a reconfiguration of Ps. 2:7 and Isa. 42:1 (Watson 2002, 199–200). Bauckham (1983, 219–21) argues that the phrase "on the holy mountain" is taken from Ps. 2:6 and indicates that the author sees the words of 2 Pet. 1:17b as an allusion to Ps. 2:7. This seems quite likely. Thus, as Watson argues, in light of Ps. 2 the author of 2 Peter views Jesus's transfiguration as God's enthronement of Jesus as eschatological king.

However, the exact words of 2 Pet. 1:17b are much closer to the words of the voice in the synoptic accounts of the transfiguration than they are to Ps. 2:7 and Isa. 42:1. This makes it seem likely that 2 Pet. 1:17b depends directly on the synoptic tradition and only indirectly on the OT passages underlying it. Thus verses 16–18 should be seen as a recitation of Mark 9:2–8 and parallels in the author's own words. One part of this recitation, the words spoken by the voice in verse 17b, can be seen as replication of the exact words of the saying found in Matt. 17:5, yet with one or more differences (Gilmour 2002, 96–97). There are four differences. In 2 Pet. 1:17b: (1) "this is" (*houtos estin*) follows rather than precedes "my beloved son" (*ho huios mou ho agapētos*); (2) "my" (*mou*) is repeated after "beloved" (*agapētos*); (3) "in whom" has been expressed differently (*eis hon* instead of *en hō*); and (4) "I" (*egō*) has been added after "in whom." Thus it is quite likely that 2 Pet. 1:16–18 exhibits dependence on at least Matt. 17:1–8 (Miller 1996).

It is noteworthy, however, that the author of 2 Peter omits many details of the synoptic account. The author does not specify who accompanied Jesus, only that he himself was present along with some others. He says nothing about their reaction to what happened or about the presence of Moses and Elijah. More significant, he mentions the transfiguration of Jesus only rather obliquely by saying that he, the author, was an eyewitness of Jesus's majesty and that Jesus received honor and glory from God. This probably refers to the transformation of Jesus as something that was seen, but it is expressed in such general terms that it could simply be a reference to the words spoken by the voice. In comparison with the Synoptic Gospels' account of Jesus's transfiguration, the author of 2 Peter lets the transformation of Jesus recede into the background of the story. The author does explicitly report the words of the voice and emphasizes that he and others heard it; this is the most important aspect of the story for the author. To emphasize the source of these words, the author adds some details not found in the synoptic accounts. He explicitly calls God "the Father," which is appropriate because the voice identifies Jesus as "my beloved Son," and mentions twice (1:17 and 18) that the voice was borne to Jesus, presumably by God.

Philo of Alexandria

Philo of Alexandria (ca. 20 BCE–50 CE) was a member of a wealthy and influential Alexandrian Jewish family, probably one of the leading Jewish families in the Roman Empire of its day. In his many surviving writings in Greek, Philo tried to show the compatibility of Judaism with Greek philosophy. He did this mainly by interpreting the Jewish scriptures allegorically. In this way the Scriptures were understood as expressing philosophical ideas, but these philosophical ideas were also modified to suit the content of the Scriptures. Philosophically, Philo was a follower of Plato (ca. 428–347 BCE), himself a follower of Socrates and teacher of Aristotle. Plato was one of the most influential Greek philosophers. He expressed his philosophical ideas in dialogues that combine literary excellence and penetrating thought.

In denying that the power and coming of Jesus derive from myths (1:16), the author makes use of a term common in first-century Greek literature. It was sometimes used positively to refer to stories that expressed truth in nonliteral form. It was also used negatively, as here, to indicate stories that were not true. Philo of Alexandria defends biblical stories against the charge that they are myths in this sense (cf. *Opif.* 2; Spicq 1966, 218–19). Josephus (*Ant.* 1.22) contrasts Moses with legislators who "followed myths" (*mythois exakolouthēsantes*), using a phrase identical to that found in 2 Pet. 1:16 (Windisch 1951, 89; Bauckham 1983, 213–14). The term is also used negatively in 1 Tim. 1:4; 4:7; 2 Tim. 4:4; Titus 1:14.

"Coming" (*parousia*, 1:16) was used as a technical term for the coming of a divinity or a person of high rank, especially kings and emperors (Schelkle 1961, 196n2; Spicq 1966, 220). When applied to Jesus, it evoked these associations. The use of the term for the second coming of Jesus was already well established among Christians when the author of 2 Peter used it (cf. Matt. 24:3, 27, 37, 39; 1 Cor. 15:23; 1 Thess. 2:19; 3:13; 4:15; 5:23; 2 Thess. 2:1, 8; James 5:7, 9; 1 John 2:28). Ceslas Spicq (1966, 220) and Henning Paulsen (1992, 118) suggest that verse 16 refers to the first coming of Jesus rather than the second. This use of the term can probably be seen in Ignatius of Antioch (*Phld.* 9.2) and is clearly found in Justin, who speaks of two comings of Jesus (e.g., *Dial.* 32). However, since "coming" clearly refers to the second coming of Jesus in 2 Pet. 3:4, it probably has the same meaning in 1:16.

The word "eyewitnesses" (*epoptai*), found in 1:16, was used to designate higher-grade initiates into mystery cults, indicating that they had seen sacred things (cf. Plutarch, *Alc.* 22.4; Kelly 1969, 318; Fornberg 1977, 123; Bauckham 1983, 215).

In describing God as Father, the passage makes use of a conception of God widespread in both Jewish and Greco-Roman culture. Likewise, in having the voice imply that Jesus is the Son of God, the passage makes use of the closely related idea that humans can be called children of God. Such presentation of Jesus as the Son of God is very common in other early Christian literature. In the Hebrew scriptures "son of God" does not imply a special ontological relationship with God. "Son of" is an idiom in Semitic languages that expresses a range of relationships in addition to that of biological descent. "Son of God" indicates a relationship with God shared by many people, including the people of Israel as a whole, the king of Israel, and the Messiah. Thus, calling someone son of God in this context does not imply that he is divine. However, in the Hellenistic world, "son of God" designated divinities who were seen as literal offspring of the gods (Cullmann 1959, 270–305; Hahn 1969, 279–346; Fuller 1965, 31–33; Hengel 1976; Callan 1994, 49–51). As we will see below, 2 Peter probably understands Jesus's being Son of God along Hellenistic lines.

This passage continues to develop the values of honor versus shame, the patron-client relationship, and purity. It imputes honor to Jesus, especially in referring to his power and coming, his majesty, and his receiving honor and glory from God. It also imputes honor to God by referring to God as the Majestic Glory. And it imputes honor to Peter by defending what he has made known to the addressees. It develops the patron-client relationship by defending Peter's mediation of the addressees' patron-client relationship with God. And it develops the topic of purity by referring to the mountain on which the transfiguration occurred as holy.

The passage introduces the theme of challenge and response. The passage is a response to some opponents' challenging the honor of Jesus and Peter (Neyrey 1993, 171–72 and elsewhere).

Argument from Prophecy (1:19–2:10a)

Second Peter continues to use the testament form in 2:1–3. In this passage, the author predicts the rise of false teachers, something often found in testaments (Grundmann 1974, 87; Bauckham 1983, 237–38; Harrington 2003, 262–63).

Duane F. Watson (2002, 200) argues that 1:19 is a recitation of Num. 24:17 with modification. It is probable that 1:19 at least alludes to this passage. Watson (1988, 107; 2002, 201) argues that 2:1–3 draws on early Christian predictions that false teachers would arise in the last days, predictions sometimes included in testaments. Second Peter 2:4–8 is a recitation that summarizes Gen. 6:1–19:29, a span of text that includes various episodes.

Beginning in 2:1 and extending through 3:3, 2 Peter recontextualizes Jude 4–18. For the most part 2 Peter has not adapted Jude by quoting it directly. Though 2 Peter contains many of the words and some phrases found in Jude, no sentence of Jude is quoted in 2 Peter. Twice, however, clauses of Jude are used in 2 Peter with little change. These passages are Jude 13b = 2 Pet. 2:17b and Jude 17–18 = 2 Pet. 3:2–3.

Jude is mainly a critique of the immoral behavior of its opponents (Bauckham 1983, 11–13; Watson 1988, 29–30; Neyrey 1993, 31–32; Thurén 1997b). However, the author of 2 Peter has adapted Jude to serve as an argument against both the teaching and the behavior of its opponents. In adapting Jude, the author of 2 Peter also changed Jude's critique of a group presently confronting its addressees into prediction of a group that will confront the addressees of 2 Peter in the future. This may have been required by the fiction that the author is Peter, writing in the past. This was not difficult to do, since it was mainly a matter of changing the past tense of the verb in Jude 4 into future tense in 2 Pet. 2:1–3.

Second Peter 2:1–3 recontextualizes Jude 4(–5). In addition to changing its tense, the author of 2 Peter made other changes in Jude 4 (and 5) while adapting it in 2:1–3. The author of 2 Peter began his condemnation of future opponents by saying that false prophets arose among the people, meaning the people of Israel. Only then does he say that false teachers will likewise appear

Chiastic

The adjective "chiastic" means "resembling the Greek letter *chi,*" a letter that looks like *X* in the English alphabet. It describes a relationship between two literary units in which the first and second elements of the first unit appear in reverse order in the second unit. If the first unit is written above the second, the lines connecting the corresponding elements form the letter *chi,* as in the following diagram.

in the future. The reference to false prophets creates a chiastic relationship between 2 Pet. 2:1–3 and 1:16–21. The false prophets of 2:1a are a negative counterpart of the true prophets mentioned in 1:19–21; the false teachers of 2:1b–3 are a negative counterpart of the apostolic teachers mentioned in 1:16–18 (Bauckham 1983, 236; Watson 1988, 106). In this way, the author of 2 Peter connects the critique of false teachers in chapter 2 with the earlier part of the letter.

The author of 2 Peter rewrote the main clause and final participial phrase of Jude 4 in 2 Pet. 2:1; he rewrote the second participial phrase from Jude 4 in 2 Pet. 2:2; and he rewrote the first participial phrase from Jude 4 in 2 Pet. 2:3. The reference to the people of Israel in 2 Pet. 2:1 and the three references to destruction of the false teachers in 2:1, 3 may have been suggested by Jude 5. This revision served to connect the material 2 Peter adapted from Jude with the earlier part of 2 Peter, to predict the coming of false teachers, and to introduce the main things for which they would be criticized in 2 Pet. 2:4–3:3.

Second Peter 2:4–10a recontextualizes Jude 5–8a. Passing over Jude 5, 2 Peter incorporates Jude 6–8a into a long conditional sentence consisting of three conditional clauses (vv. 4–8) and a conclusion (vv. 9–10a). The historical precedents cited in Jude 6–7 are fashioned by 2 Peter into two of the three conditional clauses (vv. 4, 6–7); to these the author added a third (v. 5). In this way 2 Peter creates a list of precedents supporting the conclusion that God both punishes the unrighteous and rescues the godly. Second Peter uses the first part of Jude 8 to describe the unrighteousness of the false teachers it opposes.

The passage makes reference to a number of social and cultural matters. Many of these derive from Jewish history and culture: prophetic word (1:19), prophecy of Scripture (1:20), prophecy and Holy Spirit (1:21), false prophets among the people (2:1), the way of truth (2:2), and the examples of God's past judgment and salvation (2:4–8). Some of these may also reflect Greco-Roman culture: there were prophets and prophecy in Greco-Roman culture, so 1:19 may also allude to Greco-Roman ideas (Neyrey 1993, 183–84); judgment by water and fire is found among the Greeks as well as the Jews (Neyrey 1993, 203). In addition, 2:1 may allude to sacral manumission as practiced at Delphi (setting slaves free through the god's fictional purchase of them from their previous owner), and the reference to Tartarus in 2:4 might cause the addressees to think of the Greek story of the Titans, cast into Tartarus, the lowest level of the underworld.

In addition to introducing the topics of the prophet and the teacher (in 2:1), the author further develops the topic of the master-slave relationship. In 1:1 he has referred to himself as the slave of Jesus Christ; in 2:1 he says that the false teachers deny the Master who bought them, meaning Jesus.

The passage further develops the values of honor versus shame, challenge-response, and especially purity. Denial of the Master dishonors the Master; reviling dishonors the way of truth (2:2; Neyrey 1993, 189–90). The entire passage is a second response to the challenge against Jesus's and Peter's honor mentioned in 1:16. More specifically, "counterfeit words" (*plastois logois*) in 2:3 is a response to 1:16 (Neyrey 1993, 193), and 2:4–10a is a response to 2:3b (Neyrey 1993, 195–96, 199–200). The passage develops the value of purity by referring again to the topics of holiness (1:21), piety (2:5, 6, 9), and desire (2:10). The value of purity is further developed by references to the false teachers' introduction of ruinous doctrines (2:1; Neyrey 1993, 190) and to licentiousness (2:2, 7), greed (2:3), lawlessness (2:7), and defilement (2:10; Neyrey 1993, 200–201).

The passage can be seen as introducing the theme of group orientation versus individualism. Asserting that prophecy is not of one's own interpretation (1:20) expresses a preference for group orientation (Neyrey 1993, 181–82). However, as we will see below, 1:20 should probably not be understood to mean this.

Tracing the Train of Thought

First Reply: Argument from the Transfiguration (1:16–18)

1:16–18. This passage is equally argumentative and narrative in character. Making an argumentative point, the author begins by denying that he and others have derived the power and coming of Jesus Christ from myths. **For it was not having followed cleverly devised myths that**

2 Peter 1:16–2:10a in the Rhetorical Flow

The letter opening (1:1–15)

The letter body (1:16–3:13)

▶ Two arguments against opponents (1:16–2:10a)

First reply: Argument from the transfiguration (1:16–18)

Second reply: Argument from prophecy (1:19–2:10a)

Appeal: Attend to prophecy (1:19–21)

The coming of false teachers predicted (2:1–3)

Destruction of false teachers and salvation of the righteous predicted (2:4–10a)

173

we made known to you the power and coming of our Lord Jesus Christ (1:16a). The author could be contrasting his teaching with that of his opponents by characterizing the latter as myths (Grundmann 1974, 80). However, since the author explicitly responds to arguments against his teaching in chapter 3, it seems likely that he is here rejecting someone's claim that his teaching derives from myths. This response makes explicit for the first time that the full knowledge of Jesus that the author has spoken about (1:2–3, 5–6, 8) includes belief in Jesus's second coming. The author's denial of the claim is based on the narrative of Jesus's transfiguration, of which Peter and others were eyewitnesses. They did not follow myths in making Jesus's power and coming known, **but having been eyewitnesses of his majesty. For having received honor and glory from God the Father when a voice such as this was borne to him by the Magnificent Glory: "My Son, my beloved, is this one, in whom I am well pleased." And this voice we heard borne from heaven, being with him on the holy mountain** (1:16b–18).

The author implies that what Peter and others experienced when Jesus was transfigured was a foretaste of Jesus's future **power and coming** (contra Paulsen 1992, 120, who simply sees it as a general legitimation of the author's message). Although the author's description of the transfiguration does not explicitly speak of power, seeing Jesus's **majesty** and his reception of **honor and glory from God** and hearing the words of the voice might reasonably be summarized as a vision of his power. However, in order to be an experience of Jesus's coming, the transfiguration must have been an anticipation of this future event (Neyrey 1980, 510–14). Bauckham (1983, 219–20) maintains that the author of 2 Peter understands the transfiguration as Jesus's appointment by God to the role he will exercise at his second coming, in fulfillment of Ps. 2 (so also Watson 1988, 102; cf. Vögtle 1994, 164–65). Otto Knoch (1990, 255) argues that the author understands the transfiguration, and especially the words of the voice, as God's testimony to the power of Jesus and thus the reliability of Jesus's promise to come again. Bauckham's and Knoch's explanations take account of 2 Peter's emphasis on the words of the voice.

Perhaps people have denied that Jesus will come again in glory by arguing that Jesus's earthly life was incompatible with such an expectation. If so, the story of Jesus's transfiguration might be an effective counterargument. Jesus's temporary transformation and the words of the voice reveal a dimension of Jesus that is otherwise hidden. But even if the author is not responding to this specific objection, the revelation that Jesus is the eternal son of the Father supports the idea that he will come again because Jesus has not yet acted like the Son. If this is the truth about Jesus, it is reasonable to suppose that at some time he will appear in this role and enact it more completely than he has thus far.

Second Peter 1:17 is not a complete sentence. It begins with the word **for**, showing that the verse is intended to support verse 16's denial that the author and others followed cleverly devised myths. It begins with a participial phrase that describes Jesus as "having received honor and glory from God" but does not have a main clause. Perhaps the addressees are intended to supply something like "Jesus's power and coming was revealed." The author may stop the sentence before completing it in order to emphasize the key point that he and others heard the voice, which is what he goes on to say in the next sentence (Grundmann 1974, 82).

In this brief passage **glory** is mentioned twice in 1:17, and the **voice** having been **borne** to Jesus is mentioned in verses 17 and 18. Verse 17 says that Jesus received **honor and glory from God the Father** and then refers to God as **the Magnificent Glory** (1:17). The glory that Jesus received from God was a participation in God's own glory. In 1:3 the author has said that Jesus has called him and the addressees by means of his glory; now he informs them about the origin and character of that glory. Verses 17–18 first report what the **voice borne to** Jesus said, then say that Peter and others heard the **voice borne from heaven** (1:17b, 18a).

This passage continues the emphasis on the cognitive found in the earlier sections of the letter, defending the reliability of what the author has made known to the addressees. It also develops the topic of power, first introduced in 1:3. In that verse the author referred to Jesus's divine power. Here the author defends his description of Jesus's power as divine against the charge that this is a cleverly devised myth.

The passage returns to the use of the pronoun "we" found in the opening of the letter. In 1:12–15 the author uses first-person singular verbs and pronouns for himself, and second-person plural pronouns for the addressees. (The one exception is in verse 14, where the first-person plural pronoun "our" includes author and addressees.) But in 1:16–18 he resumes the use of first-person plural verbs and pronouns. They mainly designate a group distinct from the addressees. The author says that he and others were eyewitnesses of Jesus's majesty and heard the heavenly voice. This suggests that the first-person plural refers to Peter, James, and John, who were present for the transfiguration of Jesus, according to the Synoptic Gospels (Mark 9:2–8 par.). None of them directly communicated the power and coming of Jesus to the addressees of 2 Peter, but Peter, James, and John were the ultimate source of this communication to all Christians. However, when Jesus is called "our" Lord in verse 16, this first-person plural clearly includes author and addressees.

Second Reply: Argument from Prophecy (1:19–2:10a)

Second Peter 1:19–2:10a continues the author's argument that he and others did not follow "cleverly devised myths" in making known to the addressees the "power and coming" of Jesus. The first counterargument was that the author was an eyewitness of Jesus's transfiguration. The second counterargument, announced in 1:19–20, is the prophetic word, which, the author implies, predicts the coming of Jesus.

In 1:20–2:3 the author elaborates his appeal to the prophetic word in two ways. First, it is necessary to realize that prophecy is not of one's own interpretation because prophets spoke from God (vv. 20–21). Second, in 2:1–3 the author concedes that there were false prophets among the people of Israel, just as there will be false teachers among the addressees. These false teachers will misinterpret the prophecies of Scripture and so deny the Master who bought them, in other words, deny his future coming. Many will follow them in the licentiousness that results from this denial, but their judgment is not idle and their ruin does not sleep.

In 2:4–10a the author specifies the prophecies that point to Jesus's coming. He argues that if God punished sinners and saved the righteous in the past instances he mentions, God can surely do so in the future. This is especially clear in verse 6.

1:19–21. *Appeal: Attend to prophecy.* The passage is strongly argumentative; its basic argument is that expectation of the power and coming of Jesus is in accord with the prophetic word. The author says **And we have the more secure prophetic word** (1:19a), implying that the prophetic word foretold Jesus's power and coming and that expectation of it is, therefore, well founded. It is **more secure** than the transfiguration because it predicts the power and coming of Jesus less ambiguously. The **prophetic word** consists mainly of prophecies found in the Jewish Bible (Kelly 1969, 321) but also includes those contained in Christian writings (contra Bauckham 1983, 224), at least the Letters of Paul (cf. 3:16). In the immediate context (2:4–8) the author refers only to prophecies from the Jewish Bible; in chapter 3 he refers also to prophecies found in Christian writings.

Having referred to the prophetic word, the author urges the addressees to attend to it and supports this invitation by comparing the prophetic word to a lamp shining in a dark place—**which you do well to heed like a lamp shining in a dark place** (1:19b). The word translated **dark place** is one of the rare words used by the author. The dark place is the present world (Kelly 1969, 321; cf. Bauckham 1983, 225), which is dark because day has not yet dawned. Two metaphors indicate the end of the period during which the addressees need to attend to the prophetic word: **until day dawns and the light-bearer rises** (1:19c). The dawning of day and rising of the light-bearer are metaphors for the coming of Jesus (contra Grundmann 1974, 85–86); use of two terms for one reality is hendiadys. The contrast between the shining lamp and the dark place is the figure of speech called antithesis.

"Day" is probably the first instance of an image for the end of the world later used frequently in 2 Peter (e.g., in 2:9; 3:10). The meaning of "light-bearer" is less certain. Usually it is taken to refer to the planet Venus, the morning star whose appearance heralds the dawn. If this is the meaning of "light-bearer" here, dawn and the rising of the morning star are not mentioned in chronological order. In light of 1:3, 9, and 10, this would not be surprising. However, the best interpretation of "light-bearer" may be to see it as meaning the sun. Then the rising of the light-bearer is the appearance of the sun over the horizon just after dawn. Whether "light-bearer" refers to the morning star or to the sun, it is probably an image for Christ (Callan 2006a, 145–47).

The addressees are urged to attend to the prophetic word: **in your hearts first knowing this, that all prophecy of Scripture is not of one's own explanation** (1:19c–20). Most interpreters understand **in your hearts** as modifying the preceding verb "rises." On this understanding, the coming of Jesus is at least partly a subjective occurrence, something that happens in one's heart. For an argument that it should be understood as modifying **knowing**, see Terrance Callan 2006a. On this understanding, the coming of Jesus is simply an objective event, as elsewhere in 2 Peter and other early Christian literature. **One's own** refers either to the prophet or to people in general, neither of which is explicitly mentioned in the sentence. According to Bauckham, most commentators argue that it refers to people in general and see the sentence as denying that one can give one's own interpretation to scriptural prophecy. Bauckham (1983, 229–33) argues that it refers to the prophet; he sees the sentence as denying that scriptural prophecy derives from the prophet's own interpretation. In light of the immediately following reference to false prophets (in 2:1), Bauckham's interpretation is the more likely (contra Paulsen 1992, 122–24). The author sees his opponents as having dismissed prophecy on the basis that it simply expressed the prophets' own ideas.

Second Peter 1:20–21 is an enthymeme in which verse 21 supports the contention that prophecy is not of one's own interpretation (v. 20). **For prophecy was never borne by the will of a human being, but being borne by the Holy Spirit, human beings spoke from God** (1:21). The argument can be restated:

Prophecy that derives from human will is of a prophet's own interpretation.
Prophecy of Scripture was never borne by human will, but being borne by the Holy Spirit, prophets spoke from God.
Therefore, prophecy of Scripture is not of a prophet's own interpretation.

Verse 21 has a chiastic structure in which two of the main items in its two clauses (**borne** and **human being**) are mentioned in one order in the first clause and reverse order in the second. The repetition of "borne" emphasizes the rejection of one source of prophecy and the affirmation of another. The former denies that prophecy ever arose from human will; the latter implies that while they were speaking from God, prophets were being borne by the Holy Spirit. In 1:17–18 the author has said that the heavenly voice was "borne" to Jesus; use of the same word to speak of the origin of prophecy pictures the latter as comparable to the former. Just as the voice was borne to Jesus, so prophets are borne by the Holy Spirit when they speak from God.

2:1–3. *The coming of false teachers predicted.* In 2:1–3 the author develops the reference to prophets in a more narrative fashion. He concedes that there were false prophets in Israel (along with true prophets): **But there were also false prophets among the people** (2:1a). The author then describes the parallel future existence of false teachers among the addressees: **as among you there will also be false teachers, who will secretly introduce heresies of destruction, even denying the Master who purchased them, bringing on themselves imminent destruction. And many will follow their licentiousnesses, because of whom the way of truth will be slandered. And in their greed they will buy you with counterfeit words, whose judgment long ago is not idle and their destruction does not sleep** (2:1b–3). The argumentative substrate of this may first of all be typological. The false prophets of the past are a type of the false teachers to come (Knoch 1990, 259; Paulsen 1992, 126). Second, this may be seen as an explication of the content of the prophetic word: the future appearance of false teachers and their destruction. Finally, the author implies that the teachers are false because they incorrectly dismiss the prophecies of Jesus's second coming, not recognizing the view of prophecy he has articulated in 1:19–21.

Referring to the teachers as false implies an argument against them as not presenting reliable teaching. The same view is expressed more specifically by some details of the author's description of them. Other details of this description attribute general moral failings to them and their followers. This description criticizes the ethos of the false teachers and tries to arouse the pathos of the addressees against them—emotions of revulsion against the false teachers, leading the addressees to reject them. The author of 2 Peter further develops this kind of argument in 2:10b–22.

Finally, the statement that the false teachers will be destroyed, which is repeated three times in different ways, constitutes an argument against them. Insofar as the addressees accept destruction as the destiny of the false teachers, they have reason not to follow them.

The false teachers will introduce **heresies of destruction** (2:1c). The word translated "heresies" means "school" or "sect"; here it seems to mean the opinion of a school or sect (Bigg 1901, 271–72; Bauckham 1983, 239–40). The plural is problematic because the word ordinarily refers collectively to all the views of a given group, not, as here, to the various views of a single group. The plural may indicate that the author alludes to traditional apocalyptic warnings, such as given by Justin, *Dial.* 35.3 (Bauckham 1983, 240). "Heresies of destruction" means "destructive heresies" (Bigg 1901, 272; Spicq 1966, 229). The false teaching is destructive to the false teachers, bringing on them **imminent destruction** (2:1e); their **judgment long ago is not idle and their destruction does not sleep** (2:3b). It is implied that the false teaching is also destructive for those who follow it. The denial that the false teachers' judgment is idle and that their destruction sleeps may be a rejection of what the false teachers assert (Bauckham 1983, 245). This would then be one of the specific ways they deny the second coming of Jesus (cf. 3:4 below). The author speaks of their judgment as "long ago" because it has been prophesied, as he will show in 2:4–10a (Paulsen 1992, 130).

The content of the false teaching is **denying the Master who purchased them** (2:1d), which means denying the second coming of Christ (Fornberg 1977, 36). The author goes on to speak of the false teachers' **licentiousnesses** (2:2a). This probably refers to the behavior that follows from denial of the coming of Jesus (contra Fornberg 1977, 37–38). **Many will follow** (2:2a) the false teachers in denying the coming of Jesus and in the licentious behavior that follows from this denial. In saying this, the author takes a charge that the adherents of the false teachers have apparently made against him, that he follows cleverly devised myths (1:16), and turns that charge against them. Because of the false teacher's influence, **the way of truth will be slandered** (2:2b). Their influence will bring Christians in general into disrepute. The author says that the false teachers **will buy** those who follow them **with counterfeit words** (2:3a). The opportunity for self-indulgence offered by the false teaching will procure the allegiance of those who follow the false teachers. This idea is developed more explicitly in 2:14, 18–19.

As noted above, there is a chiastic relationship between 2 Pet. 2:1–3 and 1:16–21. Also, 2:1–3 is ornamented in many other ways. The word translated **false teachers** (2:1b) seems to have been newly coined by the author. The reference to the Master's purchase of the opponents in 2:1 is a metaphor for Christ's saving activity; the metaphor of purchase is used in 2:3 to express the false teachers' reversal of Christ's saving activity. The reference to the way of truth in 2:2 is a metaphor for ethical life and behavior (Watson 1988, 109). The first two clauses of 2:1 display the figure of speech known as isocolon, since both clauses have almost the same number of syllables. In these two clauses, the use of the words translated **false prophets** and **false teachers** (2:1a–b) constitutes paronomasia. These two clauses are also arranged chiastically, with the prepositional phrase last in the first clause and first in the second.

2:4–10a. *Destruction of false teachers and salvation of the righteous predicted.* Second Peter 2:4–10a returns to direct argumentation. This supports the assertion in verse 3 that the judgment and destruction of the false teachers will ensue. Verses 4–10a narrate past instances of God's destruction of the sinful and salvation of the righteous in order to argue that God surely knows how to do this. The author says, **For if God did not spare the angels who sinned but, having cast them into Tartarus, delivered them to chains of gloom, kept for judgment; and if he did not spare the ancient world but guarded Noah, as an eighth, the herald of justice, having brought a deluge on the world of the impious; and if he condemned the cities of Sodom and Gomorrah, having reduced them to ashes in a catastrophe, having made them an example of the things about to happen to the impious, and he rescued just Lot, worn out by his life amid the licentiousness of the lawless—for by means of seeing and**

hearing, the just man dwelling among them day after day tortured his just soul with respect to their lawless works—then the Lord knows how to rescue the pious from trial and how to keep the unjust confined for the day of judgment, and especially those who go after the flesh in desire for defilement and despise dominion. The argument is an induction from a series of examples.

God has punished sinners in instance *A*.

God has punished sinners and saved the righteous in instance *B*.

God has punished sinners and saved the righteous in instance *C*.

Therefore, God knows how to save the righteous and punish sinners.

These instances all come from Scripture and thus serve to explain exactly how the prophetic word supports the author's presentation of the power and coming of Jesus. There is a strong narrative element to the section because the precedents the author cites are summaries of scriptural narratives.

The second and third instances obviously derive from the Jewish Bible—the stories of Noah and the flood (Gen. 6:5–9:29) and Sodom and Gomorrah (Gen. 18–19). This is not equally obvious with regard to the first instance. The author of 2 Peter adapted it from Jude 6, and it probably refers to Gen. 6:1–4. However, both seem to presume the elaboration of Gen. 6:1–4 in extrabiblical writings like *1 Enoch* (cf. 12.4). While Gen. 6:1–4 does not refer to angels, sin, or punishment, *1 Enoch* understands the passage as speaking about all three. The author of 2 Peter likewise seems to presume that Gen. 6:1–4 narrates the sin of angels, and he assumes that God punished them.

By referring to Gen. 6:1–4, the author evokes a picture in which angels left their proper place in heaven and consorted with human women on earth. However, the author of 2 Peter says only that the angels sinned. If the addressees do not recognize the story to which this alludes, they simply know that the angels were guilty of some unspecified wrongdoing. In consequence of their sin, God consigned the angels to Tartarus, where they await final judgment. They are kept in chains of gloom; Tartarus is a dark place. Although the author has not presented a detailed picture of the angels' sin, he gives much more information about their punishment.

Second Peter's summaries of the stories of Noah and the flood and Sodom and Gomorrah derive more directly from the Bible than does its reference to the sin of the angels. Obviously, however, these brief summaries omit most of the details of the biblical accounts. One detail of the story of Noah that is included is the reference to Noah as **an eighth** (2:5a). Noah was one of eight people saved from the flood; the other seven were his wife, their three sons, and the sons' wives (Gen.7:7).

These summaries also contain elements not found in the biblical text itself but paralleled in extrabiblical versions of the stories. For instance, Gen.

6:5–9:29 does not describe Noah as **the herald of justice** (2:5b), but this description can be found in other versions of the story of Noah (e.g., Josephus, *Ant.* 1.74). Likewise, the statement that Sodom and Gomorrah were reduced **to ashes** (2:6a) is not found in Gen. 18–19 but is found in Philo (*Migr.* 139; Grundmann 1974, 93–94). To this the author adds that in treating Sodom and Gomorrah this way, God made them **an example of the things about to happen to the impious** (2:6c).

Even more significantly, the author of 2 Peter emphasizes that Lot was oppressed by living among the wicked people of Sodom. The author pictures Lot as a just man who was **worn out by his life amid the licentiousness of the lawless** (2:7). The author elaborates this by saying that this **just man dwelling among them day after day tortured his just soul with respect to their lawless works** (2:8). In addition to evoking a picture of Lot as suffering from his contact with the wicked, this evokes a picture of the wicked as lawless and, specifically, licentious. The only thing suggestive of this in the biblical account, apart from general references to the people of the cities as wicked, is the story of how the men of Sodom tried to force Lot to hand his guests over to them (Gen. 19:4–11). The author of 2 Peter implies that this sort of thing happened repeatedly.

From all three descriptions the author concludes that God **knows how to rescue the pious from trial and how to keep the unjust confined for the day of judgment** (2:9). He further describes the unjust as **especially those who go after the flesh in desire for defilement and despise dominion** (2:10a). This implies that the sinful angels, the generation of the flood, the inhabitants of Sodom and Gomorrah, and the false teachers are all guilty of these things. It is clear how this applies to the angels who married human women and to the inhabitants of Sodom who wanted sexual relations with Lot's guests; it can easily be supposed to apply to the generation of the flood. In 2:3 the author mentioned the licentiousness of the false teachers. All despise dominion in at least the sense that they do not accept God as their Lord.

Second Peter 2:4–10a constitutes another elaborate sentence. After 1:3–7 it is the most polished sentence in 2 Peter. The sentence concludes the first argumentative section of 2 Peter. This may explain why it is the second most polished sentence in the letter. It stands second in importance to the opening of the letter for communicating the basic message of the letter. Earlier 1:3–7 made the point that in view of what the addressees have received and been promised by Christ, they should live virtuously. Now 2:4–10a makes the point that expectation of the second coming of Christ, the core of what he has promised, is in accord with scriptural prophecy and thus well founded.

Second Peter 2:4–10a is a conditional sentence (like 1:3–7), of which verses 4–8 state a set of circumstances, and verses 9–10a draw a conclusion from the existence of these circumstances (contra Gerdmar 2001, 33). Verses 4–7 consist of three parallel conditional clauses, each complex in itself; the last is followed by a parenthetical explanatory clause in verse 8. The three conditional clauses in verses 4, 5, and 6–7 constitute a notable instance of repetition and progression. In verse 4 the author refers to God's punishment of sinful angels, in verse 5 to God's destruction of the world by flood and salvation of Noah, and in verses 6–7 to God's destruction of Sodom and Gomorrah and salvation of Lot. The phrase **did not spare** is repeated in verses 4 and 5; the adjective **impious** is repeated in verses 5 and 6. These three clauses present a chronological progression of events. They also represent a progression in the character of the events. The first clause refers only to punishment of the sinful. The second and third clauses refer not only to this but also to salvation of the righteous. The third clause is followed by a parenthetical clause (v. 8) that elaborates the description of the situation from which Lot was saved. Thus there is an increasing emphasis on salvation of the righteous.

There is also a noteworthy progression in the movement from the three conditional clauses to the conclusion in 2:9–10a. The second and third conditional clauses are the basis for the conclusion that **the Lord knows how to rescue the pious from trial** (2:9a); the verb "rescue" is used in verses 7 and 9. The first conditional clause is the basis for the conclusion that the Lord also knows **how to keep the unjust confined for the day of judgment** (2:9b), since the sinful angels are explicitly said to be "kept for judgment" in verse 4. There is thus a chiastic relationship between the three conditional clauses and the conclusion; the author first draws a conclusion from the second and third clauses and then from the first clause. This brings the entire period back to its starting point. Note, however, that the author also sees the second and third clauses as the basis for this conclusion. This is explicit in the comment that what happened to Sodom and Gomorrah is an example of what will happen to the impious. The author may consider the generation of the flood and Sodom and Gomorrah "kept for judgment" in light of the interval between sin and its punishment in these cases.

In 2:10a the author specifies the unjust who will receive judgment as **especially those who go after the flesh in desire for defilement and despise dominion**. The author implies that this is a general description of the sins he has just summarized, and he undoubtedly understands it as a description of the sins of those against whom he argues in this letter. The author has specifically mentioned the licentiousness of Sodom and Gomorrah. Those who will be judged "despise dominion [*kyriotētos*]": they do not acknowledge God as the Lord (*kyrios*) who will judge the world at the coming of Jesus, who is also Lord (cf. Grundmann 1974, 95; he refers only to the latter; so also Paulsen 1992, 136). This leads to licentiousness.

The complexity of this periodic sentence is ornamental in itself. And the passage exhibits many other rhetorical ornaments. I mention some of the main ones. The parallel conditional clauses and the concluding clause each present an antithesis, something especially appropriate for a period (cf. Aristotle,

Rhet. 3.9.7–8; Demetrius, *Eloc.* 22–24). In 2:4 the author has used the rare word translated **cast into Tartarus**, as well as the metaphor **chains of gloom** (2:4). The author continues to write in the grand style.

This passage further develops four topics from earlier parts of the letter. The first is that of being established, which was mentioned earlier, in 1:10 and 12. In 1:19 the author refers to the prophetic word as more secure. Second, the author continues the emphasis on the cognitive by using the phrase "first knowing this" in 1:20 and by saying that the Lord knows how to save and to punish in 2:9. Notice also the references to the way of truth in 2:2 and disdaining authority in 2:10; "disdaining" is a way of thinking. Third, the author develops the topic of following. This was mentioned earlier, in 1:16, and is mentioned again in 2:2. Fourth, the author develops the topic of justice, mentioned earlier, in 1:1 and 13, by describing Noah as herald of justice (2:5), Lot as just (vv. 7 and 8), and those who will be punished as unjust (v. 9).

Theological Issues

Foundations of Christian Faith

Second Peter 1:16–18 argues that belief in the power and coming of Jesus is based in part on the transfiguration of Jesus. Thus one foundation for this belief is a historical event, something experienced by Peter and others. Although 2 Peter does not say so, other beliefs of Christians are similarly based on the experiences of the earliest followers of Jesus, experiences of his death and resurrection, his teaching and miracles, and events in the life of the early church.

Nevertheless, to say that Christian faith is based in part on historical events does not mean that what Christians believe is self-evident to any unbiased person. Such a person might wonder if the assertion that these events occurred was intentionally false or mistaken in at least some cases. And it might be difficult or even impossible to be sure this was not so. In the specific case of the transfiguration, it seems impossible for an unbiased person to be sure that this was an actual historical event. Nonetheless, it is significant that faith in the power and coming of Jesus is based partly on what believers understand to be a historical event.

Even if the transfiguration is accepted as a historical event, it does not in itself show that Jesus will come again. It does so only when it is interpreted as an anticipatory vision of Jesus's second coming. In a similar way, other historical events serve as the foundation for Christian faith only when they are interpreted. To take the most significant instance, the resurrection of Jesus shows that he is the Messiah only because he was crucified as a false messiah, and in this context his resurrection can be understood as God's declaration that Jesus truly was the Messiah (Callan 1994).

Second Peter 1:19–2:10a argues that belief in the power and coming of Jesus is based in part on the prophetic word. Thus another foundation for this belief is that it fulfills God's promises, found most of all in the OT but articulated by early Christian prophets as well. This is also the foundation for other beliefs of Christians. One of the main things that unifies the OT and NT is the idea that predictions from the OT are fulfilled in the NT.

It is easy to see that this idea is not necessarily probative for an unbiased person. Jews, who also affirm the inspiration and authority of what Christians call the OT, do not believe that it found its fulfillment in the NT. And the false teachers opposed by the author of 2 Peter apparently do not affirm that the predictions of Jesus's second coming are reliable.

Christian faith is thus inextricably bound up with historical events and their interpretation. And one important theme of this interpretation is understanding these events as the fulfillment of promises made by God.

Theology

Second Peter 1:16–2:10a presents elements of the author's understanding of God in himself. In this passage, we learn that the prophets were humans who spoke from God (1:21). We also learn that God did not spare the angels who sinned but sent them to hell (lit., Tartarus; 2:4). God did not spare the ancient world (cf. 3:6) but preserved Noah (2:5). God condemned Sodom and Gomorrah, reducing them to ashes and establishing them as a sign of what will happen to the ungodly (2:6), but saved Lot (2:7–8). Presuming that "Lord" in 2:9 refers to God, we also learn that God knows how to save the pious and punish the wicked, a general conclusion from the specific cases mentioned in 2:4–8.

Christology

Second Peter 1:16–18 develops the presentation of the relationship between God and Jesus first introduced in the letter opening. God and Jesus are distinct: God gives Jesus honor and glory; God is Father, and Jesus is Son. However, they are closely related. The use of the word translated "eyewitnesses" in verse 16 to designate the witnesses of Jesus's transfiguration may imply that they saw the divine Jesus. "Coming" is a term used for the epiphany of a god both in Hellenistic religion generally and in Hellenistic Judaism (Kelly 1969, 318). And the glory that Jesus received from God is so characteristic of God that God can simply be called the Majestic Glory in verse 17. This suggests that the author of 2 Peter understands Jesus's being Son of God along Hellenistic lines, as implying a special ontological relationship with God. In 1:1 the author simply called Jesus by the title "God."

The presentation of Jesus as Son of God in an ontological sense expresses the idea that Jesus is God and yet distinct from God. He is God in the sense

Tertullian

Tertullian (ca. 155–230 CE), a native of Carthage in North Africa, converted to Christianity in about 197. In 207 he became a Montanist Christian. Many of his apologetic and ethical writings in Latin have survived. Tertullian's *Apology* is directed to Roman provincial administrators and argues both that accusations against Christians are false and that Christianity is superior to other religions. In chapter 21 he explains how Christians can regard Christ as divine without disagreeing with Jews that there is only one God. Tertullian's explanation is that Christ was generated by God and is thus the Son of God, who is called God because of unity of substance with God.

that he was revealed to be Son of God at his transfiguration. He is distinct from God because he is the Son, not God himself. The author of 2 Peter does not explicitly affirm this understanding of Jesus as Son of God. Later writers did explicitly affirm it (see, e.g., Tertullian, *Apol.* 21). And this understanding became part of the doctrine of the Trinity.

Soteriology

The reference to Jesus as the Master who bought his followers in 2:1 implies an understanding of how Jesus saves: by purchasing his followers from those to whom they are enslaved (Callan 2001b). This might refer to setting free enslaved persons by purchase, something known both from the OT (cf. Lev. 25:47–55) and Greek literature (cf. Diodorus Siculus, *Hist.* 15.7.1; 36.2.2; 1 Pet. 1:18–19). As mentioned above, a particular form of this that might underlie 2 Peter is the sacral manumission practiced at Delphi; here Apollo purchased slaves for freedom (see Bartchy 1973, 87–125). However, two things make it more likely that 2 Pet. 2:1 refers to transferring ownership of slaves from one master to another. One is the use of the term "Master" for Jesus; it suggests that Jesus is the new owner of his followers. The other is the verb translated "purchase" (*agorazō*), which connotes purchase in the market. Paul uses this term in a similar way in 1 Cor. 6:19–20. When Paul speaks of manumission in Gal. 3:13; 4:5, however, he uses this verb with a prepositional prefix (*exagorazō*; see Marshall 1974, 156–57). Diodorus Siculus also uses this word in *Hist.* 15.7.1; 36.2.2. Jesus has purchased his followers from their previous owner, and they have become Jesus's slaves. Thus the author of 2 Peter refers to himself as slave and apostle of Jesus Christ in 1:1 (cf. Rom. 1:1; Gal. 1:10; Phil. 1:1; James 1:1; Jude 1). Like Paul, the author presumes that it is better to be Jesus's slave than to be slave of any other master (cf. Rom. 6:16–23; 1 Cor. 7:22–23).

Second Peter says nothing about how Jesus made this purchase. The language of purchase is also used in Rev. 14:4 without explanation of how the

---

Diodorus Siculus

Diodorus Siculus (ca. 90–21 BCE) was a Sicilian (Siculus means Sicilian) who wrote the *Library of History*, a forty-book history of the world in Greek. Only books 1–5 and 11–20 survive in their entirety. In book 15.7.1, Diodorus says that the philosopher Plato, who had gone to Syracuse in Sicily at the invitation of its ruler Dionysius, was sold as a slave when he offended Dionysius. Other philosophers joined together, purchased Plato's freedom, and sent him back to Greece.

---

purchase was made and in 1 Cor. 6:20; 7:23, where it is said only that a price was paid. Revelation 5:9 says that the purchase price was the blood of Jesus. This may be presumed wherever the language of purchase is used. If so, the author of 2 Peter regards Jesus's death as the price he paid to transfer his followers from their previous owner to his ownership.

Second Peter 2:1 does not specify the previous owner from whom Jesus purchased his followers. However, the following section of the letter, especially 2:19–20, does indicate how the author understands this.

Eschatology

As we have observed above, the eschatological views of the author of 2 Peter become more specific in this section of the letter. In the opening section of the letter, the author speaks of Jesus's promises that his followers might become sharers of divine nature and the hope that they would enter Jesus's eternal kingdom. Second Peter 1:16–18 strongly suggests that both will occur when Jesus comes again. According to 1:19–2:10a, Jesus's second coming will be the dawn of day and the rising of the light-bearer. It will mean judgment for the false teachers and their followers and rescue for the upright.

This section of the letter also makes it clear that the destiny of the false teachers and their followers is destruction. Like the whole world at the time of Noah, and like the cities of Sodom and Gomorrah, they will be completely destroyed. Right now, like the sinful angels, they are being kept for judgment. When that judgment occurs, they will be destroyed. See also 2:12; 3:7, 10–11. Thus the author does not speak of eternal punishment of the unrighteous, though neither does he explicitly deny it. Note, however, that in 2:17 the author omits the "forever" that is found in Jude 13, on which 2 Peter depends at this point. In 2:17 the author of 2 Peter says that the gloom of darkness has been kept for the false teachers. Perhaps this refers to an attenuated existence for evildoers who die before the final judgment. More likely it is an image of destruction.

The eschatology of 2 Peter is another aspect of the letter that Ernst Käsemann criticizes. Käsemann (1964, 185) contends that eschatology is not central to 2 Peter (as he thinks it should be) but is used by the author merely to solve the problem of theodicy and to encourage morality. I maintain that eschatology is central to 2 Peter; it serves as the completion of the salvation that has begun with the death and resurrection of Jesus (Callan 2001b, 557). Later in 2 Peter the author gives additional information about future expectations.

2 Peter 2:10b–22

Critique of Opponents

Introductory Matters

Second Peter 2:10b–22 is the middle part of the body of 2 Peter (i.e., 1:16–3:13). It presents an ad hominem critique of the author's opponents.

Second Peter 2:15–16 is a recitation of Num. 22 in substantially the author's own words, perhaps as interpreted in targums (Bauckham 1983, 268). Second Peter 2:20 is a recitation and recontextualization of Matt. 12:45//Luke 11:26 (Gilmour 2002, 98). Second Peter 2:22 is a recitation of a saying by using words different from the authoritative source. The author cites a double proverb, the first part deriving from Prov. 26:11, the second apparently coming from *The Story of Ahiqar* 8.15/18. Richard J. Bauckham (1983, 273) thinks the two may have been joined by Hellenistic Jews before incorporation into 2 Peter.

This passage continues the recontextualization of Jude 4–18 in 2 Pet. 2:1–3:3. Second Peter 2:10b–22 recontextualizes Jude 8b–16. This includes a verbatim recitation of Jude 13b in 2 Pet. 2:17b, omitting only "forever" (*eis aiōna*).

Second Peter 2:10b–16 recontextualizes Jude 8b–11. In 2 Pet. 2:10b–11 the author separates the final clause of Jude 8 from the preceding two clauses and joins to it a revised version of Jude 9. In 2 Pet. 2:12 the author follows Jude 10 more closely, though still making substantial changes. The author of 2 Peter adds 2:13–14, making some use of Jude 12. In 2 Pet. 2:15 the author uses one of the three elements of Jude 11. He expands on it and develops it further by the addition of 2 Pet. 2:16. From a rhetorical point of view, one can say that here and in the following section of 2 Peter, the author takes a portion of Jude that tries to prove Jude's thesis and reworks it into a digression in which the author of 2 Peter denounces his opponents (Watson 1988, 48–49, 114–15).

Second Peter 2:17–22 recontextualizes Jude 12–16. Second Peter 2:17 adapts the first and fourth of four metaphors found in Jude 12–13 but omits the second and third. Second Peter omits Jude 14–15 but adapts Jude 16 to serve as the premise for 2:17 and the introduction to a long denunciation of the false teachers for causing Christians to turn back to their pre-Christian state.

Second Peter 2:10b–22 makes reference to some items deriving from Jewish history and culture: angels (2:11; cf. 2:4), the story of Balaam (vv. 15–16), and the institution of prophecy (v. 15). As noticed above, there were also prophets in Greco-Roman culture. Dogs and pigs are unclean in both Jewish and Greek culture (Neyrey 1993, 224–25).

The passage further develops the master-slave relationship. In 1:1 the author has referred to himself as a slave of Jesus Christ, and in 2:1 he has said that the false teachers deny the Master who bought them. In 2:20 the author says that the false teachers are slaves of corruption, since one is enslaved by whatever overcomes that person (v. 19). This suggests that the author would say that humans must be enslaved to something, either to Christ or corruption. One has a choice of masters but cannot be without some master (cf. Rom. 6:15–23).

The passage also further develops the values of honor versus shame, challenge-response, and again especially purity. The first two are closely linked. The passage continues the effort to respond to the challenge of Jesus's and Peter's honor mentioned in 1:16 but does so by shaming the false teachers in order to defend God's honor (Neyrey 1993, 206–7, 218–19). One way the passage does this is by further developing the topics of glory, power, and reviling. The author says that the false teachers do not tremble while reviling the glorious ones (2:10). He contrasts this with the behavior of the angels, who are described as being greater in strength and power than the false teachers (2:11). (Earlier the author has referred to the power of Jesus in 1:3 and 16.) The angels do not bring a reviling judgment (2:11), but the false teachers revile what they do not know (v. 12). Earlier the author has said that the way of truth will be reviled because of those who follow the false teachers (2:2).

The principal way in which the passage shames the false teachers is by presenting them as impure (Neyrey 1993, 212–13, 221–23). The author does this by saying that the false teachers suffer the penalty for doing wrong (2:13): they lack the piety recommended in 1:3, 6, 7; 2:9 and are instead wrongdoers (2:9) or impious (2:5, 6). They seek pleasure and are blots and blemishes (2:13). Their eyes (v. 14), mouths (vv. 10b–12, 18–19), and genitals (v. 18) are uncontrolled. The author also shames the false teachers by further developing other topics introduced earlier. Escaping corruption, mentioned earlier in 1:4, is mentioned again in 2:12 and 19–20; here it is used to say that the false teachers have not escaped corruption. The topic of greed, introduced in 2:3, is further discussed in 2:14–15. The topic of lawlessness, seen earlier in 2:7, is also discussed in 2:16. The topic of desire, mentioned earlier in 1:4 and 2:10, appears again in 2:18. Licentiousness, critiqued earlier in 2:2 and 7, is further discussed in 2:18 (cf. also 2:14). The topic of holiness, seen earlier in 1:18 and 21, is mentioned again in 2:21; the false teachers and their followers turn away from holiness. Finally, the author compares the false teachers to dogs who return to their vomit and pigs who roll in the mud (v. 22).

Tracing the Train of Thought

Moral Failings of Opponents and Their Punishment (2:10b–17)

Second Peter 2:10b–17 is mainly descriptive. It describes the false teachers in negative terms, implying that the addressees of 2 Peter should reject the false teachers because they are bad. This is a critique of the ethos, or moral character, of the false teachers and at the same time an attempt to arouse the pathos of the addressees, to stimulate their emotional rejection of the false teachers. The following passage (vv. 18–22) presents argument from logos, or reasoning.

2:10b–11. Here the author describes the false teachers as not trembling to revile the glorious ones and contrasts this with the behavior of the angels. **Stubborn bold ones, they do not tremble, slandering the glories, where angels, being greater in strength and power, do not bear against them a slanderous judgment from (the side of) the Lord.** Glories is usually understood to refer to church (Bigg 1901, 279–80) or secular (Reicke 1964, 167) leaders or to angels, either good (Neyrey 1993, 213–14; Harrington 2003, 268; G. Green 2008, 270–71) or evil.[1] These interpretations may be too much influenced by Jude's use of the word. In the context of 2 Peter, it is most likely that the **glories** are God and Jesus, since they are the ones said in 2 Peter to have glory (God in 1:17; Jesus in 1:3, 17; 3:18). **Slandering the glories** refers to the false teachers' skepticism that Jesus will return and God will bring this world to an end.

The behavior of the angels with which the conduct of the false teachers is contrasted is far from clear, though the contrast itself can be explicated. Not only is the meaning of "glories" uncertain; it is also uncertain with whom the angels are being contrasted and against whom the angels' judgment might be directed. I suggest that it is the false teachers in both cases. Although the angels are **greater in strength and power** (2:11a) than the false teachers (so Grundmann 1974, 95; contra Schelkle 1961, 210; Kelly 1969, 338; Fornberg 1977, 54; Bauckham 1983, 262), they do not bring against the false teachers (contra Schelkle 1961, 211; Bauckham 1983, 261; Harrington 2003, 268–69) a **slanderous judgment from (the side of) the Lord** (2:11c). The angels are greater

---

1. See Wohlenberg 1915, 226; Chaine 1939, 67; Windisch 1951, 95; Schelkle 1961, 210; Kelly 1969, 337; Bauckham 1983, 261; Knoch 1990, 266; Paulsen 1992, 138–39; Vögtle 1994, 197–99.

than the false teachers and thus might be more justified in slanderous judgment but nevertheless do not engage in it.

If this is the meaning of the contrast, it remains unclear what the author understands by the idea that the angels do not bring "a slanderous judgment from (the side of) the Lord" against the false teachers. Pheme Perkins (1995, 184) thinks it means that the angels do not bring the blasphemous judgments of the opponents into the heavenly court as evidence against them. However, this understanding does not seem to supply the contrast required by the context. More likely the author is saying that the angels who stand in God's presence do not go out from that presence to bring against the opponents a judgment comparable to the judgment of the opponents against God and Jesus. It is not clear what makes the author think the angels restrain themselves in this way or why they do so. Perhaps the author is contrasting this behavior with that of the sinful angels mentioned in 2:4.

> **2 Peter 2:10b–22**
> **in the Rhetorical Flow**
>
> **The letter opening (1:1–15)**
> **The letter body (1:16–3:13)**
>   **Two arguments against opponents (1:16–2:10a)**
> ▶ **Critique of opponents (2:10b–22)**
>   Moral failings of opponents and their punishment (2:10b–17)
>   Negative effects of the opponents' teaching (2:18–22)

The phrase translated "a slanderous judgment from (the side of) the Lord" (*para kyriou*) can be understood to mean "a slanderous judgment from the Lord." Understood this way, the phrase implies that the angels are bearers of the Lord's own slanderous judgment. Obviously, it is problematic to refer to God's judgment as slanderous. Thomas J. Kraus (2000) has argued that a different reading of the text is more original: *para kyriō* (so also Windisch 1951, 95). The text could be translated "a slanderous judgment near the Lord." This may be correct, but even if it is not, the alternative text can and should be understood in a very similar way. The main difference between the two is that the text I have translated implies motion from the side of the Lord, which suits the verb "bear" rather well.

2:12–14. These three verses constitute one elaborate sentence. In this sentence the author compares the false teachers to irrational animals who are destined for corruption and further describes them in several ways that explain why they are destined for corruption. **But these, like irrational animals begotten naturally for capture and corruption, slandering things of which they are ignorant, will also be corrupted in their corruption, being wronged as the reward of wrongdoing, considering luxuriousness during the day a pleasure, spots and blemishes luxuriating in their deceits while feasting together with you, having eyes full of an adulteress and not ceasing from sin, enticing unstable souls, having a heart trained in greed, children of a curse.** Corruption is natural for irrational animals but (the author implies) not for rational animals, meaning humans. The comparison with irrational animals emphasizes the physical meaning of corruption. Both die and disintegrate and are no more. In 1:4 the author has described the addressees as having escaped the corruption in the world by desire; the false teachers have not escaped it.

The first additional description of the false teachers repeats the criticism of 2:10b–11; they are **slandering things of which they are ignorant** (2:12c). This has the same meaning as "slandering the glories" in verse 10, namely, eschatological skepticism. This description is followed by an additional description of the false teachers' future corruption; it is a matter of their **being wronged as the reward of wrongdoing** (2:13a). This is another expression of the idea that one's destiny corresponds to one's behavior. In 1:5 and 11 the author has expressed this positively, saying that those who have supplied virtue will have entry into the kingdom of Christ supplied to them. Here the idea is expressed negatively: those who do wrong will have wrong done to them. The idea is expressed this way for the sake of the play on words (paronomasia) between "being wronged" and "wrongdoing." It does not imply that the false teachers are thereby treated unjustly.

The remaining additional descriptions of the false teachers are of three kinds. With some of these descriptions, the author simply uses pejorative terms to indicate their negative character; **spots and blemishes** (2:13c) and **children of a curse** (2:14e) fall into this category. Other descriptions criticize them for specific moral failings: **luxuriousness** and **luxuriating**, seeking out an **adulteress** and **greed** (2:13–14). Finally the author criticizes them for **enticing unstable souls** (2:14c). This is a criticism he develops at some length in 2:18–22.

The charge of "luxuriousness" envisions misbehavior at meals. In part this may be a matter of holding lavish meals during the day rather than properly in the evening (cf. Eccles. 10:16; Isa. 5:11); in part it is a matter of unspecified misbehavior at the common meals of the Christian community. One possible instance of the latter is the behavior for which Paul criticizes the Corinthians in 1 Cor. 11:17–22 (Grundmann 1974, 97). It is unclear whether "adulteress" is meant literally or adultery is being used as an image for sin understood as infidelity to God. The author has accused the false teachers of "greed" in 2:3 and may develop this idea implicitly in the comparison of them to Balaam in verses 15–16.

Second Peter 2:12 begins with a similitude comparing the false teachers to animals. In verse 13 the false teachers are described metaphorically as "spots and blemishes." In verse 14 the author has used two rare words, translated **not ceasing** and **unstable**. The phrases **eyes full of an adulteress and not ceasing from sin** and **heart trained in greed** (2:14) are both instances of the trope hyperbole and the figure of thought known as emphasis, revealing a deeper meaning than is actually expressed by the words. They can also be seen as examples of the trope periphrasis because the ideas could have been expressed more directly. The latter phrase also uses the metaphor of athletic training.

Verse 14 uses another metaphor, that of catching with bait, which is used to describe the false teachers' activity.

2:15–16. Here the false teachers are compared to Balaam, and his story is briefly told, especially his being restrained by his donkey. **Abandoning the straight way, they have gone astray, having followed in the way of Balaam, son of Bosor, who loved the reward of wrongdoing. And he received a rebuke of his own lawbreaking. A voiceless donkey having spoken with a human's voice prevented the madness of the prophet.** The false teachers have followed the example of Balaam, specifically in his love for **the reward of wrongdoing** (2:15c). In 2:13 the author has said that the false teachers will receive the reward of wrongdoing; here he says that in this they are like Balaam. Bauckham (1983, 260, 268) suggests that this comparison with Balaam may develop the accusation that the false teachers are characterized by greed, since that was Balaam's sin, according to Jewish tradition. Donald Senior (1980, 125) suggests that the author may have compared the false teachers to Balaam because "his credentials as prophet and wise man fit the false teachers" (cf. Fornberg 1977, 39–40). Balaam may be one of the false prophets among the people to which the author has referred in 2:1, who are a type of the false teachers whom the author opposes (Grundmann 1974, 99).

The exact nature of the wrongdoing whose reward Balaam loved is not clear. The author may be thinking of Balaam's advice to the Moabites (Num. 31:16) to have their women lead the Israelites into idolatry (see Num. 25). The author may imply that the false teachers lead people astray through sexual misconduct; he has already accused the false teachers of sexual misbehavior in 2:1 and 14. The author may be thinking that Balaam's ultimate reward for his behavior was to be killed by the Israelites along with the Midianites (Num. 31:8); the false teachers' reward will be similar.

The references to **abandoning the straight way** and having **gone astray** (2:15) are used metaphorically to express the idea of moral failure. Verse 15 uses the same metaphor another time, in speaking of **the way of Balaam.** The reference to Balaam's love of the reward of wrongdoing may be ironic, having in view the judgment Balaam received for his activity. Verse 16 exhibits paronomasia in pairing the words translated **lawbreaking** (*paranomia*) and **madness** (*paraphronia*), and the words **voiceless** and **voice.** The word translated **madness** is a new coinage of the author; the second paronomasia is also an instance of antithesis.

2:17. This verse continues the description of the false teachers in negative terms. **These are waterless springs and mists driven by a storm, for whom the gloom of darkness has been kept.** The author describes them in two metaphors. The first, **waterless springs,** implies that they are useless. They seem to be sources of water but do not actually supply any water. According to Duane F. Watson (1988, 120), this is a traditional metaphor, as in Jer. 2:13. The second metaphor, **mists driven by a storm,** indicates that the false teachers are insubstantial and suggests that they are controlled by powerful external forces. The author describes their fate as **the gloom of darkness**, another metaphor. This metaphor describes the false teachers' undergoing destruction as entering into darkness.

Negative Effects of the Opponents' Teaching (2:18–22)

While 2:10b–17 is mainly a negative description of the false teachers, verses 18–22 argue against them.

2:18–19a. Verses 17–19a are an enthymeme in which verses 18–19a support the assertions of verse 17. **For speaking boastful words of futility, they entice with the desires of the flesh, with licentiousnesses, those who are just escaping from the people who live in error, promising them freedom while being themselves slaves of corruption.** The argument can be restated:

One who uses licentious desires of the flesh to entice people who are escaping those who live in error (etc.) is a waterless spring (etc.).

The opponents of the author of 2 Peter do use licentious desires of the flesh to entice those who have recently escaped those who live in error (etc.).

Therefore, the author's opponents are waterless springs (etc.).

The teaching of the false teachers is problematic because of the behavior it promotes. They speak **boastful words of futility** and apparently encourage indulgence in **the desires of the flesh, licentiousnesses** (2:18). They say that expectation of the power and coming of Jesus derives from cleverly devised myths, and thus there is no reason to restrain one's appetites. To accept this is to rejoin those who live in error, from which group one has just escaped; it is to negate one's salvation.

In 2:14 the author has accused the false teachers of "enticing unstable souls." Now the author repeats and elaborates that accusation. The false teachers entice [them] **with the desires of the flesh, with licentiousnesses, [by] promising them freedom** (2:18b–19a). The false teachers persuade people to abandon eschatological hope by presenting this abandonment as an opportunity to give free rein to their appetites. This is the bait they use to catch unstable souls. The false teachers are already **slaves of corruption** (cf. 2:12). They try to persuade unstable souls to join them in this slavery, but they do so by **promising them freedom** (2:19a). This contrast between freedom and slavery is an antithesis. Speaking of the false teachers as "slaves of corruption" personifies corruption. Use of **slaves** here and **enslaved** in the following sentence constitutes paronomasia. The unstable souls **are just escaping from the people who live in error** (2:18c). In 1:4 the author has described the addressees as having escaped the corruption in the world through desire, using the same verb "escaped." These are probably different ways of speaking about escape from the same thing.

The people who live in error are those enslaved to corruption in the same way as the false teachers who entice them.

2:19b. Second Peter 2:19 is an enthymeme; the assertion of verse 19a is supported by verse 19b: **For by whatever someone has been overcome, to this he has been enslaved.** This is a maxim. The argument declares:

> One is enslaved to whatever masters that person.
>
> The opponents of the author of 2 Peter are mastered by corruption.
>
> Therefore, the author's opponents are slaves of corruption even as they promise freedom to others.

2:20. Second Peter 2:18 and 20 is yet another enthymeme, with verse 20 supporting the assertion in verse 18 that the false teachers speak "boastful words of futility." **For if, having escaped the defilements of the world by full knowledge of our Lord and Savior Jesus Christ, and again having been implicated in them, people are overcome, for them the last things have become worse than the first.** This and verses 21–22 speak directly about those who follow the false teachers and indirectly about the false teachers themselves who follow their own teaching. The final clause **for them the last things have become worse than the first** is another maxim. The argument runs thus:

> Instruction that worsens one's situation is futile.
>
> The author's opponents are worsening the situation of the addressees by enticing them to return to the defilement they have escaped.
>
> Therefore, the false teachers offer futile instruction.

The contrast between **having escaped the defilements of the world** and **again having been implicated in them** (2:20a–b) is an example of antithesis. The basic meaning of the word translated **defilements** is "stain," as in a color imparted to a fabric. However, it is used almost exclusively in a figurative and pejorative sense to mean wrongful behavior of various kinds (Callan 2001b, 551–52). The author speaks of "having escaped the defilements of the world" (2:20) by using the same verb he used to speak of "escape" from the people who live in error (2:18) and from the corruption in the world through desire (1:4). These three specifications of what the addressees have escaped are probably approximately equivalent descriptions of that from which they have been saved. In 2:20 the author says that this escape has occurred **by full knowledge of our Lord and Savior Jesus Christ** (2:20a). In 1:3–4 the author says that Jesus has given the addressees all things for life and piety through full knowledge of him and later says that they have escaped the corruption in the world. In light of 2:20 we can see that this escape has occurred through full knowledge of Jesus. Seen positively, full knowledge of Jesus provides all things for life and piety; seen negatively, it is the means of escaping corruption in the world.

2:21. Second Peter 2:20b–21 is another enthymeme: verse 21 supports the conclusion of verse 20, that the last state of those deceived by the false teachers (and the last state of the false teachers themselves) is worse than the first. **For it was better for them not to have fully known the way of justice than, having fully known it, to turn away from the holy commandment delivered to them.** The argument can be restated:

Returning to a bad situation from which one has been delivered is worse than simply remaining in the bad situation.
The author's opponents are enticing those who have known the way of righteousness to turn aside from it.
Therefore, their last state is worse than the first.

Immediately after speaking about full knowledge of Jesus in verse 20, the author speaks of having **fully known the way of justice** (2:21a). This suggests that knowing Jesus is equivalent to knowing "the way of justice." Further, the author implies that turning away **from the holy commandment delivered to them** (2:21b) is equivalent to turning away from "the way of justice." The "holy commandment" is the commandment to follow "the way of justice." The "holy commandment" is the necessity of persisting in the life of holiness that has begun through one's full knowledge of Jesus. In speaking of "the way of justice," the author again invokes the metaphor he has used in verse 15.

2:22. Here the author compares those deceived by the false teachers (and the false teachers themselves) to the behavior of a dog and sow, using a double proverb that combines two maxims. **The meaning of the true proverb has applied to them: a dog having turned back to his own vomit, and a sow, having been washed, to wallowing in the mud.** The dog and sow both behave in ways that parallel the backsliding against which the author warns. Having expelled something harmful from his body, the dog returns to it. Having been washed clean, the sow makes herself dirty again; this may allude to baptism (Grundmann 1974, 101). Comparing the behavior of the false teachers' followers to the dog and the sow supports the author's argument that they are not improving their situation but, rather, are returning to a worse situation, from which they had escaped. He also tries to arouse emotions of disgust at this behavior. The word translated **vomit** is rare. Clearly the author continues to write in the grand style; 2:10b–22 is one of the most ornate parts of 2 Peter. Watson (1988, 123–24) argues that the use of metaphor and maxim in this section of 2 Peter is excessive.

Second Peter 2:10b–22 further develops ten topics from earlier parts of the letter: (1) The emphasis on the cognitive found throughout 2 Peter continues in this passage. In 2:13 the author refers to the way the false teachers regard reveling. In 2:20 full knowledge of Jesus is said to be the means by which one escapes the defilements of the world. In 2:21 full knowledge of Jesus is equated with full knowledge of the way of justice, and the author says that it would have been better not to have fully known that way than to have fully known it and then turned away from it. (2) The topic of justice, mentioned earlier (in 1:1, 13; 2:5, 7, 8, 9), appears again in the references to the wages of wrongdoing in 2:13 and 15 and to the way of justice in 2:21. (3) The topic of being established, presented earlier (in 1:10, 12, 19), reappears in 2:14, where the souls of those tempted by the false teachers are said to be unstable. (4) The metaphor of the way, introduced in 2:2, is further developed in 2:15, 21. Verse 15 contrasts the straight way with the way of Balaam; verse 21 speaks of the way of justice, which is presumably the same as the straight way. (5) The related topic of following, introduced in 1:16 and 2:2, is also developed in 2:15. (6) The topic of prophecy, previously mentioned (in 1:20–21; 2:1), is also found in the description of Balaam as a prophet in 2:16. (7) The topic of nether gloom appears in 2:4 and reappears in 2:17. (8) The related topic of keeping, introduced in 2:4 and 9, is also mentioned in 2:17. (9) The topic of promises, found earlier in 1:4, resurfaces in 2:19. (10) The topic of salvation has appeared in 1:1, 11 and is also found in the description of Jesus as Savior in 2:20.

Theological Issues

Soteriology

This passage gives much additional information about how the author understands the saving activity of Jesus (Callan 2001b). In 2:1 the author speaks of Jesus as the Master who has purchased his followers. In 2:10b–22 we learn (1) the identity of the previous owner from whom Jesus purchased his followers, (2) how they were enslaved to that previous owner, and (3) how they appropriate Jesus's purchase of them subjectively.

1. Second Peter 2:19–20 strongly suggests that before being purchased by Jesus, his followers were slaves of corruption and the defilements of the world. In this passage the author describes the false teachers he opposes as promising freedom while they themselves are slaves of corruption. He then explains that someone is enslaved by whatever overcomes that person (v. 19), clearly presuming that the false teachers have been overcome by corruption. The author says this more directly in 2:12. The false teachers are like irrational animals, begotten for capture and corruption. In the corruption of the animals, the false teachers will also undergo corruption (Bauckham 1983, 264). In 2:20 the author refers to those who follow the false teachers and to the false teachers themselves and says that if those who have escaped the defilements of the world by fully knowing Jesus are again overcome by them, their last state is worse than the first.

What does it mean to be a slave of corruption? The basic meaning of the word translated "corruption" is destruction, with a strong implication that the destruction is caused by the kind of disintegration that occurs in decay, or even when something is eaten. In addition to its use to mean physical destruction/disintegration, "corruption" can also be used to mean spiritual destruction/disintegration (like the English word "corruption").

Second Peter 2:12 clearly shows that the author of 2 Peter uses corruption to mean physical corruption. Two things suggest that the author uses the term to mean spiritual as well as physical corruption in 2:19. First, in 2:20 he implies that enslavement to corruption is equivalent to being overcome by the defilements of the world. Second, in 2 Pet. 2:18 the author implies that enslavement to corruption is equivalent to living in error and involvement in licentious desires of the flesh. Corruption and such desires are also connected in 1:4. Desire is likewise presented negatively in 2:10; 3:3.

The author of 2 Peter may understand enslavement to corruption to mean "subject to corruption," to be mortal. This seems to be the meaning of slavery to corruption in Rom. 8:21. In line with this, the author of 2 Peter mentions frequently that destruction is the end of those enslaved to corruption. The false teachers introduce heresies of destruction and by denying the Master who bought them, bring destruction on themselves (2:1). Their destruction does not sleep (2:3). However, the author of 2 Peter also understands enslavement to corruption as meaning being overcome by the defilements of the world, living in error, and being subject to licentious desires. In 2:10 the author describes those whom the Lord will punish as going after the flesh in the desire for defilement. Enslavement to this spiritual corruption leads to literal corruption.

2. The followers of Jesus, previously enslaved to corruption and the defilements of the world, have escaped this enslavement through full knowledge of Jesus as Savior. Second Peter does not explain how this enslavement to corruption and the defilements of the world came to be; however, several passages hint at an explanation that seems to be presupposed. Thus 2:18 says that the false teachers tempt people who have escaped those who live in error; they tempt these people by speaking boastful words of futility and appealing to licentious desires of the flesh. Having escaped those who live in error is probably another description of freedom from slavery to corruption. Since the false teachers tempt them with futile speech and an appeal to desire, it seems likely that this is how they originally became slaves to corruption. Since futility is the opposite of knowledge, it is easy to see how futile speech would lead people into error and thus into slavery to corruption. The causal role of desire is confirmed by 1:4, which refers to the author and addressees of 2 Peter as ones who have escaped the corruption in the world by desire. Thus the author of 2 Peter sees enslavement to corruption not as intrinsic to the human condition but as due to error, futility, and the desires of the flesh

(Bauckham 1983, 182–84). We can probably see yet another reference to Jesus's followers' having escaped slavery in 1:9, which mentions the cleansing of past sins. This suggests that enslavement to corruption derives from sin.

3. I suggested above that the author of 2 Peter understands Jesus as having purchased his followers from enslavement to corruption by his death, even though the author does not explicitly say that Jesus's death was the purchase price. However, the author does speak explicitly about the way followers of Jesus appropriate this salvation. In 1:3 the author says that Jesus's divine power has given them everything pertaining to life and piety through full knowledge of the one who called them by his glory and virtue, meaning Jesus. Jesus has done this by first calling them and then having them answer the call by fully knowing him as Savior. Likewise, 2:20 refers to escaping the defilements of the world by full knowledge of Jesus.

The first verse of 2 Peter says that the addressees have received faith from Jesus. Faith is a synonym for full knowledge of Jesus. Specifically, they have received faith equal in honor to that of Peter and others, through the justice of Jesus.

The author presupposes that Jesus's death has transferred humans from enslavement to corruption to his own service. However, this transfer does not take effect until it is known to have occurred. Prior to such knowledge, humans continue to serve their previous master because they do not know they have a new one. For the author of 2 Peter faith, meaning recognition of Jesus, is absolutely crucial.

Ethics

The fuller understanding of 2 Peter's soteriology provided by this passage also gives deeper insight into the place of ethics in Christian life for 2 Peter.

The author and addressees have received faith (1:1, 5) and have fully known Jesus as their new master (1:3; 2:20). However, as 2:20 implies, it is possible to have escaped slavery to the defilements of the world by fully knowing Jesus and then return to one's former master. Jesus's purchase of humans from their former master, and their full knowledge of him as their new Master, does not eliminate the possibility that they serve their old master. They can undo their salvation. To avoid this, their full knowledge of Jesus must be ongoing. This is why ethics is necessary. As observed earlier, this is an understanding of ethics very similar to that of Paul (see also Paulsen 1992, 143–44).

In 1:5–8 the author urges the addressees to progress in virtue (vv. 5–7) because having and increasing in these things makes them fruitful for full knowledge of Jesus (v. 8). Those who have been set free from sin by fully knowing Jesus need to persist in that freedom from sin, which is an ongoing full knowledge of Jesus. This is how they make secure their call and election (1:10), which is the starting point of their salvation (cf. 1:3). Those who do this will receive entrance into the eternal kingdom of Jesus (1:11). For 2 Peter, ethics is a matter of continuing in the full knowledge of Jesus that is the appropriation of the salvation that Jesus has accomplished. Thus the author wishes that the addressees continue their full knowledge of Jesus in 1:2. On the one hand, an immoral life is a denial of Jesus and a return to slavery. On the other hand, persisting in lives of holiness and piety is salvation.

2 Peter 3:1–13

Occasion of the Letter Restated, and Argument against Opponents Resumed

Introductory Matters

Second Peter 3:1–13 is the final part of the body of this letter (1:16–3:13). After the digression of 2:10b–22, this passage restates the letter's occasion and purpose and then resumes the direct argument against the doctrine of the false teachers. In doing so, the author also continues his use of the testament form (Bauckham 1983, 282; Harrington 2003, 284, 290).

This passage continues and concludes the recontextualization of Jude 4–18 in 2 Pet. 2:1–3:3. Here 2 Pet. 3:1–3 recontextualizes Jude 17–18. Although 2 Pet. 3:1 does not derive from Jude, 2 Pet. 3:2–3 is virtually a quotation of Jude 17–18. However, the author of 2 Peter introduces many small changes into this material to make it serve his purpose better and to reflect his stylistic preferences.

Three other passages are recited and/or recontextualized in 2 Pet. 3:1–13. Verse 8 recites and recontextualizes Ps. 90:4; verse 10 recites and recontextualizes 1 Thess. 5:2 (contra Gilmour 2002, 103–4); and verse 13 recontextualizes Isa. 65:17; 66:22.

Second Peter 3:1–2 refers to a previous letter of Peter and can be seen as a recitation of 1 Peter that summarizes a span of text. If so, this might imply that the recipients of 2 Peter are the same as the recipients of 1 Peter: the exiles of the Diaspora in Pontus, Galatia, Cappadocia, Asia, and Bithynia. We have noted above that the first five words of the greeting in 2 Pet. 1:2 are identical to the first five words of the greeting in 1 Pet. 1:2. This is the most obvious evidence that the former depends on the latter. Michael J. Gilmour (2002, 91–95; cf. also Lapham 2003) discusses other points of contact between the two including the following:

1. The use of "virtue" in reference to God in 1 Pet. 2:9 and 2 Pet. 1:3.
2. The use of "supply" (*chorēgei*) in 1 Pet. 4:11 and "supply" (*epichorēgēsate*) in 2 Pet. 1:5 (its use in 1:11—not mentioned by Gilmour—is an even closer parallel).
3. The use of "see" (*epopteuō*) in 1 Pet. 2:12; 3:2 and "eyewitnesses" (*epoptēs*) in 2 Pet. 1:16.
4. The use of "without blemish or spot" (*amōmou kai aspilou*) in 1 Pet. 1:19 and "spots and blemishes" (*spiloi kai mōmoi*) in 2 Pet. 2:13 along with "spotless and unblemished" (*aspiloi kai amōmētoi*) in 2 Pet. 3:14.
5. Both mention the fallen angels along with Noah and those saved with him (1 Pet. 3:18–20; 2 Pet. 2:4–5).

Second Peter 3:5–6 can be seen as a recitation summarizing a span of text that includes various episodes, in this case, Gen. 1–7. Richard J. Bauckham (1983, 283–85) and Duane F. Watson (2002, 203–4) argue that 2 Pet. 3:4–13 makes use of a Jewish apocalypse that is also reflected in *1 Clem.* 23.3–4; *2 Clem.* 11.2–4; 16.3; and perhaps *1 Clem.* 23.5 and 27.4 (against this is Paulsen 1992, 152–53).

Watson (2002, 205–6) suggests that the question in 3:4, introduced by "where is" (*pou estin*), is modeled on mocking questions in the OT that begin this way (e.g., Mal. 2:17). He also suggests that Hab. 2:3 may underlie 2 Pet. 3:9 and that a combination of Mal. 4:1 (3:19 LXX) and Isa. 34:4 may underlie 2 Pet. 3:10, 12 (Watson 2002, 207–9).

Second Peter 3:1–13 makes reference to some items deriving from Jewish history and culture: prophets (v. 2), ancestors (v. 4), the day of the Lord (v. 10), and the stories of creation and the flood in verses 5–6. Again, there were also prophets in Greco-Roman culture, and judgment by water and fire is known in both Jewish and Greek culture. Henning Paulsen (1992, 153–57) discusses

1 and 2 Clement

The writings called *1* and *2 Clement* are included in the collection known as the Apostolic Fathers. Neither of the writings claims to have been written by Clement. *First Clement* is a letter from the church at Rome to the church at Corinth, dating perhaps from the end of the first century CE. Some members of the Corinthian church had deposed the leaders of the church; the purpose of *1 Clement* is to restore the order of the church. *Second Clement* is an anonymous exhortation dating from mid-second century CE. It calls those it addresses to repent, live virtuous lives, and be faithful.

parallels to the views quoted in verse 4 both in Jewish tradition and among the Epicureans (cf. Neyrey 1993, 231). Verses 10–12 might remind the addressees of the Stoic idea that a conflagration ends the world and is followed by regeneration (Neyrey 1993, 241).

The passage also further develops the values of honor versus shame, challenge-response, and purity. Once again, the first two are closely linked. Much of the passage constitutes an attempt to defend the honor of God and Peter by confronting the challenge quoted in 3:4 and responding in verses 5–13 (Neyrey 1993, 227–29, 236–37). The passage develops the value of purity by referring to sincerity in verse 1. It also develops the value of purity by elaborating the positive topics of holiness (vv. 2, 11) and piety (v. 11) and treating the nega-

> **2 Peter 3:1–13 in the Rhetorical Flow**
>
> **The letter opening (1:1–15)**
> **The letter body (1:16–3:13)**
> > Two arguments against opponents (1:16–2:10a)
> > Critique of opponents (2:10b–22)
> > ▶ Occasion of the letter restated, and argument against opponents (3:1–13)
> > > Restatement of the letter's occasion and purpose (3:1–4)
> > > Resumption of argument against opponents (3:5–13)

tive topics of desire (v. 3) and impiety (v. 7). In this way the author calls the addressees to purity and accuses the false teachers of impurity.

Tracing the Train of Thought

This passage is mainly descriptive but with a strong argumentative element. Verses 1–4 again describe the writing of the letter and the reason for doing so. Verses 5–7 depict the creation of the world, its destruction by the flood, and the future destruction of the present world by fire. Verses 10–13 describe the future destruction of the world and its replacement by new heavens and earth. However, much of this description is also argumentative; verses 8–9 are the most directly argumentative part of the passage.

Restatement of the Letter's Occasion and Purpose (3:1–4)

3:1–4a. These verses constitute a single elaborate sentence: **Beloved, I now write this second letter to you, in which I arouse in your remembrance the pure understanding to remember the words spoken beforehand by the holy prophets and the commandment of your apostles of our Lord and Savior, first knowing this, that in the last days scoffers will come with scoffing, going according to their own desires and saying: "Where is the promise of his coming?"** The main clause is found in verse 1a. A relative clause (v. 1b) depends on it, and an infinitive phrase (v. 2) depends on the relative clause. A participial phrase in verse 3a continues the infinitive with an imperatival meaning[1] and introduces a noun clause (v. 3b), whose subject is modified by two participles, the second of which introduces a direct quotation in verse 4. As a resumption of the main message of the letter, the sentence is an example of two figures of thought: *aphodos* (return to the main subject after a digression) and *transitio* (brief recollection of what has previously been said, and brief indication of what is to follow).

The author here calls the addressees **beloved** (3:1a) for the first time, perhaps depending on Jude 17 (Kelly 1969, 354). He will address them the same way again in 3:8, 14, 17. He probably calls this a **second letter** (3:1a) because he regards 1 Peter as the first (Bigg 1901, 288–89; Kelly 1969, 352–53; Bauckham 1983, 286). The purpose of both letters (the Greek word translated **which** is plural) is to **arouse in your remembrance** (3:1b). This is very similar to the way the author states the purpose of this letter in 1:13.

The addressees are to remember two things: **the words spoken beforehand by the holy prophets** and **the commandment of your apostles of our Lord and Savior** (3:2). The first of these is in line with the view expressed in 1:19–2:10a that the second coming of Jesus fulfills prophecy. The commandment spoken through the apostles is the same as that mentioned in 2:21 (Kelly 1969, 354; Watson 1988, 126): the commandment that the followers of Jesus live a holy life in expectation of Jesus's return (cf. 3:11–12). The commandment is said to be of **your** apostles because it was previously communicated directly to the addressees by apostles sent to them. This communication could have occurred either orally or by means of writings such as the earlier letter of the author and the Letters of Paul. It is clear from 3:15 that the author of 2 Peter regards Paul as having written to the addressees of 2 Peter. Perhaps "your apostles" are, or at least include, Peter and Paul.

The addressees are to remember **first knowing this** (3:3a). Here the author repeats the phrase he has used in 1:20. What they are to know is that **in the last days scoffers will come with scoffing** (3:3b). The word translated **scoffing** is a new coinage; its combination with **scoffers** constitutes paronomasia. The statement that those who scoff at the coming of Jesus are themselves a sign of it is ironic. The scoffers ask a rhetorical question, **Where is the promise of his coming?** (3:4a). Use of this kind of question to express skepticism can also be seen in Mal. 2:17; Pss. 42:3; 79:10; Jer. 17:15; Luke 8:25 (Bigg 1901, 291; cf. Kelly 1969, 355; Bauckham 1983, 289). The **promise of his coming** may be one of the promises of Jesus mentioned in 1:4, where a cognate synonym of the word here translated "promise" is used.

3:4b. The scoffers support their skepticism by saying, **"For since the fathers have fallen asleep, all things continue thus from the beginning of creation."**

---

1. BDF §468; Kraus 2001, 271. Mayor (1907, liv–lv) analyzes 3:2 as an accusative-infinitive construction, and the participle in 3:3a as modifying the implied subject. On this analysis, the case of the participle is wrong, nominative instead of accusative. Gerdmar (2001, 34–35) agrees.

The identity of **the fathers** is not clear. Commentators argue that the fathers are either the patriarchs of the OT (Bigg 1901, 291) or the first Christian generation that has now died (Kelly 1969, 355–56; Bauckham 1983, 290–91; Paulsen 1992, 157), meaning the fathers of the scoffers (Schelkle 1961, 224). Neither of these fits very well with the parallel specification of time later in the verse: **from the beginning of creation**. Since the latter antedates the death of the fathers, referring to the death of the fathers seems to add nothing to the argument. An interpretation that minimizes, but does not eliminate, this problem is to see the fathers as the ancestors of the human race in general. Then the death of the fathers and the beginning of creation are roughly equivalent ways of referring to the beginning of the world's history. To say that the fathers **have fallen asleep** is a common euphemism for death (cf. Kelly 1969, 355; Bauckham 1983, 290).

The scoffers' skepticism about the return of Jesus is based on the perception that everything remains as it has been from the beginning; there is no precedent for the coming of Jesus and the end of the world, and thus no reason to think it will happen. This perception might be related to the view that the world is eternal (Bigg 1901, 292), although there is no explicit reference to it here. Bauckham (1983, 294) is skeptical about this possibility.

This restatement of the letter's occasion and purpose repeats things from earlier parts of the letter but more explicitly and pointedly. In 1:12–15 the author has spoken about making it possible for the addressees to remember his teaching in the future; 2:1–3 implies that this will be necessary when false teachers arise among them. In 3:1–4 the author explicitly says that he is making it possible for the addressees to remember by writing this letter and that the false teachers will be scoffers who question the coming of Jesus. Similarly, in 1:16–2:10a the author has replied to the idea that the power and coming of Jesus might be a cleverly devised myth; in 3:5–13 he replies to the more specific objection that this promise will not be kept because it has not been kept up to this point. In doing so, he mentions again the destruction of the world by flood, its future destruction by fire, and its replacement by a new heavens and earth. The first was explicit in 2:5, and the latter two were more generally indicated in 2:6 and 2:9–10a.

Resumption of Argument against Opponents (3:5–13)

3:5–6. These two verses form an enthymeme refuting verse 4b (Watson 1988, 129). **For it escapes the notice of those maintaining this that there were heavens long ago and an earth constituted from water and through water by the word of God, through which [water and word] the world of that time was destroyed, having been deluged with water.** The argument can be restated thus:

> One can maintain that all things have remained as they are since the beginning of creation only if the world has not previously been destroyed.

But the world was previously destroyed by the flood.

Therefore, all things have not remained as they are since the beginning of creation (and one can maintain that the world will be destroyed again).

The author says that **there were heavens long ago and an earth constituted from water and through water** (3:5b). This refers to Gen. 1:2, 6–9 and indicates that God created by first separating the primeval waters with the dome of the heavens and then gathering them together below the heavens so that earth might appear (Kelly 1969, 358–59; Bauckham 1983, 297; Paulsen 1992, 160–61). In saying that the heavens and earth were constituted **by the word of God** (3:5b), the author probably refers to the depiction of creation in Gen. 1 as having been produced by God's speech, which is also summed up as creation by the word in Ps. 33:6 (Bauckham 1983, 298). In saying that the world of that time was destroyed through water and the word, the author means that God ceased to restrain the primeval waters, and creation was undone (cf. Gen. 7:11). The word translated **having been deluged** (3:6) is a verbal cognate of "deluge" in 2:5, the author's earlier reference to the flood in the time of Noah.

3:7. Now the author draws a conclusion from the argument in verses 5–6. **And the present heavens and the earth are treasured up by the same word, kept for fire on the day of judgment and destruction of impious human beings.** The idea that the present heavens and the earth are treasured up by the same word and kept for fire probably implies that this is based on prophecy. The author sees it as predicted by the scriptural accounts of the events he has mentioned in 2:4–8. In 2:5 he presented the reduction of Sodom and Gomorrah to ashes (by fire) as a sign of what will happen to the impious. Several other passages might have been understood to predict this: Deut. 32:22; Isa. 66:15–16; Zeph. 1:18; Mal. 4:1 (3:19 LXX). Justin understands Deut. 32:22 this way in *1 Apol.* 60.8. Bauckham (1983, 301) argues that 2 Peter is immediately dependent on a Jewish apocalypse that in turn depended on these

Qumran

Qumran is a place near the northwestern shore of the Dead Sea. In 1947 scrolls were found in nearby caves; these are known as the Qumran, or Dead Sea, Scrolls. These scrolls were probably the library of a Jewish community living at Qumran, which was hidden before the Roman destruction of Qumran in 68 CE. The scrolls include a large number of texts, many of them fragmentary. Some of these are copies of biblical texts; the most notable of these is the oldest extant copy of the book of Isaiah. Other texts were composed by the members of the community. These include rules governing the life of the community, commentaries on biblical texts, and hymns.

Terrance Callan

Figure 15. Photograph of the remains near Qumran. This is one of the larger rooms in the Qumran compound, perhaps used as a refectory (dining hall). The Dead Sea is visible in the background.

passages. The idea of an eschatological conflagration can be seen in many Jewish and Christian writings, such as the Qumran *Thanksgiving Hymns* (1QH 3.19–36; Bauckham 1983, 300; cf. also Schelkle 1961, 226n1). Josephus (*Ant.* 1.70) says that Adam predicted destruction of the universe, at one time by fire, at another by water. The author of 2 Peter may also be thinking that judgment by fire is predicted by 1 Cor. 3:13–15.

The idea that the eschatological fire destroys the present heavens and earth might have been seen as implied in the prediction of new heavens and earth in Isa. 66:22 that follows the destruction by fire spoken of in 66:15–16. However, this idea also has significant parallels in Iranian and especially Stoic ideas about a conflagration that ends the world (Bauckham 1983, 300–301; Neyrey 1993, 240–41). In the Stoic view, the conflagration is followed by regeneration of the world. Bauckham (1983, 301) also mentions an idea found in Plato, *Tim.* 22C–E and elsewhere, that the world undergoes recurrent destructions by flood and fire alternately.

In saying that the present heavens and earth are **kept** for fire, the author uses the same word he used in 2:4, 9, and 17 to describe the sinful angels, wrongdoers, and his opponents, respectively, as held for future judgment. He also referred to **the day of judgment** in 2:9. The day of judgment will be the time for **destruction of impious human beings** (3:7b). According to 2:5, the first destruction of the heavens and earth was also aimed at the impious; according to 2:6 the destruction of Sodom and Gomorrah was a sign of the future destruction of the impious, in the eschatological conflagration of which the author is speaking here.

3:8. Verses 8–9 are the most directly argumentative portion of 3:1–13. Verse 8 argues that time is different for God than for humans: **And let this one thing not escape your notice, beloved, that one day with the Lord is like a thousand years and a thousand years like one day.** In 3:5 the author has pointed out that the first destruction of the world escapes the notice of the scoffers; here he warns the addressees not to let the difference between the divine and human relationship to time **escape [their] notice.** As in 3:1 the author calls them **beloved. A thousand years like one day** is quoted, with omissions, from Ps. 90:4 (89:4 LXX). To this the author has prefaced a clause stating the same equation in reverse, **one day . . . is like a thousand years,** thus creating a chiasm. He has also added **with the Lord,** reproducing the sense of "in your eyes," which he omitted from the psalm quotation. Because time is so different for God than for humans, one cannot complain that the coming of Jesus has been delayed. Although the author does not explicitly say that he is quoting Ps. 90, he presumably expects the addressees to recognize that he is. And the recognition that he is restating the teaching of an authoritative text is a reason for accepting the teaching.

Both clauses make the point that time is different for God than for humans. The first clause says that what is a short time for humans can be a long time for God; the second says that what is a long time for humans can be a short time for God. The latter point serves the author's purpose here most directly because he is arguing that from God's point of view, there has not really been a delay in the coming of Jesus.

3:9. This verse is an enthymeme arguing that God is not slow to keep his promise (Watson 1988, 130–31). **For the Lord of the promise does not delay, as some consider delay, but he is patient toward you, not wishing that any be destroyed, but that all come to repentance.** This argument presumes that "delay" means simple procrastination. If God has a reason for sending Jesus at one time rather than another, this is not delay. The argument runs thus:

> One can say that the Lord is slow to keep his promises only if there is no sufficient reason for delay in keeping them.
>
> But the Lord delays out of patience, giving all the opportunity for repentance.
>
> Therefore, the Lord is not slow to keep his promises.

In the Jewish understanding of God, patience is one of God's most prominent characteristics (e.g., Exod. 34:6; Grundmann 1974, 116).

3:10–13. This passage argues that the time of the end is unknown and that the addressees should be holy because the world is about to be destroyed. **And the day of the Lord will come like a thief, on which the heavens will pass away with a rushing noise, and the elements, set on fire, will be dissolved, and the**

earth and the works on it will be discovered. Since all these things will thus be dissolved, what sort of people is it necessary that you be with holy lives and pieties, awaiting and eagerly seeking the coming of the day of God, on account of which the heavens, burning, will be dissolved and the elements, set on fire, are melted? And we await new heavens and a new earth according to his promise, in which justice dwells. The words translated **the day of the Lord** and **like a thief** are quoted from 1 Thess. 5:2 (Fornberg 1977, 25). The **Lord** referred to here is probably God, though in 1 Thess. 5:2 it probably refers to Jesus. Bauckham (1983, 306) argues that this passage does not depend on 1 Thess. 5:2 because 2 Peter shows so little Pauline influence; I see a rather high level of Pauline influence on 2 Peter. This is the author's final response to the argument that the return of Jesus has been delayed. He says that the day of the Lord will come unexpectedly. Since no one knows when it will come, it is impossible to say that it has been delayed. If the author assumes that the addressees will recognize that he is quoting 1 Thess. 5:2, he may presume that the authority of 1 Thessalonians is a reason to accept this teaching.

Verses 10 and 12 speak about the coming of the day of the Lord in very similar terms. However, verse 10 states that the day will come like a thief, while verse 12 exhorts the addressees to wait for the coming of the day. The latter part of verse 10 consists of three cola, parallel in structure, which is the figure of speech called parisosis, and ending with the same Greek syllable (*-tai*), which constitutes the figure of speech called homoeoteleuton and at the same time homoeoptoton. The first two of these cola are repeated, with variations, in the last half of verse 12.

2 Peter 3:10	2 Peter 3:12
And the day of the Lord will come like a thief,	awaiting and eagerly seeking the coming of the day of God
on which the heavens will pass away with a rushing noise,	on account of which the heavens, burning, will be dissolved
and the elements, set on fire, will be dissolved,	and the elements, set on fire, are melted.
and the earth and the works on it will be discovered.	

Such repetition is the figure of speech called reduplication. Naturally, the last half of verse 12 also displays parisosis, homoeoteleuton, and homoeoptoton. The author uses the rare word translated **set on fire** in verses 10 and 12. It is meant metaphorically, implying that the heat to dissolve the universe is like the fever that accompanies disease. The repetition of **will be dissolved** three times in verses 10–12 is transplacement.

The **elements** (3:10c) might be either the four traditional elements of which the world is composed (earth, air, fire, and water) or the sun, moon, and stars

(Bigg 1901, 296–97; Kelly 1969, 364; Bauckham 1983, 315–16). Most interpreters argue for the latter interpretation on the grounds that it must refer to something other than the heavens and earth, which are mentioned explicitly. However, both are mentioned explicitly only in 3:10; in verse 12 the earth is not explicitly mentioned. Further, the reference to the earth in verse 10 probably means something other than simply its dissolution. Thus the former is the more likely interpretation. The author's reference to the burning elements states the means by which the earth, in contrast to the heavens, will be undone.

Bauckham (1983, 316–21) discusses variant readings of the text translated **the earth and the works on it will be discovered** (3:10d) and the proposed emendations of it and attempts to explain it. He argues that it means the earth and the works in it will be made manifest by God. Bauckham seems to approve the idea of W. E. Wilson (1920–21): "When the intervening heavens are burned away, the earth and its works, from the divine point of view, become visible" (Bauckham 1983, 319). I suggest rather that the author thinks the destruction of the universe and the revelation of earth's works are simultaneous. The slavery to corruption of the earth and some of its inhabitants will be clear when they undergo corruption. Likewise, the freedom from corruption of those who escape destruction will be clear. The dissolution of the universe at the end is thus a motive for living virtuously (3:11).

The author may evoke a picture like that presented explicitly in 1 Cor. 3:12–15. In this passage Paul says that the nature of the work a person has done in building on the foundation of Christ will be revealed by fire on the last day. Good work will survive the fire; poor work will be burned up. The author of 2 Peter uses this picture to say that the false teachers and their followers will be destroyed on the day of the Lord, and only the upright will remain.

Because all things will be dissolved, the author exhorts the addressees to **holy lives and pieties** (3:11b). The author has used the singular of the word translated **lives** in 2:7, referring to Lot's life in Sodom. The author previously emphasized the need for piety in 1:3, 6, 7. The word translated **eagerly seeking** (3:12a) might also mean "hasten" (Bigg 1901, 298; Schelkle 1961, 229; Kelly 1969, 367; Bauckham 1983, 325). Most interpreters argue for this meaning on the grounds that it expresses an idea found in Jewish texts and suits the context. However, in view of the author's frequent references to the need for eagerness (1:5, 10, 15; 3:14), "eagerly seeking" seems better.

In 3:10 comparing the day of the Lord to a thief is a simile. The author also uses the rare word translated **with a rushing noise** in verse 10. Use of this word is the trope called onomatopoeia, the sound of the word expressing its meaning.

The author and addressees **await new heavens and a new earth according to his promise, in which justice dwells** (3:13). **New heavens and a new earth** is a slightly altered quotation of Isa. 65:17; 66:22. The word translated **promise** recalls 1:4, which refers to the promises given by Jesus, as well as 3:4 and 9, which refer to the promise by using a different word. The statement that justice dwells in the new heavens and new earth parallels Isa. 32:16: "Justice will dwell in the wilderness." The reference to justice as dwelling somewhere is personification. The idea that justice will dwell in the new heavens and earth is another reason for living holy lives. One must be just if one hopes to dwell in the new creation.

Resumption of the main message of the letter in 3:1–13 involves developing a number of topics from earlier parts of the letter, some of which have already been recognized: (1) The emphasis on the cognitive found throughout 2 Peter continues in this passage. The author speaks of his purpose as reminding the addressees (3:1–2), refers to what they know in verses 1 and 3, and stresses the danger of forgetting in verses 5 and 8. (2) The topic of prophecy, mentioned in 1:20–21; 2:1, 16, is found again in 3:2. (3) The commandment mentioned in 2:21 appears again in 3:2. (4) The topic of salvation, broached in 1:1, 11 and 2:20, is also found in the reference to the Lord and Savior in 3:2. (5) The topic of promises, seen in 1:4 and 2:19, is discussed again in 3:4, 9, 13. Verse 4 reports the objection that the promise has not been fulfilled; verse 9 argues that the Lord is not slow to keep the promise; and verse 13 describes its fulfillment. (6) The topic of Jesus's coming, first mentioned in 1:16, is further discussed in 3:4 and 12. In verse 4 it is the content of the promise whose fulfillment is doubted; verse 12 speaks of the coming of the day of God rather than of Jesus, probably equating the two. (7) The metaphor of the day, used in 1:19 and 2:9, appears again in 3:7, 10, 12. In addition, the word "day" is used nonmetaphorically in 3:3 and 8, as it was earlier in 2:8. (8) The topic of eschatological destruction, introduced in 2:1 and 3, also occurs in 3:6, 7, 9. (9) Judgment by water and fire, mentioned in 2:5–6, is similarly discussed in 3:6–7, 10, 12. (10) The topic of keeping, previously seen in 2:4, 9, 17, is also found in 3:7. (11) The topic of being eager, mentioned in 1:5, 10, 15, recurs in 3:12. (12) The topic of justice, appearing in 1:1, 13; 2:5, 7, 8, 9, 13, 15, 21, reappears in 3:13.

Theological Issues

Eschatology

As we noticed in discussing 2 Pet. 1:16–2:10a, the author gradually unfolds his eschatological views in the course of the letter. The eschatological expectations of 2 Peter become most specific in 3:1–13. Here we learn that the present heavens and earth have been reserved for judgment by fire. At a time unknown to humans, like a thief, the day of the Lord will come. By fire the present heavens and earth will be dissolved and replaced by new heavens and a new earth, in which justice dwells.

As noted above, this expectation has scriptural foundations and is paralleled in contemporary Jewish and gentile thought. However, this passage is the place in Scripture where the expectation is expressed most clearly. Thus it is the principal foundation for this element of Christian belief.

Walter Grundmann (1974, 116) interprets the idea that "one day with the Lord is like a thousand years, and a thousand years like one day" (v. 8) as an abandonment of imminent expectation of the parousia. Clearly this idea could be used to argue that the parousia lies in the distant future. However, the context makes clear that the author of 2 Peter uses the idea only to explain that what some see as a delay in the arrival of the parousia is not really a delay. The author himself argues that the time of the parousia is unknown and urges the addressees to maintain a lively expectation of the parousia and to live their lives in light of that expectation. Throughout Christian history the equation of a thousand years and a day has often been used to encourage eschatological expectation, not its abandonment.

Theology and Christology

In 1:16–2:10a we have seen some of the author's portrayal of God. Now 3:1–13 adds to this portrayal. The original heavens and earth were created by the word of God (v. 5). The present heavens and earth are being treasured up by the word of God for fire on the day of judgment (v. 7); this is also the day of God (v. 12). On the assumption that "Lord" in verses 8 and 9 refers to God, the passage also tells us that time is different for God than for humans (v. 8) and that God is not slow to keep the promise of Jesus's return and all that will accompany it. Rather, God is patient, wanting all to repent (v. 9). Thus God is the Creator of all, who sustains in existence all that he has created until the time appointed for its dissolution. This implies that God directs the course of the world's history.

In 3:2 the author speaks of "our Lord and Savior," probably referring to Jesus. In 3:8, 9, and 10 the title "Lord" probably refers to God. The use of "Lord" as a title for both God and Jesus, and the frequent ambiguity about which is the referent, both in this passage and elsewhere in 2 Peter—all this is another reflection of 2 Peter's presentation of Jesus as divine (Callan 2001a).

Ethics

The passage once again speaks about the place of ethics in Christian life. It is because the present heavens and earth will be replaced with new heavens and a new earth that the addressees should live holy and pious lives (3:12). Unlike the present heavens and earth, the new heavens and earth will be ones in which justice dwells. In order to have a place in the new order, Christians must live now as ones belonging to that order. As we have seen above, this is a matter of maintaining the freedom from the old order that they have received through Christ.

2 Peter 3:14–18

The Letter Closing

Introductory Matters

Second Peter 3:14–18 is the closing section of the letter. Jeffrey A. D. Weima has identified a number of conventions that belong to the closings of ancient letters, both Greek and Semitic. The most common convention in both is the farewell wish. Greek letter closings also include the health wish, the greeting, the autograph, the illiteracy formula, the dating formula, and the postscript (Weima 1994, 28–56). The health wish, dating formula, and postscript are occasionally found in Semitic letters; Semitic letter closings regularly include a signature (Weima 1994, 63–76). However, many Greek letters simply end and have no closing formulas (Weima 1994, 30). The closing of 2 Peter does not include any ancient letter-closing conventions. However, it ends with a doxology. This serves as a closing formula, concluding previous material, but it is not a convention of letter closings (Weima 1994, 141).

This passage continues and concludes 2 Peter's use of the testament form when it refers to its addressees as "knowing these things beforehand" in 3:17 (Bauckham 1983, 336; Harrington 2003, 299).

Second Peter 3:14–15 is a recitation that summarizes a span of text: the letter(s) written by Paul to the addressees of 2 Peter. If 2 Pet. 3:1 implies that 2 Peter is addressed to the exiles of the Diaspora in Pontus, Galatia, Cappadocia, Asia, and Bithynia, the only surviving Letters of Paul that might be recited in verses 14–15 are Galatians, Ephesians, and Colossians. Of these, the letter most likely to be meant is Ephesians. Verse 14 and Eph. 4:3 both use the verb *spoudazō* and the noun *eirēnē*, though the Ephesians passage lacks the eschatological dimension of verse 14. Note, however, that 2 Pet. 3:15a most closely resembles Rom. 2:4, which was obviously not written to any of the recipients of 1 Peter. According to Michael J. Gilmour (2002, 102n39), some have seen this as reason to think that 2 Peter was written to Christians in Rome. Specifically, Gilmour mentions Joseph B. Mayor (1907, 164).

Second Peter 3:16a expands this into a recitation that summarizes all the Letters of Paul. In addition to the connections with the Letters of Paul just mentioned, we have noticed above that 2 Pet. 3:10 cites 1 Thess. 5:2. Gilmour (2002,

> **2 Peter 3:14–18**
> **in the Rhetorical Flow**
>
> The letter opening
> (1:1–15)
>
> The letter body
> (1:16–3:13)
>
> ▶ The letter closing
> (3:14–18)
>
>   Concluding exhortation (3:14–18a)
>
>   Final doxology (3:18b)

100–105) discusses this and other possible points of contact between 2 Peter and the Letters of Paul but concludes that they do not indicate literary dependence. The possible points of contact mentioned by Gilmour include the following, in the order he discusses them:

1. 2 Pet. 2:19 resembles the thought of Rom. 6:16.
2. 2 Pet. 3:9 resembles Rom. 2:4.
3. 2 Pet. 1:13–14 uses the same imagery as 2 Cor. 5:1–4.
4. 2 Pet. 3:15 refers to the wisdom given to Paul; Paul refers to himself in similar terms in 1 Cor. 3:10.

In addition, the understanding of the human predicament and its origin in 2 Pet. 2:18–20 is similar to that of Rom. 8:20–21, understood as a summary of Rom. 1:18–32. And the understanding of salvation's completion as Christians' becoming incorruptible in 2 Pet. 1:4 is similar to that of 1 Cor. 15:50–55 (Callan 2001b, 552–53, 556–57).

The passage further develops the values of purity, honor versus shame, and the patron-client relationship. The value of purity underlies the exhortations that the addressees be spotless and blameless (3:14; Neyrey 1993, 247–49), the opposite of the false teachers, according to 2:13, and that they avoid the lawlessness (3:17) that characterized the inhabitants of Sodom and Gomorrah (2:7) and Balaam (2:15–16). The value of honor versus shame is found in the description of Paul as wise in 3:15 (Neyrey 1993, 249), as well as the ascription of glory to Jesus (v. 18), a topic mentioned earlier in 1:3, 17, and 2:10b. The patron-client relationship underlies the exhortation that the addressees grow in knowledge of Jesus and thus in recognizing him as Lord and Savior. The value of group-oriented personality is reflected in the reference to the wisdom given to Paul (3:15; Neyrey 1993, 249).

Tracing the Train of Thought

Concluding Exhortation (3:14–18a)

The passage is mainly argumentative.

3:14–15a. Second Peter 3:14–15a is a double enthymeme (cf. Watson 1988, 136), arguing on the basis of verses 5–13 that the addressees should live well and consider the forbearance of the Lord as salvation. **Therefore, beloved, awaiting these things, be eager to be discovered by him spotless and unblemished in peace. And consider the patience of our Lord salvation** (3:14–15a). The argument can be restated thus:

> One who expects new heavens and earth in which justice dwells will strive to be virtuous.
>
> The addressees do expect new heavens and earth in which justice dwells.
>
> Therefore, they should be eager to be found spotless and blameless.

> One who expects the destruction of the impious on the day of judgment (3:7) will consider an opportunity for repentance to be salvation.
>
> The patience of the Lord leading to delay of the day of judgment is an opportunity for repentance (v. 9).
>
> Therefore, the addressees should regard the patience of the Lord as salvation.

As in 1:10 and 12, **therefore** indicates that the author is drawing a conclusion from what he has said previously. As in 3:1 and 8, he calls the addressees **beloved** (3:14a). In 3:10 and 12 respectively, the author has referred to **awaiting** "the coming of the day of God" and "new heavens and a new earth"; these are what the author means here by **these things** (3:14a). In 3:12 the author has urged the addressees to seek eagerly the coming of the day of God; here he tells them to **be eager** (3:14b). They are to be eager to **be discovered**, as in 3:10, **by him**, meaning God, **spotless and unblemished** (3:14c). This reverses the description of the false teachers in 2:13 as "spots and blemishes," again using these terms as metaphors for ethical behavior. They are to be discovered **in peace** (3:14c). The letter began with the wish that peace might be multiplied for the recipients (1:2). The addressees should also **consider the patience of our Lord salvation** (3:15a). This repeats the verb "consider" from 3:9 and uses a noun cognate to the verb "to be patient" that is found in that verse.

3:15b–16. Here the author appeals to the authority of Paul in support of his exhortation: **as also our beloved brother Paul wrote to you according to the wisdom given to him, so also in all his letters speaking in them about these things, in which [letters] there are some things hard to understand, which the ignorant and unstable twist, as they also do the rest of the Scriptures, to their own destruction.** The author supports the exhortation by saying that Paul wrote the same thing to the addressees (3:15b) and likewise in all of his letters (v. 16a). This then leads him to comment on the difficulty of understanding Paul's Letters in 3:16b. It is not clear whether the author appeals to Paul in support of 3:14, of 3:15a, or of both.

The author refers to Paul as **our beloved brother** (3:15b), using the adjective he has applied to the addressees in 3:1, 8, and 14 and the noun he has applied to them in 1:10. Obviously the author considers himself in complete harmony with Paul. However, the following reference to the difficulty of understanding Paul might imply that the errors the author of 2 Peter combats are at least partly based on an interpretation of Paul's Letters that differs from his.

The author refers first to what Paul has written to the addressees. Second Peter nowhere identifies those to whom it is addressed. If it can be assumed that they are the same as the addressees of 1 Peter (Christians living in Pontus, Galatia, Cappadocia, Asia, and Bithynia), the author might be thinking of one or more of Paul's Letters to the Galatians, Ephesians, and Colossians. The author further says that Paul wrote **according to the wisdom given to him** (3:15b). This may allude to Paul's frequent references to the grace given to him (Rom. 12:3; 15:15; 1 Cor. 3:10; Gal. 2:9; Eph. 3:2, 7; Col. 1:25), to those he addresses (1 Cor. 1:4), or to both (Rom. 12:6; 2 Tim. 1:9). In 1 Cor. 3:10, immediately after referring to the grace given to him, Paul describes himself as wise. Compare also the reference to the wisdom given to Jesus in Mark 6:2.

The author goes on to say that what Paul wrote to the addressees of 2 Peter, he also wrote **in all his letters** (3:16a). This indicates that the author knew of a collection of Pauline letters, which suggests a fairly late date for 2 Peter. The earliest reference to multiple letters of Paul is found in the letter of Ignatius of Antioch *To the Ephesians* (12.2), written around 108. Second Peter was probably written after this date. The author admits that some things in Paul's letters are difficult to understand and asserts that **the ignorant and unstable** deliberately misinterpret them, which leads to their **destruction** (3:16c). These people lack the knowledge that Christians must have, as the author has repeatedly emphasized. The rare word translated "unstable" was used earlier, in 2:14. This reference to the ignorant and unstable constitutes metonymy: use of qualities in place of a name. These people treat **the rest of the Scriptures** (3:16d) the same way. The author has also referred to Scripture in 1:20. Here the Letters of Paul are regarded as belonging to the same category as the Jewish Bible (contra Paulsen [1992, 175], who thinks this refers to Christian texts). This indicates an even later date than does the reference to multiple Pauline letters, because it was probably some time after they had been collected that they began to be regarded as authoritative. By about 140, Marcion had a collection of ten Pauline letters that he regarded as authoritative.

3:17–18a. The author makes a concluding appeal to avoid the errors of those who misinterpret Paul and to grow in grace and knowledge of Jesus. **Therefore you, beloved, knowing these things beforehand, be on guard in order that you**

may not fall away from your own firm footing, having been led astray by the error of the lawless. But grow in favor and knowledge of our Lord and Savior Jesus Christ. As in 3:14, the author draws a conclusion by saying **therefore** and calls the addressees **beloved**. Verses 16b–17 form another enthymeme; the argument can be restated:

> One who knows that incorrect interpretation of Scripture is dangerous will guard against it.
>
> The addressees know that the ignorant and unstable twist the meaning of the Scriptures, leading to their own destruction.
>
> Therefore, the addressees should be on guard so that they do not fall away from their own firm footing.

The author says that the addressees' foreknowledge should enable them to avoid going astray. This foreknowledge is probably their knowledge that the false teachers twist the meaning of the Scriptures (Bauckham 1983, 336–37). **Fall away** (3:17b) is synonymous with "stumble" in 1:10. The word translated **firm footing** (3:17c) is rare; it is cognate to the words used in 1:12; 2:14; 3:16. It is another metaphor for a moral state or condition. The author used the word **lawless** in 2:7 to describe the inhabitants of Sodom and Gomorrah, whose lives distressed the righteous Lot.

The author urges the addressees to **grow in favor and knowledge of our Lord and Savior Jesus Christ** (3:18a). The author began the letter by wishing that favor to be multiplied for the addressees (1:2). This imperative makes it clear that knowledge of Jesus can increase. The author also used the phrase "our Lord and Savior Jesus Christ" in 1:11; 2:20.

Final Doxology (3:18b)

3:18b. The letter ends with a doxology: **To him be glory both now and into the day of eternity. Amen.** Elsewhere in the NT this kind of doxology is reserved for God (cf. Jude 24–25). Another doxology addressed to Jesus is found in Rev. 1:5–6. In that passage Jesus is clearly subordinated to God the Father. The doxology in 2 Peter suggests that the author regards Jesus as God. The author has previously mentioned the **glory** of Jesus in 1:3, 17; and probably 2:10. He has mentioned the glory of God in 1:17 and probably 2:10.

As is appropriate for the closing of the document, 3:14–18 develops a number of topics from earlier parts of the letter. Several have already been mentioned above. Others include the following: (1) Eagerness, encouraged in 1:5, 10, 15 and 3:12, reappears in 3:14. (2) The topic of salvation, seen in 1:1, 11; 2:20; and 3:2, is found again in 3:15 and 18. (3) The emphasis on the cognitive, stressed throughout the letter, is found here in 3:16, which refers to ignorance;

in verse 17, which recognizes the addressees' foreknowledge; and in verse 18, which urges them to grow in their knowledge of Jesus. (4) The topic of being established, treated earlier in 1:10, 12, 19 and 2:14, appears again in 3:16, 17. (5) Scripture, mentioned in 1:20, appears again in 3:16. (6) Eschatological destruction, treated in 2:1, 3; 3:6, 7, and 9, reappears in 3:16. (7) The topic of wandering, discussed in 2:15, 18, is seen again in 3:17. (8) The metaphor of the day, used earlier in 1:19; 2:9; 3:7, 10, and 12, is also found in 3:18.

The development of the second and third of these topics constitutes *inclusio*, repeating at the end of the letter a word or phrase used at its beginning. Thus the topic of salvation is mentioned in 1:1 and 3:18, and the topic of knowledge is mentioned in 1:2 and 3:18. In addition, the topic of glory is mentioned in 1:3 and 3:18; favor is mentioned in 1:2 and 3:18; and peace is mentioned in 1:2 and 3:14. All of these serve to end the letter by returning to items mentioned at the beginning.

This is not one of the more highly ornamented sections of 2 Peter. However, several ornaments have been identified above. The repetition "unstable"/"firm footing" (*astēriktoi/stērigmou*) in 3:16–17 is paronomasia. In verse 18 application of "Lord" and "Savior" to Jesus is the trope called epithet. (On the style of 3:14–18, see Duane F. Watson 1988, 136–41.)

Theological Issues

Development of Canon

This section of 2 Peter contains what may be the earliest reference to development of the NT canon. As noted above, the author of 2 Peter clearly knows of a collection of Paul's Letters. This consists of at least one letter written to the addressees of 2 Peter, along with others; collectively the author calls them "all his letters."

Further, he regards Paul's Letters as comparable to what he calls "the rest of the Scriptures," probably referring to the Jewish Bible. Thus the Letters of Paul belong in the same category as what Christians now call the OT, forming at least the beginning of a NT. Earlier in the letter, the author of 2 Peter speaks of the prophecies of Scripture (1:20–21), arguing that they have their origin in the Holy Spirit. At least the prophecies of Scripture are inspired. Perhaps the author would say the same thing about all of Scripture. In speaking about the wisdom given to Paul, according to which Paul wrote his letters (3:15b), the author implies that this wisdom came from God.

The author is aware that the Letters of Paul were written to particular communities, but he regards all of them as pertinent for Christians in general. He is also aware that they can be interpreted differently and that consequently correct interpretation must be distinguished from incorrect interpretation. Probably the author implies that the false teachers have based their denial of

Jesus's coming and consequent moral laxity partly on an incorrect interpretation of Paul (see Schelkle 1961, 236–39; Bauckham 1983, 335).

Christology

The doxology with which 2 Peter ends probably implies that the author sees Jesus as God. As noted above, in the NT such a doxology is ordinarily reserved for God. Second Peter's use of such a doxology for Jesus probably indicates that the author sees Jesus as divine. This accords with what we have seen elsewhere in 2 Peter.

Summary

In the course of this commentary, I have argued that "early Catholicism" is not a helpful category for interpreting 2 Peter and have discussed the theological implications of the view that 2 Peter is pseudonymous, mentioning both in connection with the opening section of the letter (1:1–15). I have also discussed the following theological topics that are treated in 2 Peter:

- Christian faith is inextricably bound up with historical events and their interpretation (1:16–2:10a).
- God is truly revealed by the OT (1:16–2:10a; 3:1–13).
- Jesus Christ is God but distinct from God, and there is only one God. This view is reflected in every section of the letter except 2:10b–22. The Christology of 2 Peter is one of the most exalted in the NT.
- Christ has saved his followers from corruption (1:1–15; 2:10b–22), probably by means of his death and resurrection (1:16–2:10a).
- Christian ethics prescribes the appropriate response to having been saved by Christ, a response that also maintains one's status as having been saved (1:1–15; 2:10b–22; 3:1–13).
- The second coming of Christ at the end of the world will be the completion of the salvation he accomplished (1:16–2:10a; 3:1–13). Second Peter's expectation that the world will be destroyed by fire at this time is its most distinctive contribution to early Christian eschatology.
- The Letters of Paul are Scripture, like the writings of the OT (3:14–18).

Bibliography

Aageson, James W. 2004. "1 Peter 2.11–3:7: Slaves, Wives and the Complexities of Interpretation." In *Feminist Companion to the Catholic Epistles and Hebrews*, edited by Amy-Jill Levine with Maria Mayo Robbins, 34–49. London: T&T Clark International.

Abbott, E. A. 1882. "On the Second Epistle of St. Peter." *The Expositor* 2/3:49–63, 139–53, 204–19.

Achtemeier, Paul J. 1989. "New-Born Babes and Living Stones: Literal and Figurative in 1 Peter." In *To Touch the Text: Biblical and Related Studies in Honor of Joseph H. Fitzmyer*, edited by M. P. Horgan and P. J. Kobelski, 207–36. New York: Crossroad/Continuum.

———. 1993. "Suffering Servant and Suffering Christ in 1 Peter." In *The Future of Christology: Essays in Honor of Leander E. Keck*, edited by A. J. Malherbe and W. A. Meeks, 176–88. Minneapolis: Fortress.

———. 1996. *1 Peter*. Hermeneia. Minneapolis: Fortress.

Adinolfi, M. 1988. *La prima lettera di Pietro nel mondo greco-romano*. Bibliotheca Pontificii Athenaei Antoniani 26. Rome: Antonianum.

Agnew, Francis H. 1983. "1 Peter 1:2: An Alternative Translation." *Catholic Biblical Quarterly* 45:68–73.

Aland, Kurt. 1960. "Der Tod des Petrus in Rom." In *Kirchengeschichtliche Entwürfe: Alte Kirche, Reformation und Luthertum, Pietismus und Erweckungsbewegung*, 35–104. Gütersloh: Gerd Mohn.

Antoniotti, L.-M. 1985. "Structure littéraire et sens de la Première Épître de Pierre." *Revue thomiste* 85:533–60.

Applegate, Judith K. 1992. "The Co-elect Woman of 1 Peter: Symbol or Real Person." *New Testament Studies* 32:587–604. Reprinted in *Feminist Companion to the Catholic Epistles and Hebrews*, edited by Amy-Jill Levine with Maria Mayo Robbins, 89–102. London: T&T Clark International, 2004.

Arichea, Daniel C., Jr., and Eugene A. Nida. 1980. *A Translator's Handbook on the First Letter from Peter: Helps for Translators*. New York: United Bible Societies.

Aune, David E., ed. 2003. *The Westminster Dictionary of New Testament and Early Christian Literature and Rhetoric*. Louisville: Westminster John Knox.

Balch, David L. 1974. "'Let Wives Be Submissive . . .': The Origin, Form, and Apologetic Function of the Household Duty Code (Haustafel) in 1 Peter." PhD diss., Yale University. Ann Arbor, MI: University Microfilms International, 1976.

———. 1981. *Let Wives Be Submissive: The Domestic Code in 1 Peter*. Society of Biblical Literature Monograph Series 26. Chico, CA: Scholars Press.

———. 1986. "Hellenization/Acculturation in 1 Peter." In *Perspectives on First Peter*, edited by Charles H. Talbert, 79–101. National Association of Baptist Professors of Religion Special Studies 9. Macon, GA: Mercer University Press.

———. 1988. "Household Codes." In *Greco-Roman Literature and the New Testament: Selected Forms and Genres*, edited by David E. Aune, 25–50. Society of Biblical Literature Sources for Biblical Study 21. Atlanta: Scholars Press.

Bartchy, S. Scott. 1973. *Mallon Chresai: First Century Slavery and 1 Corinthians 7:21*. Society of Biblical Literature Dissertation Series 11. Missoula, MT: Scholars Press.

Batten, Alicia. 2009. "Neither Gold nor Braided Hair (1 Timothy 2.9; 1 Peter 3.3): Adornment, Gender and Honour in Antiquity." *New Testament Studies* 55:484–501.

Bauckham, Richard J. 1983. *Jude, 2 Peter*. Word Biblical Commentary 50. Waco: Word.

———. 1988. "2 Peter: An Account of Research." In *Aufstieg und Niedergang der römischen Welt: Geschichte und Kultur Roms im Spiegel der neuren Forschung*, edited by H. Temporini and W. Haase, part 2, *Principat* 25.5:3713–52. Berlin: de Gruyter.

———. 1990. *Jude, 2 Peter*. Word Biblical Themes. Dallas: Word.

———. 1992. "The Martyrdom of Peter in Early Christian Literature." In *Aufstieg und Niedergang der römischen Welt: Geschichte und Kultur Roms im Spiegel der neuren Forschung*, edited by H. Temporini and W. Haase, part 2, *Principat* 26.1:539–95. Berlin: de Gruyter.

Beare, Francis Wright. 1970. *The First Epistle of Peter: The Greek Text with Introduction and Notes*. 3rd ed. Oxford: Blackwell.

Bechtler, Stephen R. 1998. *Following in His Steps: Suffering, Community, and Christology in 1 Peter*. Society of Biblical Literature Dissertation Series 162. Atlanta: Scholars Press.

Best, Ernest. 1969. "1 Peter II 4–10—A Reconsideration." *Novum Testamentum* 11:270–93.

———. 1970. "1 Peter and the Gospel Tradition." *New Testament Studies* 16:95–113.

———. 1971. *1 Peter*. New Century Bible. London: Oliphants; Grand Rapids: Eerdmans.

Bigg, Charles A. 1901. *A Critical and Exegetical Commentary on the Epistles of St. Peter and St. Jude*. International Critical Commentary. New York: Scribner.

Black, C. Clifton. 1994. *Mark: Images of an Apostolic Interpreter*. Columbia: University of South Carolina Press.

Boismard, Marie-Émile. 1961. *Quatre hymnes baptismales dans la première épître de Pierre*. Paris: Cerf.

Boring, M. Eugene. 1999. *First Peter*. Abingdon New Testament Commentaries. Nashville: Abingdon.

Bradley, Keith R. 1984. *Slaves and Masters in the Roman Empire: A Study in Social Control*. Oxford: Oxford University Press.

———. 1994. *Slavery and Society at Rome*. Key Themes in Ancient History. Cambridge: Cambridge University Press.

Bratcher, Robert G. 1984. *A Translator's Guide to the Letters of James, Peter, and Jude*. New York: United Bible Societies.

Brown, Jeannine K. 2006. "Just a Busybody? A Look at the Greco-Roman Topos of Meddling for Defining *Allotriepiskopos* in 1 Peter 4:15." *Journal of Biblical Literature* 125:549–68.

Brown, Raymond E. 1968. *Jesus, God and Man: Modern Biblical Reflections*. Impact Books. London: Chapman.

———. 1994. *An Introduction to New Testament Christology*. New York: Paulist Press.

Brown, Raymond E., Karl P. Donfried, and John Reumann, eds. 1973. *Peter in the New Testament: A Collaborative Assessment by Protestant and Roman Catholic Scholars*. Minneapolis: Augsburg; New York: Paulist Press.

Brown, Raymond E., and John P. Meier. 1983. *Antioch and Rome: New Testament Cradles of Catholic Christianity*. New York: Paulist Press.

Brox, Norbert. 1975. "Zur pseudepigraphischen Rahmung des ersten Petrusbriefes." *Biblische Zeitschrift* 19:78–96.

———. 1978. "Tendenz und Pseudepigraphie im ersten Petrusbrief." *Kairos* 20:110–20.

———. 1981. "'Sara zum Beispiel': Israel im 1. Petrusbrief." In *Kontinuität und Einheit: Für Franz Mussner*, edited by P.-G. Müller and W. Stegner, 484–93. Freiburg: Herder.

———. 1986. *Der erste Petrusbrief*. 2nd ed. Evangelisch-katholischer Kommentar zum Neuen Testament 21. Zurich: Benzinger; Neukirchen-Vluyn: Neukirchener Verlag. [1st ed. 1979.]

Callan, Terrance. 1994. *The Origins of Christian Faith*. New York: Paulist Press.

———. 2001a. "The Christology of the Second Letter of Peter." *Biblica* 82:253–63.

———. 2001b. "The Soteriology of the Second Letter of Peter." *Biblica* 82:549–59.

———. 2003. "The Style of the Second Letter of Peter." *Biblica* 84:202–24.

———. 2004. "Use of the Letter of Jude by the Second Letter of Peter." *Biblica* 85:42–64.

———. 2005. "The Syntax of 2 Peter 1:1–7." *Catholic Biblical Quarterly* 67:632–40.

———. 2006a. "A Note on 2 Peter 1:19–20." *Journal of Biblical Literature* 125:143–50.

———. 2006b. *Dying and Rising with Christ: The Theology of Paul the Apostle*. New York: Paulist Press.

———. 2009. "Comparison of Humans to Animals in 2 Peter 2:10b–22." *Biblica* 90:101–13.

Calloud, J. 1980. "Ce que parler veut dire (1 P 1,10–12)." In *Études sur la première lettre de Pierre*, by Association catholique française pour l'étude de la Bible, 175–206. Lectio divina 102. Paris: Cerf.

Campbell, Barth L. 1998. *Honor, Shame, and the Rhetoric of 1 Peter*. Society of Biblical Literature Dissertation Series 160. Atlanta: Scholars Press.

Campbell, D. N., and Fika Van Rensburg. 2008. "A History of the Interpretation of 1 Peter 3:18–22." *Acta patristica et byzantina* 19:73–96.

Carrez, M. 1980. "L'esclavage dans la première épître de Pierre." In *Études sur la première lettre de Pierre*, by Association catholique française pour l'étude de la Bible, 207–17. Lectio divina 102. Paris: Cerf.

Carter, Warren. 2004. "Going All the Way? Honoring the Emperor and Sacrificing Wives and Slaves in 1 Peter 2:13–36." In *Feminist Companion to the Catholic Epistles and Hebrews*, edited by Amy-Jill Levine with Maria Mayo Robbins, 14–33. London: T&T Clark International.

Casurella, Anthony. 1996. *Bibliography of Literature on First Peter*. New Testament Tools and Studies 16. Leiden: Brill.

Cavallin, H. C. C. 1979. "The False Teachers of 2 Pt as Pseudoprophets." *Novum Testamentum* 21:263–70.

Chaine, Joseph. 1939. *Les épîtres catholiques: La seconde épître de Saint Pierre, les épîtres de Saint Jean, l'épître de Saint Jude*. 2nd ed. Paris: Gabalda.

Charles, J. Daryl. 1997. *Virtue amidst Vice: The Catalog of Virtues in 2 Peter 1*. Journal for the Study of the New Testament: Supplement Series 150. Sheffield: Sheffield Academic Press.

Chase, F. H. 1900. "Peter, Second Epistle of." In *Hastings Dictionary of the Bible*, 3:796–818. Edinburgh: T&T Clark.

Chevallier, M.-A. 1978. "Israël et l'église selon la première épître de Pierre." In *Paganisme, Judaïsme, Christianisme: Influences et affrontements dans le monde antique; Mélanges offerts à Marcel Simon*, 117–30. Paris: de Boccard.

Chin, Moses. 1991. "A Heavenly Home for the Homeless: Aliens and Strangers in 1 Peter." *Tyndale Bulletin* 42:96–112.

Combrink, H. J. B. 1975. "The Structure of 1 Peter." *Neotestamentica* 9:34–63.

Cothenet, Édouard. 1980–81. "Le réalisme de l'espérance chrétienne selon 1 Pierre." *New Testament Studies* 27:564–72.

Cross, Frank Leslie. 1954. *1 Peter: A Paschal Liturgy*. London: Mowbray.

Cullmann, Oscar. 1959. *The Christology of the New Testament*. Translated by S. C. Guthrie and C. A. M. Hall. Philadelphia: Westminster.

Dalton, William Joseph. 1979. "The Interpretation of 1 Peter 3,19 and 4,6: Light from 2 Peter." *Biblica* 60:547–55.

———. 1989. *Christ's Proclamation to the Spirits: A Study of 1 Peter 3:18–4:6*. 2nd rev. ed. Analecta biblica 23. Rome: Pontifical Biblical Institute.

Danker, Frederick W. 1978. "2 Peter 1: A Solemn Decree." *Catholic Biblical Quarterly* 40:64–82.

―――. 1982. *Benefactor: Epigraphic Study of a Graeco-Roman and New Testament Semantic Field*. St. Louis: Clayton.

Davids, Peter H. 1990. *The First Epistle of Peter*. New International Commentary on the New Testament. Grand Rapids: Eerdmans.

―――. 2006. *The Letters of 2 Peter and Jude*. Pillar New Testament Commentary. Grand Rapids: Eerdmans; Cambridge: Apollos.

Deissmann, Adolf. 1901. *Bible Studies*. Translated by A. Grieve. Edinburgh: T&T Clark.

Donelson, Lewis R. 2010. *I & II Peter and Jude: A Commentary*. New Testament Library. Louisville: Westminster John Knox.

Dryden, J. de Waal. 2006. *Theology and Ethics in 1 Peter: Paraenetic Strategies for Christian Character Formation*. Wissenschaftliche Untersuchungen zum Neuen Testament 2.209. Tübingen: Mohr Siebeck.

Dubis, Mark. 2006. "Research on 1 Peter: A Survey of Scholarly Literature since 1985." *Currents in Biblical Research* 4:199–239.

Elliott, John H. 1966. *The Elect and the Holy: An Exegetical Examination of 1 Peter 2:4–10 and the Phrase βασίλειον ἱεράτευμα*. Novum Testamentum Supplements 12. Leiden: Brill.

―――. 1970. "Ministry and Church Order in the New Testament: A Traditio-Historical Analysis (1 P 5,1–5 plls.)." *Catholic Biblical Quarterly* 32:367–91.

―――. 1980. "Peter, Silvanus and Mark in 1 Peter and Acts: Sociological-Exegetical Perspectives on a Petrine Group in Rome." In *Wort in der Zeit: Neutestamentliche Studien; Festgabe für Karl Heinrich Rengstorf zum 75. Geburtstag*, edited by W. Haubeck and M. Bachmann, 250–67. Leiden: Brill.

―――. 1990. *A Home for the Homeless: A Social-Scientific Criticism of 1 Peter, Its Situation and Strategy, with a New Introduction*. Minneapolis: Fortress. [1st ed. 1981.]

―――. 1995. "Disgraced yet Graced: The Gospel according to 1 Peter in the Key of Honor and Shame." *Biblical Theology Bulletin* 25:166–78.

―――. 2000. *1 Peter*. Anchor Bible 37B. New York: Doubleday.

―――. 2008. "Elders as Leaders in 1 Peter and the Early Church." *Hervormde Teologiese Studies* 64:681–95.

Exler, Francis Xavier J. 1923. *The Form of the Ancient Greek Letter of the Epistolary Papyri (3rd c. B.C.–3rd c. A.D.): A Study in Greek Epistolography*. Washington, DC: Catholic University of America.

Feldmeier, Reinhard. 1992. *Die Christen als Fremde: Die Metapher der Fremde in der antiken Welt, im Unchristentum und im 1. Petrusbrief*. Wissenschaftliche Untersuchungen zum Neuen Testament 64. Tübingen: Mohr Siebeck.

Fitzmyer, Joseph A. 1979. "Aramaic Epistolography." In *A Wandering Aramean: Collected Aramaic Essays*, 183–204. Chico, CA: Scholars Press.

Forbes, Greg. 2005. "Children of Sarah: Interpreting 1 Peter 3:6b." *Bulletin for Biblical Research* 15:105–9.

Fornberg, Tord. 1977. *An Early Church in a Pluralistic Society: A Study of 2 Peter*. Coniectanea biblica: New Testament Series 9. Lund: Gleerup.

225

Foster, Ora Delmar. 1913. *The Literary Relations of the "First Epistle of Peter" with Their Bearing on Date and Place of Authorship.* Transactions of the Connecticut Academy of Arts and Sciences 17. New Haven: Yale University Press.

Francis, James. 1980. "'Like Newborn Babes'—The Image of the Child in 1 Peter 2:2–3." In *Studia Biblica 1978: Sixth International Congress on Biblical Studies, Oxford, 3–7 April 1978,* vol. 3, *Papers on Paul and Other New Testament Authors,* edited by E. A. Livingstone, 111–17. Journal for the Study of the New Testament: Supplement Series 3. Sheffield: JSOT Press.

Fuller, Reginald H. 1965. *The Foundations of New Testament Christology.* New York: Scribner.

Gärtner, Bertil. 1965. *The Temple and the Community in Qumran and the New Testament: A Comparative Study in the Temple Symbolism of the Qumran Texts and the New Testament.* Society for New Testament Studies Monograph Series 1. Cambridge: Cambridge University Press.

Gerdmar, Anders. 2001. *Rethinking the Judaism-Hellenism Dichotomy: A Historiographical Case Study of Second Peter and Jude.* Coniectanea biblica: New Testament Series 36. Stockholm: Almqvist & Wiksell.

Gilmour, Michael J. 2002. *The Significance of Parallels between 2 Peter and Other Early Christian Literature.* Academia Biblica 10. Atlanta: Society of Biblical Literature.

Golebiewski, R. P. E. 1965. "Dieu nous console dans l'épreuve (1 P 5,6–11)." *Assemblées du Seigneur* 57:17–23.

Goppelt, Leonhard. 1993. *A Commentary on 1 Peter.* Edited by Ferdinand Hahn. Translated and augmented by John E. Alsup. Grand Rapids: Eerdmans.

Green, Gene L. 2008. *Jude and 2 Peter.* Baker Exegetical Commentary on the New Testament. Grand Rapids: Baker Academic.

Green, Joel B. 2007. *1 Peter.* Two Horizons New Testament Commentary. Grand Rapids: Eerdmans.

Green, Michael. 1987. *The Second Epistle General of Peter and the General Epistle of Jude.* Tyndale New Testament Commentaries 18. Grand Rapids: Eerdmans.

Gross, Carl D. 1989. "Are the Wives of 1 Peter 3.7 Christians?" *Journal for the Study of the New Testament* 35:89–96.

Grundmann, Walter. 1974. *Der Brief des Judas und der zweite Brief des Petrus.* Theologischer Handkommentar zum Neuen Testament 15. Berlin: Evangelische Verlagsanstalt.

Hahn, Ferdinand. 1969. *The Titles of Jesus in Christology: Their History in Early Christianity.* Translated by H. Knight and G. Ogg. London: Lutterworth.

Harrington, Daniel J. 2003. "Jude and 2 Peter." In *1 Peter, Jude and 2 Peter,* by Donald P. Senior and Daniel J. Harrington, 159–299. Sacra pagina 15. Collegeville, MN: Liturgical Press.

Harris, Murray J. 1992. *Jesus as God: The New Testament Use of "Theos" in Reference to Jesus.* Grand Rapids: Baker.

Harvey, Robert, and Philip H. Towner. 2009. *2 Peter & Jude.* The IVP New Testament Commentary Series. Downers Grove, IL: InterVarsity.

Haselhurst, R. S. T. 1926. "Mark, My Son." *Theology* 13:34–36.

Hemer, Colin J. 1978. "The Address of 1 Peter." *Expository Times* 89:239–43.

Hengel, Martin. 1976. *The Son of God*. Translated by J. Bowden. Philadelphia: Fortress.

Hiebert, D. E. 1984. "Selected Studies from 2 Peter, Part 2, The Prophetic Foundation for the Christian Life: An Exposition of 2 Pet. 1:19–21." *Bibliotheca sacra* 141:158–68.

Himmelfarb, Martha. 1993. *Ascent to Heaven in Jewish and Christian Apocalypses*. New York: Oxford University Press.

Hofmann, J. Chr. K. von. 1875. *Der zweite Brief Petri und der Brief Judä*. Part 7.2 of *Die heilige Schrift Neuen Testaments zusammenhängend untersucht*. Nördlingen: Beck.

Horrell, David G. 2002. "The Product of a Petrine Circle? A Reassessment of the Origin and Character of 1 Peter." *Journal for the Study of the New Testament* 86:29–60.

———. 2003. "Who Are 'the Dead' and When Was the Gospel Preached to Them? The Interpretation of 1 Pet 4.6." *New Testament Studies* 49:70–89.

———. 2007. "The Label *Christianos*: 1 Peter 4:16 and the Formation of Christian Identity." *Journal of Biblical Literature* 126:361–81.

Hort, Fenton John Anthony. 1898. *The First Epistle of St. Peter, I.1–II.17: The Greek Text with Introductory Lecture, Commentary, and Additional Notes*. London: Macmillan.

Hunzinger, Claus-Hunno. 1965. "Babylon als Deckname für Rom und die Datierung des I. Petrusbriefes." In *Gottes Wort und Gottes Land: Hans-Wilhelm Hertzberg zum 70. Geburtstag am 16 Januar 1965*, edited by H. Graf Reventlow, 67–77. Göttingen: Vandenhoeck & Ruprecht.

James, Montague R. 1912. *The Second Epistle General of Peter and the General Epistle of Jude*. Cambridge Greek Testament for Schools and Colleges. Cambridge: Cambridge University Press.

Jobes, Karen H. 2002. "Got Milk? Septuagint Psalm 33 and the Interpretation of 1 Peter 2:1–3." *Westminster Theological Journal* 64:1–14.

———. 2005. *1 Peter*. Baker Exegetical Commentary on the New Testament. Grand Rapids: Baker Academic.

Johnson, Luke T. 1989. "The New Testament's Anti-Jewish Slander and the Conventions of Ancient Polemic." *Journal of Biblical Literature* 108:419–41.

———. 2001. *The First and Second Letters to Timothy*. Anchor Bible 35A. New York: Doubleday.

Johnson, Sherman E. 1971. "Unresolved Questions about Early Christianity in Asia Minor." In *Studies in New Testament and Early Christian Literature: Essays in Honor of Allen P. Wikgren*, edited by David E. Aune, 181–93. Novum Testamentum Supplements 33. Leiden: Brill.

———. 1975. "Asia Minor and Early Christianity." In *Christianity, Judaism, and Other Greco-Roman Cults: Studies for Morton Smith at Sixty*, edited by Jacob Neusner, part 2, *Early Christianity*, 77–145. Studies in Judaism in Late Antiquity 12. Leiden: Brill.

Käsemann, Ernst. 1964. "An Apologia for Primitive Christian Eschatology." In *Essays on New Testament Themes*, translated by W. J. Montague, 169–95. Studies in Biblical Theology 41. Naperville, IL: Allenson.

Kelly, J. N. D. 1969. *The Epistles of Peter and of Jude.* Harper's New Testament Commentaries. New York: Harper & Row.

Kendall, Daniel W. 1986. "The Literary and Theological Function of 1 Peter 1:3–12." In *Perspectives on First Peter*, edited by Charles H. Talbert, 103–20. Macon, GA: Mercer University Press.

Kiley, Mark. 1987. "Like Sara: The Tale of Terror behind 1 Peter 3:6." *Journal of Biblical Literature* 106:689–92.

Klumbies, Paul-Gerhard. 2001. "Die Verkündigung unter Geistern und Toten nach 1 Petr 3,19f. und 4,6." *Zeitschrift für die neutestamentliche Wissenschaft* 92:207–28.

Knoch, Otto. 1990. *Der erste und zweite Petrusbrief; Der Judasbrief.* Regensburger Neues Testament. Regensburg: Friedrich Pustet.

Knox, John. 1953. "Pliny and 1 Peter: A Note on 1 Pet 4:14–16 and 3:15." *Journal of Biblical Literature* 72:187–89.

Kraus, Thomas J. 2000. "Παρὰ κυρίου, παρὰ κυρίῳ oder *omit* in 2Petr 2,11." *Zeitschrift für die neutestamentliche Wissenschaft* 91:265–73.

———. 2001. *Sprache, Stil und historischer Ort des zweiten Petrusbriefes.* Wissenschaftliche Untersuchungen zum Neuen Testament 136. Tübingen: Mohr Siebeck.

Kümmel, Werner Georg. 1973. *Introduction to the New Testament.* Translated by H. C. Kee. Nashville: Abingdon.

Langkammer, H. 1987. "Jes 53 und 1 Petr 2,21–25: Zur christologischen Interpretation der Leidenstheologie von Jes 53." *Bibel und Liturgie* 60:90–98.

Lapham, F. 2003. "The Second Epistle of Peter." In *Peter: The Myth, the Man and the Writings; A Study of Early Petrine Text and Tradition*, 149–71. Journal for the Study of the New Testament: Supplement Series 239. London: Sheffield Academic Press.

Légasse, Simon 1988. "La soumission aux authorités d'après 1 Pierre 2.13–17: Version spécifique d'une parénèse traditionelle." *New Testament Studies* 34:378–96.

Lips, H. von. 1994. "Die Haustafel als 'Topos' im Rahmen der urchristlichen Paränese: Beobachtungen anhand des 1. Petrusbriefes und des Titusbriefes." *New Testament Studies* 40:261–80.

Lohse, Eduard. 1963. *Märtyrer und Gottesknecht: Untersuchungen zur urchristliche Verkündigung vom Sühntod Jesu Christi.* 2nd ed. Forschungen zur Religion und Literatur des Alten und Neuen Testaments 64. Göttingen: Vandenhoeck & Ruprecht.

Lyall, Francis. 1984. *Slaves, Citizens, Sons: Legal Metaphors in the Epistles.* Grand Rapids: Zondervan.

Malherbe, Abraham J. 1986. *Moral Exhortation: A Greco-Roman Sourcebook.* Library of Early Christianity 4. Philadelphia: Westminster.

———. 1988. *Ancient Epistolary Theorists.* Society of Biblical Literature Sources for Biblical Study 19. Atlanta: Scholars Press.

Malina, Bruce J. 1993. *The New Testament World: Insights from Cultural Anthropology.* 2nd ed. Atlanta: Westminster John Knox.

Marshall, I. Howard. 1974. "The Development of the Concept of Redemption in the New Testament." In *Reconciliation and Hope: New Testament Essays on Atonement and Eschatology*, edited by R. Banks, 153–69. Grand Rapids: Eerdmans.

Martin, Ralph. 1994. "1 Peter." In *The Theology of the Letters of James, Peter, and Jude*, edited by Andrew Chester and Ralph P. Martin, 87–133. New Testament Theology. Cambridge: Cambridge University Press.

Martin, Troy W. 1992. *Metaphor and Composition in 1 Peter*. Society of Biblical Literature Dissertation Series 131. Atlanta: Scholars Press.

———. 1999. "The TestAbr and the Background of 1 Pet 3,6." *Zeitschrift für die neutestamentliche Wissenschaft* 90:139–46.

Mayor, Joseph B. 1907. *The Epistle of St. Jude and the Second Epistle of St. Peter*. London: Macmillan.

McCartney, D. 1991. "*Logikos* in 1 Peter 2:2." *Zeitschrift für die neutestamentliche Wissenschaft* 82:352–59.

Michaels, J. Ramsey. 1988. *1 Peter*. Word Biblical Commentary 49. Waco: Word.

Miller, Robert J. 1996. "Is There Independent Attestation for the Transfiguration in 2 Peter?" *New Testament Studies* 42:620–25.

Mills, Watson. 2000. *1 Peter*. Bibliographies for Biblical Research: New Testament Series 17. Lewiston, NY: Mellen Biblical Press.

Minear, Paul S. 1982. "The House of Living Stones: A Study of 1 Peter 2:4–12." *Ecumenical Review* 34:238–48.

Molthagen, J. 1995. "Die Lage der Christen im römischen Reich nach dem 1. Petrusbrief." *Historia* 44:422–80.

Moo, Douglas J. 1996. *2 Peter and Jude*. The NIV Application Commentary. Grand Rapids: Zondervan.

Mounce, Robert H. 1982. *A Living Hope: A Commentary on 1 and 2 Peter*. Grand Rapids: Eerdmans.

Murphy-O'Connor, Jerome. 1995. *Paul the Letter-Writer: His World, His Options, His Skills*. Good News Studies 41. Collegeville, MN: Liturgical Press.

Nauck, Wolfgang. 1955. "Freude im Leiden: Zum Problem einer urchristlichen Verfolgungs-tradition." *Zeitschrift für die neutestamentliche Wissenschaft* 46:68–80.

Neyrey, Jerome H. 1980. "The Apologetic Use of the Transfiguration in 2 Peter 1:16–21." *Catholic Biblical Quarterly* 42:504–19.

———. 1993. *2 Peter, Jude*. Anchor Bible 37C. New York: Doubleday.

Norden, Eduard. 1898. *Die antike Kunstprosa vom VI. Jahrhundert v. Chr. bis in die Zeit der Renaissance*. Leipzig: Teubner.

Osborne, Thomas P. 1983. "Guide Lines for Christian Suffering: A Source-Critical and Theological Study of 1 Peter 2,21–25." *Biblica* 64:381–408.

Ostmeyer, Karl-Heinrich. 2000. *Taufe und Typos: Elemente und Theologie der Tauftypologien in 1. Korinther 10 und 1. Petrus 3*. Wissenschaftliche Untersuchungen zum Neuen Testament 2/118. Tübingen: Mohr Siebeck.

Parker, D. C. 1994. "The Eschatology of 1 Peter." *Biblical Theology Bulletin* 24:27–32.

Paulsen, Henning. 1992. *Der zweite Petrusbrief und der Judasbrief*. Meyer Kommentar. Göttingen: Vandenhoeck & Ruprecht.

Perdelwitz, Richard Emil. 1911. *Die Mysterienreligion und das Problem des 1. Petrusbriefes: Ein literarischer und religionsgeschichtlicher Versuch*. Religionsversuche und Vorarbeiten 11/3. Giessen: Töpelmann.

Perkins, Pheme. 1995. *First and Second Peter, James, and Jude*. Interpretation. Louisville: John Knox.

Perrot, C. 1980. "La descente aux enfers et la prédicaton aux morts." In *Études sur la première lettre de Pierre*, by Association catholique française pour l'étude de la Bible, 231–46. Lectio divina 102. Paris: Cerf.

Piper, John. 1980. "Hope as the Motivation of Love: 1 Peter 3:9–12." *New Testament Studies* 26:212–31.

Prasad, Jacob. 2000. *Foundations of the Christian Way of Life according to 1 Peter 1,13–25: An Exegetico-Theological Study*. Analecta biblica 146. Rome: Pontifical Biblical Institute.

Reese, Ruth Anne. 2007. *2 Peter and Jude*. Two Horizons New Testament Commentary. Grand Rapids: Eerdmans.

Reicke, Bo. 1946. *The Disobedient Spirits and Christian Baptism: A Study of 1 Peter iii.19 and Its Context*. Acta seminarii neotestamentici upsaliensis 13. Copenhagen: Munksgaard.

———. 1964. *The Epistles of James, Peter, and Jude*. Anchor Bible 37. Garden City, NY: Doubleday.

Richard, Earl. 1986. "The Functional Christology of 1 Peter." In *Perspectives on 1 Peter*, edited by Charles H. Talbert, 121–40. National Association of Baptist Professors of Religion Special Studies 9. Macon, GA: Mercer University Press.

———. 2004. "Honorable Conduct among the Gentiles: A Study of the Social Thought of 1 Peter." *Word and World* 24:412–20.

Richards, E. Randolph. 2000. "Silvanus Was Not Peter's Secretary: Theological Bias in Interpreting διὰ Σιλουανοῦ . . . ἔγραψα in 1 Peter 5:12." *Journal of the Evangelical Theological Society* 43:417–32.

Rigato, M. L. 1990. "Quali i profeti di cui nella 1 Pt 1,10?" *Rivista biblica* 38:73–90.

Robbins, Vernon K. 1996. *Exploring the Texture of Texts: A Guide to Socio-Rhetorical Interpretation*. Valley Forge, PA: Trinity Press International.

Rose, H. J. 1959. *Outlines of Classical Literature*. Cleveland: World.

Ruppert, Lothar. 1972a. *Jesus als der leidende Gerechte? Der Weg Jesu im Lichte eines alt- und zwischentestamentlichen Motivs*. Stuttgarter Bibelstudien 59. Stuttgart: Katholisches Bibelwerk.

———. 1972b. *Der leidende Gerechte: Eine motivgeschichtliche Untersuchung zum Alten Testament und zwischentestamentlichen Judentum*. Forschung zur Bibel 5. Würzburg: Echter.

———. 1973. *Der leidende Gerechte und seine Feinde: Eine Wortfelduntersuchung*. Würzburg: Echter.

Schelkle, Karl H. 1961. *Die Petrusbriefe; Der Judasbrief*. Herders theologischer Kommentar 13/2. Freiburg: Herder.

Schmidt, Karl M. 2003. *Mahnung und Erinnerung im Maskenspiel: Epistolographie, Rhetorik und Narrative der Pseudepigraphen Petrusbriefe*. Freiburg: Herder.

Schubert, Paul. 1939. *Form and Function of the Pauline Thanksgiving*. Berlin: Töpelmann.

Schutter, William L. 1989. *Hermeneutic and Composition in First Peter*. Wissenschaftliche Untersuchungen zum Neuen Testament 2/30. Tübingen: Mohr Siebeck.

Schwank, P. Benedikt. 1962. "Diabolus tamquam leo rugiens." *Erbe und Auftrag* 38:15–20.

Schweizer, Eduard. 1992. "The Priesthood of All Believers: 1 Peter 2:1–10." In *Worship, Theology, and Ministry in the Early Church: Essays in Honor of Ralph P. Martin*, edited by Michael J. Wilkins and Terence Paige, 285–93. Journal for the Study of the New Testament: Supplement Series 87. Sheffield: JSOT Press.

———. 2000. "Glaubensgrundlage und Glaubenserfahrung in der Kirche des allgemeinen Priestertums: 1 Petr 2,1–10." In *Kirche und Volk Gottes: Festschrift für Jürgen Roloff zum 70. Geburtstag*, edited by Martin Karrer, Wolfgang Kraus, and Otto Merk, 272–83. Neukirchen-Vluyn: Neukirchener Verlag.

Selwyn, Ernest G. 1947. *The First Epistle of St. Peter: The Greek Text with Introduction, Notes, and Essays*. 2nd ed. London: Macmillan; New York: St. Martin's.

Senior, Donald P. 1980. *1 and 2 Peter*. New Testament Message 20. Wilmington, DE: Glazier.

———. 2003. "1 Peter." In *1 Peter, Jude and 2 Peter*, by Donald P. Senior and Daniel. J. Harrington, 1–158. Sacra pagina 15. Collegeville, MN: Liturgical Press.

Sidebottom, E. M. 1967. *James, Jude, and 2 Peter*. New Century Bible. London: Nelson.

Siegert, Folker. 2004. "Christus, der 'Eckstein,' und sein Unterbau: Eine Entdeckung an 1 Petr. 2:6f." *New Testament Studies* 50:139–46.

Smith, Terence V. 1985. *Petrine Controversies in Early Christianity: Attitudes towards Peter in the Christian Writings of the First Two Centuries*. Wissenschaftliche Untersuchungen zum Neuen Testament 2/15. Tübingen: Mohr Siebeck.

Snodgrass, Klyne R. 1977. "1 Peter II.1–10: Its Formation and Literary Affinities." *New Testament Studies* 24:97–106.

Soards, Marion L. 1988. "1 Peter, 2 Peter, and Jude as Evidence for a Petrine School." In *Aufstieg und Niedergang der römischen Welt: Geschichte und Kultur Roms im Spiegel der neuren Forschung*, edited by H. Temporini and W. Haase, part 2, *Principat* 25.5:3827–49. Berlin: de Gruyter.

Spicq, Ceslas. 1966. *Les Épîtres de Saint Pierre*. Sources bibliques 4. Paris: Gabalda.

———. 1969. "La place ou le rôle des jeunes dans certaines communautés néotestamentaires." *Revue biblique* 76:508–27.

Spitta, Friedrich. 1885. *Der zweite Brief des Petrus und der Brief des Judas*. Halle: Waisenhaus.

———. 1890. *Christi Predigt an die Geister (1 Petr. 3,19ff.): Ein Beitrag zur neutestamentlichen Theologie*. Göttingen: Vandenhoeck & Ruprecht.

Starr, James M. 2000. *Sharers in Divine Nature: 2 Peter 1:4 in Its Hellenistic Context*. Coniectanea biblica: New Testament Series 33. Stockholm: Almqvist & Wiksell.

Stowers, Stanley. 1986. *Letter Writing in Greco-Roman Antiquity*. Library of Early Christianity 5. Philadelphia: Westminster.

Talbert, Charles H. 1986a. "Once Again: The Plan of 1 Peter." In *Perspectives on First Peter*, edited by Charles H. Talbert, 41–51. National Association of Baptist Professors of Religion Special Studies 9. Macon, GA: Mercer University Press.

———, ed. 1986b. *Perspectives on First Peter*. National Association of Baptist Professors of Religion Special Studies 9. Macon, GA: Mercer University Press.

Thiede, Carsten P. 1986. "Babylon, der andere Ort: Anmerkungen zu 1 Petr 5,13 und Apg. 12,17." *Biblica* 67:532–38. Reprinted in *Das Petrusbild in der neueren Forschung*, edited by Carsten P. Thiede, 221–29. Wuppertal: Brockhaus, 1987.

Thomas, J. 1968. "Anfechtung und Vorfreude: Ein biblisches Thema nach Jakobus 1,2–18 in Zusammenhang mit Psalm 126, Röm 5,3–5 und 1 Petr. 1,5–7 formkritisch untersucht und parakletisch ausgelegt." *Kerygma und Dogma* 14:183–206.

Thurén, Lauri. 1990. *The Rhetorical Strategy of 1 Peter with Special Regard to Ambiguous Expressions*. Åbo: Åbo Academy Press.

———. 1995. *Argument and Theology in 1 Peter: The Origins of Christian Paraenesis*. Journal for the Study of the New Testament: Supplement Series 114. Sheffield: Sheffield Academic Press.

———. 1996. "Style Never Goes out of Fashion: 2 Peter Re-evaluated." In *Rhetoric, Scripture and Theology: Essays from the 1994 Pretoria Conference*, edited by S. E. Porter and T. H. Olbricht, 329–47. Journal for the Study of the New Testament: Supplement Series 131. Sheffield: Sheffield Academic Press.

———. 1997a. "The General New Testament Writings." In *Handbook of Classical Rhetoric in the Hellenistic Period: 330 B.C.–A.D. 400*, edited by S. E. Porter, 587–608. Leiden: Brill.

———. 1997b. "Hey Jude! Asking for the Original Situation and Message of a Catholic Epistle." *New Testament Studies* 43:451–65.

Tite, Philip K. 2009. "Nurslings, Milk and Moral Development in the Greco-Roman Context: A Reappraisal of the Paraenetic Utilization of Metaphor, 1 Peter 2:1–3." *Journal for the Study of the New Testament* 31:371–400.

Trobisch, David. 1994. *Paul's Letter Collection: Tracing the Origins*. Minneapolis: Fortress.

Unnik, W. C. van. 1979. "Le role de Noé dans les épîtres de Pierre." In *Noé, l'homme universel*, edited by Jacques Chopineau, 207–39. Colloque de Louvain 1978. Brussels: Institutum Judaicum Bruxelles.

Van Rensburg, Fika J. 2004. "Sarah's Submissiveness to Abraham: A Socio-Historic Interpretation of the Exhortation to Wives in 1 Peter 3:5–6 to Take Sarah as Example of Submissiveness." *Hervormde Teologiese Studies* 60:249–60.

———. 2005. "Metaphors in the Soteriology in 1 Peter: Identifying and Interpreting the Salvific Imageries." In *Salvation in the New Testament*, edited by J. G. Van der Watt, 409–35. Leiden: Brill.

Villiers, J. L. de. 1975. "Joy in Suffering in 1 Peter." *Neotestamentica* 9:64–86.

Vögtle, Anton. 1994. *Der Judasbrief; Der 2. Petrusbrief*. Evangelisch-Katholischer Kommentar zum Neuen Testament 22. Solothurn and Düsseldorf: Benziger; Neukirchen-Vluyn: Neukirchener Verlag.

Wagner, J. Ross. 2008. "Faithfulness and Fear, Stumbling and Salvation: Receptions of LXX Isaiah 8:11–18 in the New Testament." In *The Word Leaps the Gap*, edited by J. Ross Wagner, C. Kavin Rowe, and A. Katherine Grieb, 76–106. Grand Rapids: Eerdmans.

Warden, Duane. 1989. "The Prophets of 1 Peter 1:10–12." *Restoration Quarterly* 31:1–12.

Watson, Duane F. 1988. *Invention, Arrangement, and Style: Rhetorical Criticism of Jude and 2 Peter*. Society of Biblical Literature Dissertation Series 104. Atlanta: Scholars Press.

———. 2002. "The Oral-Scribal and Cultural Intertexture of Apocalyptic Discourse in Jude and 2 Peter." In *The Intertexture of Apocalyptic Discourse in the New Testament*, edited by D. F. Watson, 187–213. Society of Biblical Literature Symposium Series 14. Atlanta: Society of Biblical Literature.

Webb, Robert, and Betsy J. Bauman-Martin, eds. 2007. *Reading First Peter with New Eyes: Methodological Reassessments of the Letter of First Peter*. Library of New Testament Studies 364. London: T&T Clark.

Weima, Jeffrey A. D. 1994. *Neglected Endings: The Significance of the Pauline Letter Closings*. Journal for the Study of the New Testament: Supplement Series 101. Sheffield: Sheffield Academic Press.

Westfall, Cynthia Long. 1999. "The Relationship between the Resurrection, the Proclamation to the Spirits in Prison and Baptismal Regeneration: 1 Peter 3:19–22." In *Resurrection*, edited by Stanley E. Porter, Michael A. Hayes, and David Tombs, 106–35. Sheffield: Sheffield Academic Press.

Wilson, W. E. 1920–21. "Εὑρεθήσεται in 2 Peter iii.10." *Expository Times* 32:44–45.

Windisch, Hans. 1951. *Die katholischen Briefe*. 3rd ed. Handbuch zum Neuen Testament 15. Tübingen: Mohr Siebeck.

Winter, Bruce W. 1988. "The Public Honouring of Christian Benefactors: Romans 13:3–4 and 1 Peter 2.14–15." *Journal for the Study of the New Testament* 34:87–103.

Witherington, Ben, III. 2007. *Letters and Homilies for Hellenized Christians*. Vol. 2, *A Socio-Rhetorical Commentary on 1–2 Peter*. Downers Grove, IL: IVP Academic; Nottingham: Apollos.

Wohlenberg, G. 1915. *Der erste und zweite Petrusbrief und der Judasbrief*. Leipzig: Deichert.

Index of Subjects

Index of Modern Authors

Index of Scripture and Ancient Sources